LITERATURE, LANGUAGE
AND SOCIETY IN ENGLAND 1580–1680

LITERATURE, LANGUAGE AND SOCIETY IN ENGLAND 1580–1680

David Aers · Bob Hodge · Gunther Kress

GILL AND MACMILLAN
DUBLIN
BARNES & NOBLE BOOKS
TOTOWA

First published 1981 by
Gill and Macmillan
Dublin
with associated companies in
London, New York, Delhi, Hong Kong,
Johannesburg, Lagos, Melbourne
Singapore, Tokyo

© David Aers, Bob Hodge, Gunther Kress 1981

Published in the USA 1981 by
Barnes & Noble Books
81 Adams Drive
Totowa, New Jersey 07512

SBN 7171 0978 X   (Gill and Macmillan)
ISBN 0-389-20198-7   (Barnes & Noble)

Contents

Introduction

In this study we concentrate on works by five English writers from the late sixteenth to the late seventeenth century. These years saw important developments in English society and art. We have not attempted a survey of these, because that would miss what is most crucial at the present stage: understanding the complex nexus of relationships between literature and society. That general relationship describes a set of possibilities, rather than a static dualism of 'texts' and 'background' in which the background exists as a constant which is relevant equally and in the same way to all writers and all texts. Writers write out of the milieu in which they live, drawing on forms of language and ideology which are given by their society and which are essential not only to writing but to the very possibility of a fully human consciousness. But within these forms, within specific historical circumstances and problems, writers undertake their own construction of meanings. Some works may simply echo or mirror the dominant inherited paradigms of thought and practice. But others are the product of a more active and dynamic relationship, in which the writer works over given material, subjecting it to processes of criticism and transformation.

Clearly, works of this kind are important objects of study if one wishes to grasp the possibilities of an age. Terms like "major" beg many questions—who is the judge, and on what grounds are the judgments made—but some writers *have* emerged as especially significant figures, as 'major' writers. Such claims need to be looked at critically. We might have expected that writers who have been designated as "major" by a particular tradition would prove to be the most conformist; but this seems not to be the case. Here it is worth quoting Marcuse, whose words point towards central preoccupations in our book, while commenting on the relation between significant art and the dominant culture:

There is no work of art which does not break its affirmative stance by the "power of the negative", which does not, in its very structure, evoke the words, the images, the music of another reality, of another order repelled by the existing one and yet alive in memory and anticipation, alive in what happens to men and women, and in their rebellion against it. Where this tension between affirmation and negation, between pleasure and sorrow, higher and material culture no longer prevails, where the work no longer sustains the dialectical unity of what is and what can (and ought to) be, art has lost its truth, has lost itself. And precisely in the aesthetic form are this tension, and the critical, negating transcending qualities of bourgeois art—its antibourgeois qualities.

(Counter Revolution and Revolt, Allen Lane 1972, 92–3*)*

Most of the texts we explore are by writers who fit the 'heroic' role in which Marcuse casts the artist: writers who wrote out of an acute sense of crisis or ideological dislocation, and whose works manifest aspects of the tension Marcuse points to. As we attempt to demonstrate, such tension does indeed turn out to be an inextricable part of their most impressive achievements. The presence of 'the power of the negative' is what gives their work its comprehensiveness for its age, its adequacy to what is *not* as well as what *is*. Conversely, to recognise this quality requires a grasp of the social context of literary creativity as a dynamic process constituted by its conflicts and antagonisms and not solely by its commanding orthodoxies.

This needs insisting on because most of the critical and scholarly studies of this period which are taught in our schools and institutions of higher learning seem unable to focus on this dimension of literary works and their twofold relationship to dominant norms and practices in the culture. Whatever their personal views, such critics write as though they had a commitment to the established order of the writer's present, the dominance of which is legitimated by a belief in the essential conformity of writers of the past. This belief is then projected onto the reading and interpretation of the great works of the past, absorbing them into a tradition of orthodoxy, imposing a mythology of coherence onto writers, texts, and contexts. An interpretation which departs from this orthodoxy is labelled unhistorical. Yet this containment of the radical and subversive moments of literature can utterly falsify the historical meaning and resonance of past works. We have no wish to enlist these works in a static and uniform counter-orthodoxy, characterised by rebellion and rejection of the existing order. The point is to be able to trace the open, active relationship between works of literature, ideological forms and aspects of social organisation, and to situate individual writers and works in terms of such a process.

Prerequisite to the study of this relationship, and the under-standing of particular works in terms of it, is an adequate concept of the nature and role of language. The historian of forms of consciousness from the past has only texts to work on, as records of what men thought and felt, written in forms of language of the age. Language itself is a social activity which is constantly in a state of change, expressing forms of life and consciousness evolved by specific social beings and groups. Different forms of language articulate different forms of life and outlook, and writers express their attitudes towards inherited ideology in the minute particulars of language. The linguistic structures carry important meanings which are so habitual as to be beneath the level of consciousness. Words and sentences work at different levels of meaning, allowing subtle but sensitive contradictions and confu-sions to coexist in seemingly smooth and innocuous surface forms. Language is used to present meaning, or to evade it. It presents persuasive images of reality, constructing a conscious-ness of self and world which can become a second reality. A study of works in summary or paraphrase would miss a rich and vital source of insight into contemporary forms and processes of thought.

From this follows what we believe is the necessary strategy for an enquiry of this kind: a movement from the most detailed and close analysis of the language of texts outwards to relevant contexts (social, ideological, personal) and back to a renewed scrutiny of details of the text. Such a study cannot be totally neutral or value-free. Inevitably it will set itself to answer some questions and not others, because these seem the crucial ques-tions in terms of more fundamental principles and commitments. An assertion of priorities is essential for any purposive study. For us the aim of the study of literature is to generate a further, more precise understanding of particular texts and writers, and of the culture within which writers lived, worked and wrote. Such understanding leads to an enhanced enjoyment of the texts, and to a deeper grasp of the historical process. The writers we look at include some of the greatest writers in English, and the period they wrote in formed a crucial stage in the evolution of the society we live in today.

We are aware that our use of a term like 'greatest' will make certain Marxist readers wince—is not the use of such traditional evaluations a naïve acceptance of the 'bourgeois canon' of English literature and its ideological standpoint? We registered this question in the second paragraph of the Introduction, and gave our own response, but it is worth expanding that, however briefly. Our own critical enterprise in this book revolves around a pre-existing selection of writers, valued in 'bourgeois' cultural tradition and still studied in contemporary institutions where the writing of the period in question is taught. Our purpose, as we have observed, is to examine certain writers in that canon, to explore the complex ways in which received ideology functions in the texts under discussion, and to enhance understanding of texts, writers and culture. We also hope to encourage certain directions within the critical traditions whose business is the study of the canon in question. We are aware that our approach could have bearings on the arguments among English Marxists centred on E.P. Thompson's *The Poverty of Theory* (Merlin 1978) and the uses of L. Althusser in Marxist aesthetics. But ours is definitely neither a study of critical ideology nor an attempt at 'Theory'—capital 'T'. Although the methods of analysis and the specific evidence in this book may offer some contribution to current theoretical debate, as we have emphasized in this Introduction, the present book is a study of specific discourses, their ideology and function, from Marlowe to Milton.

In writing the book we have gained much from different quarters. The editors of *Literature and History* were generous with advice concerning several chapters, and in their encouragement of the project; we wish to thank them for that as well as for permission to reprint chapters 2 and 8 which first appeared in their journal, vols. 8 and 7 respectively. We also wish to thank the editor of *Milton Studies*, XIII (1979), published by University of Pittsburgh Press, for permission to reprint chapter 6. Professor Christopher Hill gave encouragement to a part of our project early on; but more than that, the debt we owe to his work will be apparent in much of the book, even where we do not make an overt acknowledgment. One of the authors, David Aers, has benefited immeasurably from the constant friendship and intellectual support of the late Elizabeth Salter, the most generous of scholars and teachers. Dr Barry Reay gave us valuable comments on chapter 7; and Tania West gave one of the authors some penetrating insights into *King Lear* which appear in transmuted form in chapter 4. We would like to record our thanks to Hartley College of Advanced Education, which made it possible for one of the authors to spend some weeks working on this project. The authors also wish to thank Peter Brooks, for his extremely shrewd and constructive criticism was a great help to us: we hope we have benefited from his generous commentaries, even though much remains with which he will probably disagree. Jill Brewster typed the manuscript—impeccably—under the constant pressure of a demanding job. She managed to preserve her good humour and the authors from some embarrassing errors. For all that we wish to express to her our thanks and warmest gratitude.

Though it is conventional to say this it is nevertheless true that those from whom we have benefited had no part in whatever errors we may in the end have committed.

1

Marlowe, Marx and Machiavelli: Reading into the Past

BOB HODGE

In understanding any historical period, we need to understand the meanings it held for individuals who lived it. These meanings are often elusive, and nowhere more so than when they are carried through literary works. A play by Marlowe or Shakespeare represents people saying and doing things in particular situations with particular outcomes. It is not a treatise or an essay. Yet audiences and readers regard these texts as carrying important meanings which are nowhere definitively stated. Critics gloss these meanings with phrases like 'Shakespeare/ Marlowe says/sees/believes/shows profound understanding of X', where the X is a range of general truths about man and society. In effect, the critical essay is an explication which turns implicit meanings into explicit ones, translating a work of art into what is claimed to be a fully explicit corresponding treatise.

There are obvious dangers in this process. Literary works are highly vulnerable to ideological interpretation. Students recognise this, and often resist what they call 'reading things into' literary works. They see, uneasily, how a literary text is made the pretext for an improving homily, and the art of criticism comes to seem the ability to discover such morally edifying treatises within the text itself. Yet in spite of the inherent dangers, there is no simple solution. There is never a neutral and self-evident reading to appeal to. All reading involves 'reading into', an effort to reconstruct meanings which are implied by the text. The reader must take an active role in this process. What the reader is trying to do is to project the meanings the work has. Not all such projections have the same status. Of all the meanings a text might have, the meanings which we guess it had for its author and/or its original audience have a special importance; this is certainly the case in a historically based inquiry. Consequently scholars are perhaps most persuasive when they invoke the authority of an entity such as 'the sixteenth/seventeenth-century mind' or 'the average Elizabethan' or 'what Shakespeare/Marlowe's audience believed/thought', to rule out an interpretation as anachronistic. This strategy is often an illegitimate one. The 'sixteenth-century mind' is not a self-evident fact which can be known by a scholar. Scholars, at best, can know a number of surviving texts, literary works and other treatises. They can read and interpret these but can never do more than guess what meanings these works had for some or all of their original readers.

To see how complex the relation between a literary text and a treatise can be, consider Brecht's observations on his early plays.

> When I read Marx's *Capital* I understood my plays . . . it wasn't of course that I found I had unconsciously written a whole pile of Marxist plays: but this man Marx was the only spectator for my plays that I had ever come across.[1]

The paradox which Brecht brings out here has important implications. Brecht does not have a treatise (Marx's *Capital*) which he has translated into dramatic form. On the contrary, he wrote his plays and then, when he had read the treatise, began to understand the plays. He insists that the plays are not equivalent to the treatise. The treatise is the catalyst which enables meanings, which the play had for the author himself, to become visible to him for the first time. They become visible because Marx is projected as an ideal spectator, not simply someone who wrote *Capital* but someone who understood what Brecht felt were the meanings implicit in that work. The meanings which Brecht says he now understands, are therefore still elusive, still implicit both in his plays, and in Marx's treatise, but they have a different status in his own mind. They are more conscious, and so they are more available for inspection and criticism and action.

Althusser, in *Reading 'Capital'* makes some valuable observations about the complex processes involved in reading a text like Marx's, understanding that text itself as evidence for Marx's own reading of other theoretical works, such as Adam Smith's *Wealth of Nations,* the eighteenth-century classic work on political economy, which Marx acknowledged as an important influence on his own theory. Althusser looks at Marx's way of reading such predecessors, as this can be gleaned from his comments on them:

> In the *first reading,* Marx reads his predecessor's discourse (Smith's for instance) through his own discourse. The result of this reading through a grid, in which Smith's text is seen through Marx's, projected onto it as a measure of it, is merely a summary of concordances and discordances, the balance of what Smith discovered and what he missed, of his merits and failings, of his presences and absences.[2]

But if Marx had only stayed at this level, he could only have catalogued Smith's omissions, not understood him. But Marx 'sees' more than a set of omissions, he sees in Smith things that were invisible to Smith: not things that Smith accidentally did not see, but things which in principle he could not see, which nonetheless can be detected in his text, as answers to problems he had not posed, requiring terms which were not available to him.

> These new objects and problems are necessarily *invisible* in the field of the existing theory, because they are not objects of this theory, because they are *forbidden* by it—they are objects and problems without any necessary relations with the field of the visible as defined by this problematic.[3]

This second reading is arrived at by reflection on the first. In it Marx understands the inner necessity for the omissions revealed by juxtaposition. It is also a new way of seeing, a shift in terrain, as Althusser puts it. Yet this shift is not simply a difference between Smith and Marx. Marx perceives the contradictions to Smith in Smith's own work: an intimation of Marx, discovered in his opponent.

Althusser then proposed to read Marx in the same spirit, although in this case he does not want to say that Marx himself failed to 'see' the invisible problems and objects.

And if, as I have dared to suggest, there is undoubtedly in Marx an important *answer* to a *question that is nowhere posed,* an answer which Marx only succeeded in formulating on condition of multiplying the images required to render it . . . it is surely because the age Marx lived in did not provide him, and he could not acquire in his lifetime, an adequate concept with which to think what he had produced.[4]

Even with Marx, then, there are important meanings implicit, which Marx 'produced' but did not 'think'. That is an obscure and dangerous distinction, but it brings out the difficulties of attributing this kind of meaning in a particular case.

From Althusser, we can suggest some distinctions in the kinds of meaning which he calls 'invisible': what the writer sees, but does not state (intended implications); what he does not realise he has seen (unconscious meanings); what he is forbidden to see, which is negatively implied by his text (specific absences); and what is irrelevant to his text. We can represent this structure in a diagram, as follows:

$$
\text{meanings}
\begin{cases}
\text{presences}
\begin{cases}
\text{explicit} \\
\text{implicit}
\begin{cases}
\text{intended} \\
\text{unconscious}
\end{cases}
\end{cases} \\
\text{absences}
\end{cases}
$$

$$
\text{non-meanings}
\begin{cases}
\text{adjacent} \\
\text{non-adjacent}
\end{cases}
$$

STRUCTURE OF MEANINGS

This diagram shows the status and kinds of meanings for a given person or class of person at a given time. It is a relative schema, not an absolute one, as it applies to a given text. Brecht, for instance says he 'understood' his plays after reading Marx: in other words, meanings which previously were implicit and un-available to consciousness, became visible to him. It may also mean that he now noticed 'absences', meanings which at an earlier stage he was not just accidentally but intrinsically unable to produce: blind spots or shadows in the meaning of his plays. No doubt there would still be 'absences' which were unavailable to him even after he had read Marx. And though he does not mention it here, we can presume that certain experiences would help him to see some absences, or fail to see others.

The point of the schema is that it provides distinctions which help to organise the meanings hypothesised by a reader for a text, in terms of different levels of understanding of the author. With the help of these distinctions we can talk more precisely about what we suppose an author or his audience may have understood, as well as the ways in which we think the meanings were understood and how available they were as a basis for consciousness and action. The schema enables us to articulate more clearly the nature of the communication that might have occurred or failed to occur in any particular reading: as when an artist like Marlowe read a theorist like Machiavelli, or as when members of Elizabethan society might have read both Machiavelli and Marlowe.

What follows is a reading of one play, Marlowe's *The Jew of Malta*, seen as a possible reading of Machiavelli's *The Prince*, with this relationship being 'read' through the grid of Marx, which is itself of course a particular reading of Marx. The use of Marx should not suggest that this is an anti-historical reading, however. It is generally agreed that Marlowe read Machiavelli's work, in some form. But the all-important question remains: what did he make of that work? Marx can help us answer that crucial question if we can maintain the distinctions between the various works and their meanings within different periods for different people.

The words of Machiavelli's text survive, but it is clear that there are at least two different interpretations of that text. One was the conventional moralistic view, which saw him as a cynical purveyor of evil advice to rulers, advice which was scorned by the virtuous and God-fearing rulers of England. As a 'reading' of *The Prince*, this is biased and selective, but it is probably the set of meanings many Elizabethans derived from the text which they had read or heard about. We can call this treatise *Prince A*. But radicals could read him to very different effect. Here is Lillburne, one of the leaders of the Levellers, writing half a century later than Marlowe:

(Machiavelli) is one of the most judicious, and true lovers of his country, of Italy's liberties, and the good of all mankind that ever I read of in my days . . . who though he be commonly condemned . . . by all great state politicians . . . yet by me his books are esteemed for real usefulness in my straights to help me clearly to see through all the disguised deceits of my potent, politic . . . adversaries.[5]

Turning to Marlowe's play, there is one point where Machiavelli's name is clearly relevant. The prologue to the play is put into the mouth of 'Machevill'. This character presents the kind of parody of Machiavelli that I have labelled *Prince A:*

I count religion but a childish toy
And hold there is no sin but ignorance
(lines 14–15)

We can show that Machiavelli's text did not contain this meaning, since Machiavelli insisted many times that religion was not a 'childish toy' but a potent instrument of rule. The prologue is Marlowe's most explicit reference to Machiavelli. It seems to provide evidence that Marlowe 'read' *Prince A*. In fact, it has been known for a long time that Marlowe took most of the sentiments in the prologue from an epigram by Gabriel Harvey, a contemporary Cambridge academic of no great intellectual distinction.[6] So from this evidence, Marlowe might not even have read Machiavelli at first hand. Or the possibility exists that Marlowe did not write the prologue at all. A prologue is easy to add to a play. Heywood composed some specifically for his revival and edition of Marlowe's play, and might well have composed this one also. We see how unreliable the words of a text can be as the basis for judgment about how Marlowe read Machiavelli, and what meanings he saw in him.

But dramatists also communicate through the plot they create, and Marlowe can be taken to have 'meant' the implications of this plot, the generalisations that make sense of the events he describes. These generalisations are in total contrast to the statements contained in the prologue.

The play follows the career of Barabas, the Jew of the title, with a dispassionate eye for political reality and for the discrepancy between actions and words that could be seen as Machiavellian. The Jews in Malta are aliens, allowed to trade, but without political rights. Barabas is an extremely successful merchant. The play opens with him at the height of his economic power, shown in his counting room counting his wealth, and brooding about the prospects of more. But economic power is soon shown to be vulnerable on its own. Malta is subject to the Turks, who demand tribute. Fernese, the Christian governor of Malta, tries to raise the money by confiscating the property of the Jewish merchants: half their property if they give the money immediately, all of it if they protest. Barabas does protest, and loses everything except what he has hidden away. State power triumphs easily over mere wealth.

One major discrepancy between prologue and play lies in the identification of the play's Machiavel. The prologue announces Barabas as Machiavelli's disciple, but it is Fernese the governor who is the real Machiavellian prince. He is a consummate user of conventional pieties to cloak ruthless action on behalf of the state. For instance, after he has appropriated all Barabas's property, and left him without capital or even means of subsistence, Fernese says sanctimoniously

Be patient, and thy riches will increase.
Excess of wealth is cause of covetousness,
And covetousness, O, 'tis a monstrous sin!
(I. 2. 123)

Barabas bitterly exposes the hypocrisy here:

Aye, but theft is worse

and he labels it as 'policy', which to the Elizabethans was almost the same as 'Machiavellianism'. Barabas himself, though, is Machiavellian only in seeing so clearly what is going on. He is the helpless victim of this act of legal theft, not a prince.

But Barabas recovers from this early set-back, and nearly manages to become the ruler of Malta. He takes advantage of a division among the rulers. Fernese tries to win total control in Malta, and defies the Turks, who are led by Calymath, son of the Turkish Emperor. Barabas first betrays Malta, leading Calymath and his troops by a secret route into the fortress, where Fernese is overpowered. Calymath then offers Barabas the governorship of Malta: control of state power at last. But Barabas prefers wealth to political power, a decision that proves fatal. He tries to double-cross Calymath, making a deal with Fernese, but Fernese is too clever for him. Calymath is captured, and Barabas dies in the trap he himself had prepared for the Turk.

This sequence can be seen as a distinctively Machiavellian kind of analysis, a cool, objective study of the errors of rulers, judged purely by results. In the play, Barabas, Fernese, and Calymath are all potential rulers. All of them make mistakes which Machiavelli specifically discusses, and all suffer the consequences which Machiavelli predicted. Fernese is the closest to an exemplary prince, since he survives at the end in a more powerful position than he was at the beginning. He does make one serious mistake, however. He takes Barabas's property, but does not kill him (cf. *Prince,* chapter 17). Calymath makes two mistakes. He trusts Barabas, who owes him nothing (cf. chapter 3) and he separates himself from his own troops (cf. chapters 12, 14). Barabas makes a number of errors of judgment, climaxed by his misplaced faith in Fernese.

This far, the logic of events in the play corresponds very closely to Machiavelli's analysis of political reality. But some events in Marlowe's play require explanatory categories which are largely absent from Machiavelli. One such concept is ideology as false consciousness. Such a concept is an important 'invisible' in Machiavelli's work. His whole theory takes it for granted, yet he never deals with it directly. Religion and conventional morality in his account act as a kind of false consciousness, but only for the populace. Machiavelli sees clearly how it serves the interests of the rulers, but he does not begin to explain why it works so well. More interestingly, he keeps urging his aspiring Princes not to be taken in by conventional morality, as though he is afraid they might very easily lapse fatally into virtue, and become victims of their own ideology.

This is a real problem because his Prince is not as totally amoral and individualistic as is often supposed.

> So let a prince set about the task of conquering and maintaining his state; his methods will always be judged honourable, and will be universally praised.
>
> *(The Prince,* chapter 18)

The end here will justify the means, but the end itself is not simply individual gratification. The Prince must maintain 'his state'. Fernese, for instance, ruthlessly expropriated the Jews of

Malta, but he did so on behalf of 'Malta', or at least on behalf of the ruling class, not out of private self-interest alone. The successful Prince, according to Machiavelli, must rely on 'his own people' and 'his own arms'. What makes these 'his own' is never made clear but Machiavelli insists that it is important.

Marlowe's fullest study of how false consciousness works is contained in the figure of Barabas. Barabas fails in the end because he is psychologically not prepared to be a ruler. He has power within his grasp but renounces it, seemingly having forgotten that the word of a ruler is not to be trusted, so that the governor once re-instated will engage again in legal theft. But why does Barabas miscalculate so badly? The grounds of the miscalculation can be seen early in the play. In his second soliloquy (I. 1. 101) he sees himself as a Jew, a member of a 'scattered nation', and he takes pride in listing his great co-religionists. This is race-consciousness acting as a kind of class consciousness, since the Jews in Malta are also a distinct economic and social group. But he specifically renounces any ambition to rule:

Crowns come either by succession,
Or urged by force; and nothing violent,
Oft have I heard tell, can be permanent.
Give us peaceful rule, make Christians kings,
That thirst so much for principality.

(lines 133–7)

The basic distinction here corresponds to Machiavelli's initial distinction between hereditary principalities and new ones (chapter 1), with 'new' glossed by reference to the necessary use of force. But Barabas immediately opts out of princely aspirations by rejecting the use of force. His reason is highly conventional, in both form and content. 'Nothing violent/Oft have I heard tell, can be permanent'. The half-rhyme, 'violent/permanent', gives a jingling quality to the aphorism. Its source is explicitly conventional wisdom: 'oft have I heard tell'. That is, Marlowe makes Barabas give the source of the text he is producing: a conventional comment on a fragment of Machiavelli. *Prince A* is being used to define Barabas's limitations not Marlowe's own meanings. This conventional wisdom represents a failure of understanding, a failure which is contained in the contradiction of the single line: 'Give us peaceful rule, make Christians kings.' In the world of the play, Jews will never have peace while Christians are kings. The ambiguity of 'Give us peaceful rule' seems even to toy with the idea that Jews can, through their wealth, be the real rulers, while Christians fight it out for irrelevant crowns. But the play's action is based on the irreconcilable antagonism between Jews and Christians, which Barabas consistently underestimates, for all his outbursts of invective. And merely economic power proves to be of little use against state power controlled by the Christians.

There is, here, an important difference of emphasis between Machiavelli and Marlowe. Machiavelli notes a constant struggle between *i grandi*, the powerful noble families, and *i popoli*, the populace, in fact the middle classes since Machiavelli assumes they own property. The prince can be the creation of either class, but is more likely to be the defender of the populace (chapter 9). But class struggle was not at the centre of Machiavelli's analysis, as it was for Marx and Engels: 'The history of all hitherto existing society is the history of class struggles' *(Manifesto of the Communist Party)*. In Machiavelli, the class struggle seems like a background noise, constantly there but something that a prince must minimise. It would seem plausible in Machiavelli's account that a citizen should hope for 'peaceful rule', and remain safely obscure. So Barabas's wisdom is unprincely in Machiavelli's terms, but is a possible option. In Marlowe's play, class conflict cannot be ignored, and Barabas cannot opt out. On this point, Marlowe's text implicitly disagrees with both *Prince A* and *Prince B*.

Immediately after this soliloquy, three Jews enter, representatives of the Jewish community who clearly look to Barabas as their natural leader. Turkish galleys have been seen in the harbour, so they come to ask his advice about what this might mean. He gives an explanation which is deliberately and pointlessly misleading, as his asides and a following soliloquy show. So he imposes on them the illusion he has just imposed on himself, the illusion of 'peaceful rule', a conflict-free state:

> Fond men, what dream you of their multitudes?
> What need they treat of peace that are in league?

The Turks and those of Malta are in league:
Tut, tut, there is some other matter in't.
(lines 160–63)

In fact, the relation between Malta and Turkey is similar to that
between the Jews and the Christians in Malta. Malta pays tribute
to Turkey, and in order to meet this, Fernese will exact tribute
from the Jews. Barabas thinks that the Turks have deliberately let
the tax accumulate, so that they would have an excuse to seize
the lot. Fernese's plan is to find a pretext for doing the same to
Barabas. Barabas at this stage could not know how close the
analogy will be, but he certainly knows that he has tried to
mislead his compatriots, to lull them into the same false sense of
security that he has in relation to the Maltese establishment.

Barabas really has an ambiguous role here, as potential ruler
and as an egoistic individual incapable of rule. The duality is
conveyed starkly through his asides. For instance, he under-
takes to go to the Senate-house meeting to look after Jewish
interests:

If anything shall there concern our state,
Assure yourselves I'll look—unto myself *(Aside)*
(lines 175–6)

It is asides like this that have made some readers suppose that the
play is technically crude. But the aside here can be taken as more
than an expository device. It is a dramatic image of an essential
split in Barabas. 'Our state' is close to Machiavelli's *lo stato*, our
condition, our interests, and Barabas presents himself as the
Jews' prince. But the aside renounces this role in favour of crude
self-interest. The action of the play implies a double critique of
this simple egoism. In practice it proves poor policy. 'However
the world go, I'll make sure for one' Barabas hopes (189) but his
fate and that of the Jews, and Malta, are inextricably related. In
any case, Barabas psychologically cannot sustain pure egoism.
The sense of Jewish solidarity that he displayed in his exchange
with the three Jews was not merely a pose. In the next scene,
when Fernese announces his punitive new tax of half the goods of
all Jews, with total confiscation the penalty for anyone refusing,
the three Jews speak as one man:

> Oh my lord, we will give half!
>   (I. 2. 80)

Barabas seems to react spontaneously to this, in spite of himself:

> O earth-mettled villains, and no Hebrews born!
>   (line 81)

He repudiates his fellow Jews in the name of the Jewish race, even though it is financially disastrous to do so. He has been briefly betrayed into being a John Hampden to the Jewish community, trapped by his sense of racial solidarity into acting against his egoistic interests. Fernese immediately swoops, and Barabas tries to retract, but too late. Barabas has not been totally imprudent. He has hidden some of his stock against such an eventuality. But even so, his action involves him in considerable loss, and is heroic in its way. So he can justly rebuke his fellow Jews for their collective selfishness:

> Why did you yield to their extortion?
> You were a multitude, and I but one
>   (I. 2. 180–81)

If they had joined together to act in the interests of their class, they might have prevailed. In other terms we could say that they lacked sufficient class-consciousness. But the form of Barabas's criticism shows his fundamental egoism. He still thinks of himself as apart from the other members of his class—'I but one'. Marx's comments apply to Barabas's contradictory response: 'In their relations as a class the bourgeoisie act together, but in relation to each other their interests are opposed.' Barabas shows a version of this split. The Jews have a kind of herd-instinct which is very different from class consciousness. Their response to Barabas's criticism is a piety as glib as Fernese's:

> *First Jew:*   Yet, brother Barabas, remember Job
>   (line 183)

This is religion used crudely to reconcile a victim to his exploitation. Farnese's 'Be patient, and thy riches will increase' might have used Job as a text. The Jews have become the purveyors of ideology on behalf of their rulers, out of gratitude that they have not been totally dispossessed. Their piety is an attempt to neutralise Barabas's indignation, which has a disturbing impact on them, and it also cocoons them from thinking of themselves as victims too. Class consciousness must be the consciousness *of* a class. Neither Barabas nor his fellow Jews are capable of it.

So the relation between speech and aside in Barabas is not an opposition between what he says and what he thinks. He 'thinks' both: he sees himself as both Jew and isolated individual. Similarly, he can sometimes see through the dominant ideology and sometimes he is trapped by it. He is a brilliant study in confused consciousness, destroyed by forces that hardly enter into the Machiavellian analysis.

There is one feature of Marlowe's application of Machiavelli that counts as a radical change of terrain, in Althusser's sense. Machiavelli's analysis is purely political, and his primary classes are political classes, rulers and ruled. Marx stressed the importance of economic classes, which he termed the bourgeoisie, feudal landowners, and the proletariat. Marlowe's Jew is merchant-as-Machiavel. In Machiavelli's terms, this would be at best an analogy. In Marx's, it sets the phenomenon into proper focus. For him, a Jew and a merchant would represent a pure type of the bourgeoisie. Barabas's Jewishness is obviously Marlowe's way of representing the quintessential merchant. Here is Marx making the same connection.

> The practical Jewish spirit, Judaism or commerce, has maintained itself and even reached its highest development in Christian society . . . The Jew who is a particular member of civil society is only the particular appearance of the Judaism of civil society.
>
> *(On the Jewish Question)*

Fernese is not so clearly a member of the bourgeoisie, but the Malta he is governor of gets its wealth largely through trade. He is not as isolated as Barabas, but he, too, is a lonely figure. In the play he has no wife and no friends, only subordinates. He has one son, Lodowick, who is slain by Don Mathias, lover of Barabas's daughter Abigail, in a duel engineered by Barabas. His reaction to this death is curiously contrived and formal. Don Mathias is killed too, and both he and Lodowick are lying dead on the stage, when Fernese and Katherine, the mother of Mathias, enter together, and engage in a stiffly formal exchange of grief:

Kath. Lend me that weapon that did kill my son
         And it shall murder me
Fern. Nay Madam, stay: that weapon was my son's
         And on that rather should Fernese die

(III. 2.23)

But Katherine quickly turns her thoughts to revenge, and this seems to pacify her:

Kath. Hold; let's enquire the causers of their deaths,
         That we may venge their blood upon their heads.

Fernese is attracted by this double prospect of ratiocination and revenge, and he closes the scene with a pious couplet:

Come, Katherine, our losses equal are,
Then of true grief let us take equal share.

This all sounds utterly unlike 'true grief'. There are two possible judgments we could make on this. One is that Marlowe was, on this occasion, writing very stiff dialogue out of mere incompetence. Another possibility is that this stiffness is intentional, acting as a satiric comment on the inadequacies of Fernese and Katherine. Fernese's conclusion establishes a specious equation between their respective griefs. Katherine is comforted by all this, and so is Fernese, if he felt anything in the first place. His seemingly extravagant offer to die on his son's sword is in fact calculated to prevent any excessive response by Katherine. The form of reasoning that they both use is literally calculating. Katherine thinks that she should die on the sword because it killed her son. Fernese counters by pointing out that *he* should die on it (if anyone should) because it *belonged* to Lodowick, who belonged to him. Possession, owning a thing, a sword or a son, establishes a stronger motive and higher right. Katherine respects this principle too. She only asks to be 'lent' the sword. The calculating modes of thought seem incompatible with real feeling, yet there is no reason to think that Fernese is being insincere here. There is no other emotion that he 'really' feels: it is just that he is incapable of real feelings, or is unable to express them. He can only manipulate the conventions of grief, in order to achieve aims which are not unbenevolent, since he is comforting Katherine.

Machiavelli's prince is often seen as a kind of monster. The deformities of a Fernese are less dramatic, less remote from everyday life. Again, words from Marx and Engels articulate the implied criticism:

> The bourgeoisie, wherever it has got the upper hand, has put an end to all feudal, patriarchal, idyllic relations. It has pitilessly torn asunder the motley feudal ties that bound man to his 'natural superiors' and has left remaining no other nexus between man and man than naked self-interest, than callous 'cash payment' . . . The bourgeoisie has torn away from the family its sentimental veil, and has reduced the family relation to a mere money relation.
>
> *(Manifesto of the Communist Party)*

For Fernese and Katherine, the potentially rich world of social relations has been reduced to a system of commodities. They are not here engaged in selling children or friends, of course: the deformity lies deeper, in their inability to conceive or express genuine feelings about the most basic human relationships in any other currency.

What Marlowe seems to be doing here has the harsh economy of caricature. Barabas is studied in far greater depth, by a variety of methods, in an early study of what Marx called alienation. Sometimes Marlowe makes his points with powerful brevity, as with Barabas's famous cry:

> O girl! O gold! O beauty! O my bliss!
>
> (II. 1. 58)

This comes after Abigail has thrown him down his bags of gold, which he had concealed in his house to protect them from Fernese's edict. The main judgment implicit in this comes through the juxtaposition of 'girl' and 'gold', but the whole judgment is more complex. This can be seen by comparing Barabas's line with Shakespeare's re-use of the trick in his *Merchant of Venice*. Salanio repeats Shylock's cry of

> My daughter! O my ducats! O my daughter!

and describes this as

> a passion . . . so confused
> So strange, outrageous and so variable.

He sees the reaction as simply perverse and outrageous, a departure from a norm which Christian merchants (like Antonio) achieve easily enough, in which daughters are more important than ducats, or are not confused with ducats. Shylock is an aberration—for Salanio if not for Shakespeare.

Barabas's exclamation, however, hovers on the edge of being the proclamation of a new religion. For the Jew/Capitalist, in Marx's words:

> Money is the jealous god of Israel, before whom no other god can stand . . . Money is the universal, self-constituted value of all things. It has therefore robbed the whole world, human as well as natural, of its own values. Money is the alienated essence of man's work and being, this alien essence dominates him and he adores it.
>
> *(On the Jewish Question)*

Shylock conflated his daughter and his ducats, but at least his daughter won by two exclamations to one. In Barabas's exclamation, 'beauty' and 'bliss' are concentrated in the gold, so that aesthetic, erotic and religious impulses are given a momentary illusory satisfaction. The judgment on the deformity is far more disturbing because it is not a temporary 'confusion', the ravings of a distraught father, but the achieved transference of all value into the gold, intensely felt, insidiously attractive, an ideal which briefly feels almost valid.

Barabas himself is intermittently aware of how money has deprived his world of all value. While he is waiting for Abigail to appear at the window with the money, he paces anxiously outside the house, and in a soliloquy he realises his true condition, the loss of his humanity:

> Now I remember those old women's words,
> Who in my wealth would tell me winter's tales,
> And speak of spirits and ghosts that glide by night
> About the place where treasure hath been hid:
> And now methinks that I am one of those:
> For whilst I live, here lives my soul's sole hope,
> And, when I die, here shall my spirit walk.
>
> (II. 1. 24–30)

He sees himself as a ghost already, his obsession a kind of living death. He has drawn on popular wisdom again, but instead of accepting religious categories to distance social and psychological realities, he has reversed this movement, to achieve a measure of self-knowledge. This is the route that Feuerbach followed, according to Marx:

Feuerbach starts out from the fact of religious self-alienation, the duplication of the world into a religious one. His work consists in the dissolution of the religious world into its secular basis. He overlooks the fact that after completing this work, the chief thing still remains to be done.

(IVth Thesis on Feuerbach)

For Barabas too, the chief thing still remained to be done: and he only intermittently glimpsed the preliminaries. The point to make is not that he had full understanding, but that such understanding as he has is in its way extraordinary. In spite of his obsession, he is not so totally deformed that the pursuit of money really can satisfy him. The famous opening soliloquy, delivered 'in his wealth', while he was actually engaged in trying to count it all up, conveys the kinds of dissatisfaction that co-exist with his perverse delight in his wealth:

> The needy groom that never fingered groat
> Would make a miracle of thus much coin;
> But he whose steel-barred coffers are crammed full,
> And all his lifetime hath been tired,
> Wearying his fingers' ends with telling it,
> Would in his age be loth to labour so,
> And for a pound to sweat himself to death.
>
> (I. 1. 12–18)

'Thus much coin' is no longer a miracle for him. The spell is gone as soon as the money becomes physically real. 'Fingered groat' makes the action of counting seem grossly sensual and faintly disgusting. A sense of weariness, nausea and futility is inseparable from the fullest possible achievement of his aim, which turns out to be intrinsically self-defeating in the end (and this is the beginning of the play).

The syntax gives further insight into the dissipation of energies necessarily involved in his activity, implying important judgments on the quality of his consciousness. The subject 'he' is mimetically separated from its verb, the agent from any purposive action. In between come the 'steel-barred coffers crammed full', the packed stresses clogging the movement of the line, the coffers an image of constraint on fecundity, the 'cramming' an act of violence against container and contained. But the cramming is in the past. What follows is mere accountancy, tedious and wearisome. He acts now not directly on anything, but on himself, on his 'fingers' ends', which seem divorced from him, not quite part of himself. The complement of 'he', when it comes, is not an action but a disgust with action: 'Would in his age be loth to labour so'. Barabas is dimly aware that he is alienated from his own labour and from himself, that the money which he worships 'confronts him as an alien being', but he slides away from this insight, into his famous celebration of effortless wealth, sensuous and exotic and immensely potent, a world in which both workers and accountants disappear. His meditation ends in the magnificent image, 'Infinite riches in a little room'. The words blasphemously echo the birth of Christ, implying again the fusion of secular and religious value as his deity is incarnated in the form of a blank cheque.

Marlowe shows Barabas's capacity for basic human relationships to be stunted, yet he still has a residual humanity, which emerges in twisted and perverse forms. So although he can conflate Abigail and his money, and regard her as a commodity and as the means to other commodities, she is also as important to him personally as he claims. This does not make him a model of paternal affection, but nor is he merely prudent and calculating. In one brilliant scene, Marlowe explored the psychic consequences of the reduction of human relationships to a system of commodities. The main action of the scene is precisely that. Fernese's son Lodowick wants to marry Abigail, so he approaches Barabas for his permission. But the whole business proceeds indirectly. Abigail is never mentioned by name. The two men discuss her as though she were a diamond, and complete the transaction without either of them acknowledging that they are dealing in human trade. The wider context of this process is given by the background action. The scene opens with officers entering with slaves, and a slave-auction continues throughout in the background, as sardonic commentary on the main action. Marlowe makes the point about sexual relationships in a commodity society far more directly and brutally than Shakespeare was to do in *Lear,* two decades later. It is interesting that modern critics on Marlowe do not mention that this point is being made here, in spite of the savagely explicit form Marlowe has used.

But there is more than this going on in the scene. Barabas does not really intend to 'sell' his beloved daughter to the hated Christian, though he does mean to use her for his own purposes.

There is a split in consciousness here which is again represented dramatically through the device of the aside. The systematic ambiguity of the diamond-metaphor has split Abigail into the two aspects she has for Barabas, as person and commodity. His overt speech shows his complicity with the reductive process, while his asides reveal his complex reactions to this complicity.

It is Lodowick who initiates the diamond metaphor, having first crudely reminded Barabas of his superior rank: 'Barabas, thou knowst I am the governor's son'. Barabas's resentment of this is unmistakable but Lodowick chooses to ignore it:

> *Lod.* Well, Barabas, canst help me to a diamond?
> *Bara.* O, sir, your father had my diamonds.
> Yet I have one left that will serve your turn.
> *I mean my daugher; but, ere he shall have her,*
> *I'll sacrifice her on a pile of wood:*
> *I ha' the poison of the city for him,*
> *And the white leprosy* (Aside)
>
> (II. 3. 49–55)

'I mean my daughter' he begins, in the crudely expository fashion of a stock villain. But it was Lodowick who started the diamond-metaphor. Strictly Barabas should say '*he* means my daughter'. He has accepted the depersonalising metaphor from outside, from the hated Christian, accepting with it the role of mere agent in the sale of his daughter. So for him to say 'I mean' is an illusion, the illusion that he is in control of his meanings.

The aside allows him to express feelings of resentment and hostility that had to be suppressed from the surface of the exchange. Lodowick's arrogant insensitivity is sufficient reason for Barabas's virulence, but curiously, much of the hostility is deflected onto the innocent Abigail. 'Here he shall have her/I'll sacrifice her on a pile of wood' he swears, with irrelevant intensity. There is a similar irrelevance in his first mention of Abigail, in a soliloquy in Act 1. He holds her as dear, he claims

> As Agamemnon did his Iphigen
> (I. 1. 140)

But Agamemnon, too, sacrificed his daughter on a pile of wood. And later in the play, Abigail rejects him, becoming a Christian and a nun, carrying out in practice what he wanted her to pretend to do. Barabas's revenge is savage and indiscriminate. He poisons the whole nunnery, killing his own daughter as well. So although 'I ha' the poison of the city for him' seems directed at Lodowick, it is to be Abigail and her whole community who will receive poison in his revenge: and what Barabas strictly 'has' for Lodowick is Abigail. The connection between Abigail and poison is also hinted at in the final image, 'white leprosy'. Whiteness usually connotes the purity of Abigails and diamonds; here it stands for disease. And leprosy is the disease that makes a person untouchable—like Jews in an anti-Semitic state. Abigail's transformation into an object of barter, forced on Barabas but accepted as his own action, leaves feelings of resentment and disgust, which ought to be directed against the enemy but are attached illogically to her image. Barabas's most important human relationship has been literally poisoned.

Immediately after this exchange, Barabas buys a slave called Ithamore, thus himself treating another human as an object of barter. But again Barabas's motives are complex. He has a curious emotional dependence on this slave. He continually expresses a grotesquely exaggerated affection for him, which he will typically retract immediately in an aside, in which he promises a well-deserved revenge. This is the same ambivalence as he feels towards Abigail, but in a more incoherent form. Barabas even establishes Ithamore as his heir—for policy, he pretends, but the point of the policy is never clear. Ithamore acts as a bought child and lover, servant and friend. But Barabas's attempt to establish a bond by act of purchase is predictably hopeless. The cash-nexus breaks at a touch, and Barabas is left in helpless isolation, seeking to build a real human relationship out of the processes that have made him incapable of one. The object of his perverse affections finds his real affinities with a courtesan and a thief, low-life parasites on the fringes of Maltese society, degraded members of the lumpen proletariat, whose deformity however is not as total or crippling as that of Barabas. Ithamore betrays his master's secret to these two criminals, who proceed to blackmail Barabas. With enemies both above and below, Barabas's position is finally untenable.

Barabas and Fernese are members of the same class, and their different fates represent alternative verdicts on that class. Barabas is destroyed, unable to grasp power because of his egoism and complicity with ruling-class ideology. Fernese triumphs over both Barabas and Calymath, the ineffectual representative of the old order. In the person of Barabas, a bourgeois revolution seems disastrous but impossible: in Fernese, the disaster has already happened. The opposition between these two figures conflates two stages of history in the Marxist scheme, announcing and repudiating the victory of the bourgeoisie. For all the insight, the vision is deeply pessimistic, because the only alternatives we are given are Barabas, Fernese and Calymath. Marx could be more optimistic because in his own pious faith he looked forward to the ultimate victory of an emancipatory class, the 'proletariat', who have no separate existence in Machiavelli, and are present only in a degraded form in Marlowe.

This has been a reading, not a demonstration. A properly nuanced judgment would of course require more material in support. In fact similar preoccupations and insights can be seen to be implicit in other works of the period. Marx read a passage from Shakespeare's *Timon of Athens* as showing an understanding of the alienating role of money, equivalent to his own. L. C. Knights found a similar critique of a commodity society in Jonson, especially in *Volpone.*[7] Marlowe's concern with revolution and the political process began with his first play *Tamburlaine,* where a base-born Scythian shepherd rose to supreme power with an effortless ease that showed how facile Marlowe's political understanding was at that stage. With *Edward II* he undertook a serious study of the bases of political power and its human consequences. Shakespeare's history plays and his Roman plays continued that project, using Marlowe's plays as a major source of motifs, structures and ideas. So the kind of understanding that I have suggested is present in *The Jew of Malta* is not without analogues elsewhere in the period, though none of these works make identical statements.

However, even supposing that a substantial number of other words would also sustain such a reading, we are left with the problem of what consequences follow for our understanding of the age. In what way did Marlowe or his audience 'know' the meanings that can be derived from the play? We noticed the prologue, with its simplified version of Machiavelli. The play ends with Barabas falling into a cauldron that he himself had prepared for his enemies. This can be read as an image of hell fire guarded by devils, prepared for sinners. Quite a different treatise would be implied, a conventional Christian judgment on events, which is also implied by other sequences in the play. So the one text, like *The Prince,* generates two incompatible and antagonistic treatises, each a radical critique of the other, coexisting within the one text or battling for total possession of it. Marlowe ended the play as he did, giving traditional morality the last word. Does that mean that he could not really sustain a radical perspective? Or did he feel that it would have been too imprudent to leave it unambiguous? Or was he attracted by radical critique of society but ultimately rejected it as too one-sided and immature? Or—a different way of putting a similar judgment—that the end of the play was his capitulation, a betrayal of his insights, which involved a turning away from them and a conscious endorsement of conventional morality? The same problem arises with Shakespeare, whose texts often legitimate several contrary readings, and whose conclusions are more likely than the body of the play to seem to endorse the status quo.

In spite of these important uncertainties, however, such an analysis still allows us to make significant statements about the age. The implied treatises located in this reading go well beyond what was possible for a treatise as notoriously subversive as *The Prince.* Literary texts seemingly could carry far more radical contents than any treatise could at that period—perhaps because of the merely potential existence of such contents. Through a study of literature, then, we can project a kind of high water mark of potential consciousness, and also its mode of existence: how conscious it was and how available for action. Texts themselves become the meeting point for different treatises, different perspectives endorsed by different social groups, with the overt meanings generally corresponding to what the artist regarded as the views of the dominant group. The coexistence of these treatises in the one text mirrors social conflict, carried on in the plane of ideas. Marlowe's judgment as to what was sayable reflects his sense of the power of the upholders of conventional morality. His capacity for understanding is another matter. But if the continuities projected between Marlowe and Marx are valid, it would suggest the possibility of a radical tradition stretching further back into the past than many intellectual historians, Marxists and others, have supposed.

2

'Darke Texts Needs Notes': Versions of Self in Donne's Verse Epistles

DAVID AERS and GUNTHER KRESS

Donne's verse epistles have not received much notice from the awesome critical industry centred on his work. Any explanation of this surprising fact might make reference to an assumed lack of poetic richness in these poems, the assumption that patronage poetry is too conventional to merit serious critical attention, and perhaps even some embarrassment at a deification of living patronesses.[1] But we believe that the most significant factor is unrecognised: namely the lack of a descriptive and theoretical framework within which the real interest of these poems can be perceived and analysed. In this chapter we attempt to establish such a framework and carry out an analysis which will locate, describe, and account for versions of the self emerging within these verse letters. In the course of our critical inquiry we shall build on John Danby's hints about the explicitly social basis of so much that seems, on first sight, to be purely metaphysical speculation.[2] We hope to develop an approach which, through its very attention to the minute movements of a particular text, reveals how these become intelligible only when inserted in a wider context which includes the writer's precise social situation.

In 1608 Donne wrote a poem beginning, 'You have refin'd mee', a verse epistle to his new patroness Lucy, Countess of Bedford, in what seems to have been the most personally testing period of his life.[3] Although Donne himself includes the comment that 'darke texts need notes', his editors and critics do not seem to have found this a particularly interesting poem. However, we think it both demands and rewards scrutiny. These are the first two stanzas:

> MADAME,
> You have refin'd mee, and to worthyest things
>   (Vertue, Art, Beauty, Fortune,) now I see
> Rarenesse, or use, not nature value brings;
> And such, as they are circumstanc'd, they bee.
>   Two ills can ne're perplexe us, sinne to'excuse;
>   But of two good things, we may leave and chuse.
>
> Therefore at Court, which is not vertues clime,
>   (Where a transcendent height, (as, lownesse mee)
> Makes her not be, or not show) all my rime
> Your vertues challenge, which there rarest bee;
>   For, as darke texts need notes: there some must bee
>   To usher vertue, and say, *This is shee*.[4]

Editorial glosses on these stanzas treat them as fairly unproblematic. Grierson finds Donne's introduction of himself in 'as, lownesse mee' (stanza two), 'quite irrelevant' (and is more unsettled than Milgate), yet he assumes that he has solved any minor enigmas, and the lines seem not to need extended commentary.[5] However, there are important and unresolved tensions in these lines. The countess is alchemist, a near creator (as lines 21–22 of the poem make explicit) through whose agency the poet can now perceive things as they *really* are. This sets up a dichotomy between things as he perceives them now and things as he perceived them before. *Now* he sees that value is the product of contingent social relationships. Already there may be hints, which are clarified later in the poem, that value, being generated by rareness or use, is an aspect of market transactions. Even seemingly transcendent, platonic forms, Vertue, Art, Beauty, 'worthyest things' indeed, get their worth in this way and so have to be placed in the same category as the thoroughly contingent sub-lunar abstraction, Fortune. But before his 'refinement' the poet had assumed, in good idealist (platonic or stoic) fashion, that value transcended the contingent placings of social practice; he had assumed that value was a reflection of the object or person's intrinsic nature—that, in his own words, 'nature value brings'.

Such relativising attitudes, which are of course quite appropriate to a 'market-society', may not surprise readers today. But when we recall that the poem is addressed to Lucy, and that Donne is overtly talking about her, the worthiest thing whom he is both worshipping and elegantly asking for patronage, it is, at the very least, a strange and rather risky compliment. After all, the poem implies that she is not inherently valuable, that her worthiness is a product of contingent social circumstances, and that her refining has given him perceptions of this kind. (The second stanza is connected to the first by the logical connector 'Therefore', thus removing any lingering doubts that the first stanza is also about Lucy.) The countess's value as one of the 'worthyest things' paradoxically *depends* on her being 'circumstanc'd' in a social situation where her attributes (virtues, it so happens) are most valuable precisely because they are rare, the court rather conspicuously not being the 'clime' of virtue.

This does have a rationale and can be resolved once we see the structure of Donne's argument. He is actually working with a model which assumes the existence of two worlds or 'climes'. One is a platonic clime in which Lucy exists with platonic forms, and which her usher-exegete has knowledge of. (This world of essences transcends all contingency and relativity, and so supersedes all notions of value deployed by social man.) A second clime is the present historical world, the world of the court, of Mitcham and of Donne's frustrated daily existence, a world where value is a function of contingent market relations, supply and demand, mere 'circumstance'. It is in this second world that the countess is 'worthyest', most valuable, and it is here that Donne so desperately wishes to find employment as the official usher of the valued one. His role is to introduce the myopic courtiers to the rare (and useful?) worthy one. In this he himself gains value as the indispensable spectacles through which courtiers can perceive the rare and hidden riches of that dark text, Lucy. The 'alienated intellectual' overcomes his alienation, finds community, wins employment and use as an essential mediator between the two climes.[6] However, Donne fails to show us why the lower climes should value virtue, why this particular rare commodity should be desired by courtiers at all. The unexamined gap in his argument here is simply leapt over as he assumes, optimistically, that the second clime must find use and market value for representatives of the higher world.

Donne does not resolve the paradox in the way we have been doing, but wisely leaves it in its highly compressed form, with only hints that the very absence of virtue at the court makes the countess 'worthyest' and endows both her and her usher-exegete with value. It is understandable enough that Donne should not have wanted to express these views in such plain form, so we already have sound reasons for his wish to darken the text. Of course Donne need not have introduced the double-edged paradoxical compliment to the countess, and could have avoided the danger of relativising the countess's virtue. But this would not have permitted him to introduce the important self-reference, so well worked into a complex image of the relations between poet, patroness, society and ethical idealism. Here we have a non-trivial explanation for his desire to keep the text dark, one which offers an account of verbal processes and of relevant social and psychological motivations.

We mentioned the significant degree of self-reference in the poem; this invites some further consideration, especially in the light of Donne's 'egocentricity', widely commented on by critics.[7] The expression of this egocentricity is inevitably more complex here than in many of the *Songs and Sonnets,* where the poet-lover focuses on himself and his relations with a lover. This poem, however, is focused on the patroness, and since he delicately seeks patronage the relationship is one which needs most careful handling; not the time, one would think, for an overt display of egocentricity. And yet the poem begins with a reference to himself. It certainly bestows credit on the countess—she, as alchemist, has succeeded in refining him. But the image turns Donne into the central object of attention, just as the alchemist's attention focuses on the materials he desires to transform. And as the success of the alchemist is defined by his success in refining the material, so the countess's success is defined in terms of her effectiveness in working on the present material, the poet. Thus at the very opening of the poem the overt focus on the patroness has been inverted and become part of a rather complicated self-referring process. Lines two and eight (the self-mentioning, which Grierson found 'irrelevant') again refer to him; so do lines nine, eleven and twelve. Without doubt there is a large enough amount of self-reference in the opening stanzas at least to attract one's curiosity.

In addition there are some peculiarities of reference, predominantly in the pronouns. Line one contains the two pronouns, 'you' and 'mee': in the same line there is the 'pronoun' 'worthyest things'. Its reference is ambiguous: Donne has just been refined, so that one possible reference is 'mee'. If he is included in the category of 'worthyest things', then he belongs to the same class as Lucy ('you'), another possible referent of this phrase. 'Worthyest things' is plural in number, and so it can indeed refer to both Lucy and the poet. Presumably Donne intended the reference to be ambiguous; at any rate it is not immediately clear, and in searching for an appropriate and permitted referent, the reference to the poet will arise and need to be assessed, and decided on. The fact that in the next line Donne glosses 'worthyest things' as 'Vertue, Art, Beauty, Fortune' shows that he acknowledged the need to provide a gloss. As we pointed out above, this list collapses platonic categories into the social and contingent clime of 'Fortune', relativising and undercutting the platonic model. By the time we reach the end of the second line 'worthyest things' has accumulated a wide range of possible references: 'you', 'mee', 'you and mee', 'Vertue, Art, Beauty, Fortune'. All of these lead into 'Fortune' and are placed in the same category as Fortune, so that the relativising tendency has become thoroughly pervasive.

The fourth line of the poem continues to draw on this multiple ambiguity: 'And such, as they are circumstanc'd, they bee'. Here 'they' may refer to all the referents mentioned. Another pronoun, 'such', is introduced. It in turn may refer to all three and to 'they'; or it may pick up just one of these. If the latter, then we at least the following readings: (1) Lucy (such → worthiest things → You), the countess, such as she is circumstanced so she is—as she is placed in the contingent social market of fortune, so she is valued, worthiest. (2) Donne (such → worthiest thing → me → refined), the poet, such as he is circumstanced so he is—as he is placed in Lucy's platonic world, as a new creature, so he is valued, worthiest. As he is placed in the contingent social market, so he is valued, as nothing. His appeal to Lucy is therefore that she should 'translate' his worth in her platonic world, into a recognised use and hence value in the market, in the appropriate place; as an indispensable usher. The countess is well able to do this. So the reading as it stands is: I, as I am circumstanced so I am, as I am *now* placed in the social market of fortune so I am currently valued—as nothing.[8] At this point the paradox, deploying the model of two climes, functions to give line four another, Donne's real, though covert, reading: I am (not as I *am,* but) as I am *circumstanced.* The paradox enables Donne to present simultaneously two versions of the self here: one, the platonic one covertly (I am as I am regardless of social valuation and placing); the other, the one constructed according to market values overtly (I am as I am circumstanced). He puts one against the other in a most complex and rather disturbing form, and asks Lucy to realise his worth in one 'clime', the platonic, as 'value through use' in the other 'clime', that of contingent social situation and of fortune.

On the surface the statement is of course less complicated: the countess has refined him and now he sees that either rareness or use (being used by or of use to someone) brings value. It is precisely the patronage relationship which makes the poet useful to someone who can use him, and therefore valuable. Until he is used his identity is bestowed by his circumstances and, through no fault of his, or of nature, he is circumstanced such that he has no value.

Stanza two now becomes clearer. It refers to the countess but it also refers to Donne. At court he does not appear (either he is physically absent through having no position, or, if there, is not noticed) because he currently has no value. He places himself in a revealing structural relationship with the countess: her value does not appear at court owing to transcendent height, while his does not appear at court owing to *lownesse.* So the structural opposition links him firmly with her, in a link which comes close to an equation. This provides a perfect explanation for the difficulty Grierson recorded, and indeed it would be most odd if such a phrase appeared in one of Donne's patronage poems without precise significance and motivation. The concluding couplet gives us a final confirmation: this is about her and about him. She is the 'darke text' (as is the poem, as is his motivation) and 'darke texts need notes'.

We should ask what or whose need this is. As we noticed earlier, it is most obviously a need of the potential audience of the text, the benighted courtiers. It is also the countess's need; she who is the 'darke text' needs to be explicated if she is to be truly valued in the lower 'clime'. She needs an exegete, like Donne. Lastly, it is Donne's need: exegetes need 'darke texts', and above all Donne needs to be an exegete, he needs to be of specific use to the countess and the community. Just as the 'need' has to be explained, so too with the 'must' in the same line. 'Some must bee' refers to the exegete, implicitly Donne himself, so that this 'must bee' seemingly has the force of an existential imperative, and it echoes the 'not be' of line nine. That 'not be' takes in both Lucy and Donne; how does the non-existent poet of line nine come into existence as the necessary exegete-usher of line eleven? By being employed: and this employment not only brings him into existence, creates him indeed (as lines 21–2 make explicit),[9] but also brings the countess's virtue into the social world, thus indirectly giving her existence and, as we saw earlier, value. This is an astonishingly delicate combination of begging and self-assertion, and the relations hinted at are very complex.[10] Donne is the created creature, she the creator; he low, she high; he patronised, she patron; he exegete, she dark text; he usher, she virtue; he excluded, she included. Yet she too is excluded until he realises her social potential and value for her. Structurally Lucy and Donne are opposed and yet equated, transforms of each other creating each other from shared invisibility into apparent existence and social value.

We have by now accounted for the text's darkness. It lies in the double-layered model Donne uses to understand his complex relationship with the patroness and their mutual relations to the social world and to value. But we need to go further. On this level the explanation has entailed an account of the supplicant's perception of himself, and we now wish to explore this perception in more depth. We have made clear the way the first two stanzas offer distinct and contrasting versions of the self. To recapitulate.

One version of self refers an autonomous self to inherent values which would doubtless be recognised in a platonic utopia or by stoic and platonic individuals who have detached themselves from existing societies and are strong enough to pursue a Crusoe-like existence (without dog or man Friday of course). The other version of self sees it as socially constructed and dependent, either through equal relationships (as those between friends) or through the social relations of the market based on rareness, use and contingency. It is not difficult to believe that Donne could see these two versions of the self as competing and contradictory. But then, it is also plausible to see them as complementary, so that only those who do have inherent worth, participating in the platonic forms, *ought* to be usable, find employment and value. Such, however, is obviously not the case in the world which Donne strove so hard to convince about his marketable potential and use. For Donne these competing versions of self-identity became highly problematic and a constant, often agonised, preoccupation, in the period before his ordination.

The two stanzas with which we opened our discussion are thus legitimately seen as explorations of the self. The question of the poet's consciousness of this exploration is one which we have not treated here. Nor do we exclude a range of other possible readings of these stanzas, or for the rest of the patronage poems. But we are suggesting that this reading goes to the heart of these poems and points up their place in Donne's central preoccupations and problems. We believe these neglected poems have much to teach us about these preoccupations and the poetic and intellectual strategies with which Donne confronted them.[11]

The double version of self certainly connects most of the verse epistles, for they are attempts to work out self-identity, polarising or clustering around one or other of these two basic stances. Above all, it invites us to link abstract metaphysical problems with the concrete reality and pressures of the poet's existence.

One important feature that we have touched on in our depiction of the versions of the self in 'You have refin'd mee' can now be brought into prominence. We noted that in presenting contrary versions of self-identity and evaluation Donne envisaged his own level of being in a necessarily equivocal way. He does exist in some mode, but he needs refining, and even creation, by a patroness-alchemist; he does not exist or is not visible (lines 7–12) at court, yet he, or some, 'must bee To usher vertue'. Later in the poem he defines himself as one of Lucy's 'new creatures', part of a 'new world' created by her (lines 21–2). In other poems to patronesses this tendency becomes an overt assertion by Donne: that he is nothing. In 'T'have written then' he says (again to the Countess of Bedford), *'nothings,* as I am, may/Pay all they have, and yet have all to pay' (lines 7–8). Of course, line seven is paradoxical: the 'am' asserts existence, 'I am'; and syntactically the verb *to be* functions to relate entities to other entities or to qualities. That second function is prominent here: the classification of an individual, though he exists, as *a nothing.* Classifications are culturally and socially given, conventional and subject to historical change. But for an individual they tend to assume the force of external, changeless forms. This is particularly so as the syntactic form X is Y is used to make classifications which are established by changing cultures and conventions (e.g. 'I am a ratepayer'), as well as those relating to the impersonal, natural order (e.g. 'The sun is a star'). In this way language blurs the distinction between the two kinds of statements and their reality-status. But over and above that, any member of a society is socialised into sets of value systems which become 'reality'. In other words, if we look at Donne's 'actual' situation, even at this, his worst time, we cannot by any stretch of the imagination see him as nothing: a reasonably comfortable house in Mitcham, one or two servants, frequent trips to London, to influential friends who remain loyal and help in a host of ways, access to books, writing poetry which has an appreciative audience, no hunger . . . To the landless labourer in Mitcham Donne would have seemed the opposite of 'nothing'. But this only confirms the strength of the conventionally given perception, which meant in Donne's case that not being of the court group was not being at all. For Donne therefore these lines do not have the force of paradox: *being* is defined in terms of membership of the group to which he aspires: creation is therefore a social act, the act of admitting, drawing in the individual to the group.

Nevertheless, no sooner has Donne offered a negative version of self reflecting his present social situation than he proposes a contrary version of the self as having a transcendental and valuable identity:

> Yet since rich mines in barren grounds are showne
> May not I yeeld (not gold) but coale or stone?
>
> (lines 11–12)

Donne is certainly barren ground at the moment, in so far as he is anything at all. Yet in the same breath he *assumes* that he is also a rich mine. This draws, precisely in the ways we have shown before, on the versions of the self as having intrinsic value, whatever the social market value. But the image is most subtly chosen, for it also informs the patron of the self's potential market value, however hidden that may be. The intrinsically valuable platonic, private and independent self turns out to be as much the property of the patron as the public social self. In specifying the kind of rich mine (line 12) it may be that Donne loses confidence, moving from coal to stone. But whatever the exact market value, this hidden self is certainly cashable. Indeed, he suggests the most valuable kind of mine: a gold mine (negation being the permissible way of articulating the nearly forbidden). Still, however high his self-estimation, however much he feels he has a self beyond the *nothing* which he is socially, the clash between secret hidden core and apparent social identity forces him to invoke an external agent to strip away this surface (where before it was to burn away impurities), to dig up the riches, so that he may 'yeeld' the riches to someone else. Syntactically *yield* always occurs in forms such as '*yielded* something for/to someone', where the *someone* is never *I*. Thus the image and the syntax are tied absolutely into *use*, commerce and markets. The social creator is revealed as a potential and willing social user and exploiter, while creation turns out to be the discovery of market value in the human being. Conversely, the sense of nothingness, negation, has a social origin—namely the absence of such exploitive use. Again, the metaphysics of annihilation, of being and of nothingness, the fundamental questions of identity raised in these poems, find very tangible social explanation.

'Creation' becomes a specific term here, meaning admission to the desired social group. Some present members of such groups had membership from the beginning and did not need creation. But the process is a general one and may apply to any individual at any social level in relation to any coveted group. The only exception to this is the king—hardly surprising in the time of James I, Donne's ultimate patron—who proclaimed that kings 'are not onely Gods Lieutenants vpon earth, and sit vpon Gods throne, but even by God himselfe they are called Gods'.[12] In the poem 'To Sir H.W. at his going Ambassador to *Venice*', the king fulfils the role of creator for Wotton:

> And (how he may) makes you almost the same,
> A Taper of his Torch, a copie writ
> From his originall . . .
>   (lines 4–6)

This view of the individual and society encourages one to ask whether it was a common mode of perception at that time, or especially found in any specific group; or whether, for example, Donne's origins in an institutionally excluded group—the community of Roman Catholics—disposed him to view self in this way. Much more work on the lines we are suggesting will be necessary before satisfactory answers can be given.

The source of the creator's credentials could become problematic for anyone who is not totally content to accept the social order and the processes maintaining it. This is in fact a constant concern in the epistles, and is the obverse of his anxiety about his own lack of being, his own lack of credentials. In the light of this consideration, lines such as these from the opening of 'You have refin'd mee' take on a peculiarly bitter and ironic tone:

>   now I see
> Rareness, or use, not nature value brings;
> And such, as they are circumstanc'd, they bee.

It is the removal of his blindness which makes him see this unpalatable truth; the countess is indeed creator, though not because of her inherent virtues or nature but because this is how she happens to be circumstanced. The removal of his own blindness makes him see the more massive blindness of the social system to which he seeks admission. Donne's reiteration of the theme that the countess's virtue might go unrecognised (and so her value diminish) except for his good offices takes on a somewhat darker note in this context; Donne covertly assumes for himself the role of creator. The situation is complex enough for Donne to see himself as nothing, as inherently valuable, and possibly as creator, all simultaneously. All these involved shifts are firmly related to a highly specific set of social relationships. Discussions which perpetually divorce the literary language, the psychological, and the social, will inevitably introduce grave distortions and prove limiting in disabling ways.

We have space to glance at only one more patroness poem, 'To the Countess of Salisbury' in 1614. The first half of this poem ('Faire, great, and good') uses material from 'A nocturnall upon S. Lucies day' and the two Anniversaries for Elizabeth Drury. Donne argues that 'all is withered, shrunke, and dri'd/All Vertues ebb'd out to a dead low tyde', with all striving for universal annihilation, 'to draw to lesse,/even that nothing, which at first we were' (lines 1–21). In this state the patroness, like the Countess of Bedford or Elizabeth Drury, is the female creative deity: 'you come to repaire/Gods booke of creatures' (lines 7–8).[13] And as we saw in 'You have refin'd mee', however much Donne may negate his being in response to the social situation, he simultaneously presents himself as an intrinsically valuable self, as her seer and exegete (lines 31–6, 65–74). Yet, once more, this stage is superseded as he acknowledges that it is the countess herself who (like God here too) illuminates the dark text he is able to study. The poem concludes with a similar movement worked out in terms of a socially given blindness (lines 75–84) which is contrasted with an intuitive angel-like vision, transcending the lack of 'social eyes' through inner illumination. Characteristically, Donne does not leave the matter there. Just as the angelic intuition is actually dependent on a higher power, so Donne's illumination depends on a higher power—the Countess of Salisbury—within the profane, social world (lines 71–4, 79–82).[14] Again Donne uses metaphysical language and imagery to mediate and transform specific social relationships. To understand and describe this process is not reductive of Donne's art or his metaphysical strategems: quite the reverse, we follow the full implications and subtlety of the art and metaphysics Donne is using to manage, under grave difficulties, the social situation which was central to his psychic, intellectual and poetic development.

One way of grasping Donne's situation is in the terms proposed by Mark Curtis and Michael Walzer in their studies of intellectuals and their employment in Donne's England. Both historians point out that during the early Stuart period a group of intellectually trained people was unable to find a 'place' either in the church (on which both concentrate) or in the state. Walzer and Curtis see them as 'alienated' from the society's leading groups, to which they felt they had a right to belong. The origins of the exclusion were complex, due in part to an overproduction of graduates, in part to continued pluralism and non-residency which decreased the number of livings for those leaving university, and in part to disadvantageous changes in the patterns of patronage. The subject needs detailed study, though it seems clear that this group was large in terms of the total number of intellectuals in the community. Curtis sees them as 'an insoluble group of alienated intellectuals who individually and collectively became troublemakers in a period of growing discontent with the Stuart regime'.[15] Puritan leaderships offered one important oppositional institution for at least some members of this group, but Curtis presents them as essentially isolated in their alienation, though they did 'exhibit an *esprit de corps* that both originated in their peculiar specialised function and marked their self-conscious alienation from the rest of the clergy'.[16] Here Walzer's study differs seriously from Curtis's. He agrees that this group bred 'troublemakers' who were absolutely central in the development of radical politics in Stuart England, but he sees these 'advanced intellectuals', these 'free men', as specifically *Puritan* intellectuals, men 'capable of organising themselves voluntarily on the basis of ideological commitment', men committed to 'enthusiastic and purposive activity' in new associations *outside* the traditional patterns, ties and institutions of Elizabethan England.[17] In his *The Revolution of the Saints* he offers an acute and nuanced account of the wider group of 'alienated intellectuals', providing essential ideological and psychological discriminations which allow deeper insight into the varied processes and causes of this alienation and radicalisation. Walzer's richer model allows us to understand the position of Roman Catholic clerics and intellectuals—a very necessary factor when one is concerned with Donne, a member of a Romanist family which included martyrs. Catholics were estranged from the established institutions, just as the saints were, and Walzer notes 'significant parallels' between the two groups of alienated clerics: 'the priests had taken the lead in the Catholic struggle and their new power—somewhat like that of the Puritan clergy—was related to the collapse of the traditional lay leadership. Among the Catholic clerics the Jesuits especially resembled the Puritan ministers both in their impatience with episcopal control and their willingness to experiment politically.' But, and in Walzer's view this is vital, the Catholic experience was not formed by a radical ideology, for they were 'closely bound to the traditional social order and were most often willing to work within the limits of the feudal connection of lord and chaplain. The ultimate effect of their labour was to create a pariah culture, an enclave of secure traditionalism.' This formed a strong contrast to Calvinist intellectuals who depersonalised and objectified social and ideological conflicts and tended towards organisation 'outside the traditional structure of authority, placing less emphasis upon great personalities'.[18]

If we look at Donne in this light, certain of the complex, contradictory features which we have been highlighting become more intelligible. As Walzer's work illustrates so well, the processes which lead to the formation of such specific groupings inevitably mark the individuals involved psychologically and ideologically.[19] Donne, in this period, provides a classic example of an excluded intellectual. Structurally, he *started* from an excluded position as a Roman Catholic, a member of a group exiled from the political nation. This initial exclusion was not based on the kind of self-consciously acquired and held ideological commitment which Walzer described in Calvinist intellectuals. Quite the contrary, he was born into this situation, so that his struggle from the very beginning was to overcome an exclusion forced on him by an inherited ideological position for which he seems to have shown very little conviction.[20] His aim was *incorporation,* not opposition to established church, court and state. In gaining employment with Egerton he seemed to have succeeded, and could look forward to a secure career within traditional institutions. However, his secret marriage to a social superior led to a new exile. Again the exile was not based on ideological commitment, so that even that sustaining force was not available to him.

Thrown back into the position of the alienated intellectual,

Donne's feelings and ideas were complex, as we have seen in our discussion of the patroness poems. There he explored the new position in which he found himself; indeed, he constructed a complicated metaphysics in which a platonic model of eternal value was set off against a market model of use. Donne's critical attitude to the world which excluded him, and his self-estimation were bound up with the former model; yet he clearly wanted a place in the market and so had to assert his use as a secular servant, as usher/ideologue. Hence in his version of self the subtle sycophant[21] was always accompanied by the critical 'troublemaker' who deployed the platonic model subversively against the values of the leading social groups into which he longed to be incorporated. Whereas the Puritan alienated intellectuals developed an ideology exalting their alienation, which they saw as a kind of freedom, and which enabled them to organise against the powerful established groups excluding them, Donne had no such sustaining ideological support, and hence could not see his exclusion as 'freedom'. All his efforts were directed towards inclusion in the traditional established group. While his use of the platonic model helped him to cope with the despair of his exile, and thus worked analogously to the Puritan intellectual's view of 'freedom', it was never intended as a programme for social change: Donne wanted inclusion in the securely established traditional order, and in this he was therefore not all that far from the political tendencies of the Roman priests.

We now have a dual model of alienation: on the one hand the radical 'free man', with an ideologically buttressed programme for social change, on the other hand the sycophantic seeker for admission to a securely established traditional order. We have shown some of the forces which lead to either position. We now need to ask whether those who belong to either group show any traces of the other position. In terms of our methodology and hypothesis we need to look at the poetry of those who had gained admission to see if there are signs of alienation. Of course some of Donne's earlier poems will do here, and in fact some of his 'stoic' poems which we discuss below, are an excellent case in point, as some of these were written while he was with Egerton. We intend to show that they offer a social critique, but an unconvincing one, with the ring of a rote performance to them, as though it was the fashionable 'thing to say' among a group of people. If this is so,

then we have an example of people who are included, but who
nevertheless deplore what Curtis described as 'galloping venality
and creeping monopoly [which] had combined to poison the
sources of patronage. They were not only distasteful but fre-
quently revolting to some well-intentioned, prospective servants
of the State. Complaints about the Court and the indignities of
waiting on patrons and winning influence . . . took on in these
years overtones of disillusionment and even disgust that formerly
had been less obvious.'[22] Curtis places this in the reign of James I,
and clearly this is too late; furthermore we should note that not
just prospective but some actual servants of the state found these
things unsavoury. So one question that arises from Curtis's
remarks, and which relates very closely to our analysis of
Donne's position, is whether the attainment of a place did in fact
overcome and do away with the indignities of the situation at
court or in patronage.

Donne's early stoic poems suggest that it did not. Other
evidence is provided by such apparently untroubled work as
Jonson's *To Penshurst*. We do not have the space here for a
detailed analysis, but a brief look at the negations in the poem will
quickly reveal disturbances beneath the seemingly untroubled
classical surface. The negations permit Jonson to call up—in
denied form—the positive forms of assertions which it would be
difficult, prohibited or even dangerous for him to make. He uses
two types of negation, overt negation—forms with *not, no, un-;*
and covert negations—forms which have a semantically negative
content: 'these *grudg'd* at'; and forms which work by 'replacing'
a form which should or might have been more appropriate. The
negations cluster around four topics: the history of the house, the
present state of the house, the position of the patronised poet,
and the place and function of this house in relation to others like
it. We will give some illustrative quotations, and indicate in
outline how the negations work. First then the history of the
house. Line 1: 'Thou are not, Penshurst, built to envious
show'—where a past action (the building of the house) is presented as a present state (the judgment about the house), and that
present state is contrasted with that of all other houses; line 6:
'these grudg'd at [thou] art reverenc'd the while'—the denial of
that general rule applies in this case; lines 45–7: 'thy walls . . . are
rear'd with no mans ruine, no mans grone,/There's none, that

dwell about them, wish them downe';—here again we find the overt negation of a state that applies to all other houses and, more tellingly, a straightforward rewriting of the history of the house, which, according to Raymond Williams, *was* built on the ruins of an enclosed village.[23] This is a revealing insight into the use of negation: a troubling reality which the poet wishes, somehow, to control and to transcend, and which surfaces in the form of the negation of that reality. The negations surrounding the present state of the house concern, as Williams again has pointed out, the complete transformation of social and human processes into natural ones. This process is perhaps best described as negation by transformation; human agents, human labour, social relations are presented instead as thoroughly and unquestionably natural ones. The major examples of this are in those passages where nature of itself, unasked, provides its riches for the house; natural entities act as agents providing for the depersonalised house. Two examples will show the process—lines 19–20: 'Thy copp's . . . never failes to serve thee season'd deere.'; line 24: 'The middle ground thy mares, and horses breed'. In fact this process extends to the production of exotic fruits: fig, grape, peach, apricot grow without any human effort.

The situation of the patronised poet is shown mainly in terms of negatives: this serves to call up what may be regarded as the normal situation, one in which a nervousness regarding the poet's own situation also shows—

Where the same beere, and bread, and self-same wine,
That is his Lordships, shall be also mine.
And I not faine to sit (as some, this day,
At great mens tables) and yet dine away.
Here no man tells my cups; nor, standing by,
A waiter, doth my gluttony envy:
But gives me what I call, and lets me eate . . .

(lines 63–9)

This passage calls up starkly and vividly the humiliation of situations which Jonson must have known and, judging by the immediacy of the language, felt himself. Last but not least there is the negation, implicit in this text, of all those poems that could and should have been written about the reality of the country house period. The prohibition on that, however, was so strong as to amount to total self-censorship by any poet who wanted patronage.

We are forced to ask about this intellectual, who in Curtis's terms is *not* alienated, is he undisturbed, untroubled? What is his motive for his production of a patronage poem, a poem which involves such a massive re-ordering and reclassification of the social world, and of known history? Is not the act of producing a poem as a commodity to be exchanged for the 'lord's own meate . . .' the very sign of alienation? Not now, of course, alienation in the sense of Curtis and Walzer, but in that classic sense where the producer sells his labour-power as a commodity to a master who unilaterally determines in what commodity his labour-power shall be manifested.[24] Of course, this is the situation, within the marxist model, of all labour until the coming of the socialist millenium; however, it is the starkly apparent application and working of this model in the sphere of poetry which we find revealing here; and it may be both useful and necessary to add this notion of alienation to the dual model outlined above.

Donne sees the patronage situation in this way, at least in part. In his quest for incorporation he reluctantly accepts the necessity of turning himself, his abilities, and certain of his poems which are overt tokens of exchange—witness the usher and mine images—into commodities. Alienated and critical intellectual that he was, he had no wish to be excluded from the traditional ruling circles, and no ideology to encourage an oppositional stance which would entail action with new associations; and he certainly had no wish to be a 'troublemaker'. Our approach to Donne from this perspective suggests to us that the whole issue of 'the alienated intellectual' in this period needs considerably more research done on it. Such research would develop the lines of inquiry and methods of analysis which we are applying to Donne's verse epistles in a collective enterprise bringing together historians, linguists, and literary critics. One important general question which would be focal in such an inquiry would be at what times certain intellectuals became alienated *and* sufficiently organised to form radical, highly critical groups, acting for change against the reigning hegemony.[25]

We conclude this study by looking at three verse epistles which were *not* written to patronesses. The first two we consider, 'Sir, more then kisses' ('To Sir Henry Wotton') and (Like one who in her third widdowhood' ('To Mr Rowland Woodward') were probably written around 1597–1598, a decade before the poems which we have just considered and, significantly, before Donne was dismissed by Egerton and ejected into the social wilderness inhabited by the various 'alienated' intellectuals.

It is striking that in these two poems Donne assumes a simple version of the self, one having a virtually autonomous existence, identity without social relationships, and certainly without 'creators'. The disturbing issues about alternative versions of the self and its value, central in the later patronage poems are, at least on the surface, conspicuous by their absence. Donne assumes that the individual can retreat into a safe, inherently and unproblematically valuable core. The world around may be obnoxious but the individual has his own mental and moral edifice into which he may retreat, like the snail ('To Sir Henry Wotton', lines 49–52).

Given this stance, it is not surprising that Lawrence Stapleton, one of the few critics to attend to the verse epistles with seriousness, should claim that in those letters, written before 1600, Donne reveals 'the assumptions by men of his circle, of a stoical attitude of detachment . . . man must dwell in himself, to house his spirit, as the snail his body'.[26] Nevertheless, the same critic registers something odd about these apparently stoic poems:

> The reader feels indeed that in such verses as this Donne is but conning over, genuinely enough, the social lessons of self-mastery . . . Donne had not, of course retired to any of the uncongenial country residences that he later owed to the help of relatives or friends and resorted to through necessity. He was fashioning an attitude of detachment which might save him from corruption in the world of affairs.[27]

Stapleton leaves the issue there; in the context of our study we wish to look more closely at the 'stoical attitude' and the stoic self which Donne seems to be cultivating here.

Having roundly abused the whole social world, countries, courts and towns, Donne offers Henry Wotton the following advice:

> Be thou thine owne home, and in they selfe dwell;
> Inne any where, continuance maketh hell.

And seeing the snaile, which every where doth rome,
Carrying his own house still, still is at home.
Follow (for he is easie pac'd) this snaile,
Bee thine owne Palace, or the world's thy gaile,
And in the world's sea, do not like corke sleepe
Upon the waters' face; nor in the deepe
Sinke like a lead without a line; but as
Fishes glide, leaving no print where they passe,
Nor making sound; so closely thy course goe,
Let me dispute, whether thou breathe, or no.

(lines 47–58)

Stapleton's feeling that Donne is here 'but conning over . . .
social lessons of self-mastery' seems to be a response to the
flaccid, simpleminded version of the self informing this passage.
There is no recognition that the self may well have internalised
unpleasant aspects of the social world which Donne attacks (but
inhabits—and ambitiously so), no acknowledgment of the individual's complicity in the state of the society to which he owes his
continuing work and existence, no sign that there is any tension
between participation and retreat.[28] In Christian terms, one might
add, such 'stoical' stances are surprisingly blind to the effects of
the fall—the corruption of the will and blindness of the intellect.
There are one or two hints of these vital problems: 'Let no man
say there, Virtues flintie wall/shall locke vice in mee, I'll do none
but know all' (lines 35–6); and at line forty-eight: 'Inne any
where, continuance maketh hell'. This suggests that retreat into
the self will have to come to terms precisely with evil inside. But
this hint is not developed and these earlier poems are innocent of
the real difficulties involved in questions of identity discussed
above.

Nevertheless, while the surface suggests no complexities,
when we look at the poems more closely they reveal movements
which make us doubt that the stoic stance was ever at all
congenial to Donne, let alone seriously held as a conviction to
live by.

The version of self in the poem 'To Sir Henry Wotton'
advocates retreat leading to stasis and peace. The external
world's instability does provide a threat, and we noted the hinted
threat from internal vice. But no change of self is envisaged or
demanded: the snail remains a snail within the house, the fish

glides along leaving no print and remains exactly the fish it has always been. In the poem to Mr Rowland Woodward, the beginnings of an analysis of self are evident. It has been spatialised so that 'wee' may turn into 'our selves';

> So wee, if wee into our selves will turne,
> Blowing our sparkes of vertue, may outburne
> The straw, which doth about our hearts sojourne.
>
> (lines 22–4)

That is, the self has become an inner and outer self, with the inner seen as the heart around which there is the straw of the outer self. The latter can be burned off. Here then is an advocacy of change.

However, if we consider the interactional structures of the poem to Sir Henry Wotton we find the stasis we described rather undercut. The whole poem is organised as a dialogue. Overtly it begins with an address to a friend, in a formal tone; it ends in a gently earnest plea for the friend's love. The overall frame of the poem is thus address and plea, an interaction, and the overt content of the poem needs to be read within this context: retreat which is in tension with the interaction of the friend. Contained within this overall frame are the linguistic forms of interaction: commands, questions, statements, mirroring the alternating forms of conversation. Furthermore, they are conducted in the form of intimate address: thou, thine, thy.

In other words, in its formal structure the poem is the very antithesis of retreat: it is constructed around the core forms of the language of social interaction, and whatever version of self is depicted in the apparent stoic pose, there is a deeper version where the self is defined in interaction with others. The others are friends, intimate, and the poet seeks their love, which seems essential to him. With this in mind we can see how the disturbance at lines thirty-five, thirty-six and forty-eight reflects the way the retreat is a very limited one, with the continuing and sought after support of friends. So the two versions of self in the poem to Wotton are straightforwardly contradictory.

Yet we are struck by the amazing confidence with which, despite this, Donne's poem exhorts his friend to behave and act in ways which seemingly follow from an uncomplicated stoic stance towards the world. This combination of confusion and confident advice urges us to examine the underlying view of social processes that allows such contradictions and even makes them seem unproblematic. To do so we shall look at the syntactic forms, first pointing out the agents operating in the poem. A selection serves to indicate the kind of agents they are. Initially, some non-human ones: *They* (Rockes, Remoraes) break or stop ships (lines 7–9); *Virtue's flintie wall* shall lock vice in me (lines 35–6). Then some human ones: *men* play princes (lines 23–4); *men* retrieve and greet themselves (lines 43–5). Some passives, with the agent deleted: two temperate regions *girded in* (line 13); you, *parch'd* in court, in the country *frozen* (line 15); shall cities *be chosen* (line 16); falsehood *is denizon'd* (line 34). In the first group, non-human agents act concretely on other entities; the actions are physical ones, 'making', 'breaking', 'curing', 'locking'. In the second list, human agents act, but significantly the actions are not direct, concrete, nor do these agents act on other entities. Instead the actions are reflexive (e.g. 'retrieve and greet themselves') or non-physical actions, 'see', 'know', ('play-actions' literally, such as 'playing princes'). In the last group, the passives, we have no way of recovering who the agents were—who 'froze', 'parch'd', 'built', 'denizon'd' whom.

Without further analysis we think it sound to claim that *men* are perceived and presented as peculiarly inactive, passive, reflexive; the real agents are non-human, concrete or abstract. The imperatives from line forty-seven onwards ('Be thou thine owne home, and in thy selfe dwell . . . Follow . . . this snaile . . . Bee thine owne Palace . . .') are no exception, for while they do advocate actions by human agents they are figurative actions which are difficult to understand precisely or to perform: they exhort the addressee to be in a certain kind of state, rather than indicating the processes which would lead someone to be in that state. The poem discloses a failure to grasp specific and relevant agents, an inability to specify the processes and agents by which or by whom the new state is to be implemented. In short, there is a marked lack of understanding of processes, agents, and causation in the social world. Yet Donne has superimposed a seemingly confident stoic stance on this uncertainty. His shaky perception of agency and process explains the presence of the non-stoic formal frame and the plea for friendship, a call for support. The underlying content of this poem might then be described as being about interaction, but one which proceeds without clear grasp of the 'ground rules' of processes in the social world.

The second of the pre-1600 poems we are considering is to Mr Rowland Woodward, 'Like one who'in her third widdowhood'. It has many elements in common with the poem to Sir Henry Wotton just discussed and is open to very similar comment. Donne advises, 'Seeke wee then our selves in our selves' (line 19). We see that the active self is still envisaged as unproblematic in its autonomy, the complicated perceptions of the patroness poems are absent. Lines thirty-one onwards may appear to contradict our judgment:

> Wee are but farmers of our selves, yet may,
> If we can stocke our selves, and thrive, uplay
> Much, much deare treasure for the great rent day.

Farming, thriving, stocking and uplaying treasure may seem to be the very stuff of known social practice and relationships. We believe not, for the field and its cultivation is figured as purely individualistic and autonomous while the market in which the produce can be cashed for payment of rents is a heavenly one, located outside society and beyond history, at the Last Judgment. Despite the apparent Christian dimension here, and despite the explicit mention of original sin and the doctrine of imputed merit (lines 13-18), the self is again envisaged in such a way that the problems about corruption of the will and intellect, or the need for grace in farming the self, let alone questions about the complex interactions between individual and society, cannot arise. Nevertheless, as in the poem to Sir Henry Wotton, the poem has an interactional structure. It begins with a form of address which assumes shared knowledge and belief between speaker and addressee, '*You know*, Physitians, when they would infuse' (line 25, our italics) and ends not only with the assurance of Donne's love for Woodward, but a strong statement of his need for Woodward's love in return: 'But to know, that I love thee'and would be lov'd' (line 36). The intense need for love is expressed in a command to Woodward to love him, a most un-stoic conclusion.[29]

Clearly, there are continuities between the poem to Wotton and this one; the version of the self is a little more elaborate here and the 'stoicism' a little more openly uncertain. If we look at agency, as we did in the other poem, interestingly enough we find a large number of the human agents involved in real, physical processes (though 'metaphorically' used to indicate psychological processes): gathering the sun's beams, blowing sparks, outburning straw (lines 20-24). There are far fewer passives, and the deleted agent is in all cases Donne himself (or one of his attributes): *tyed* to retiredness (line 2); seeds *were sown* (line 6); *betroth'd* (line 8). The imperatives are commands to perform actions: manure thy self; with vain outward things be no more moved; to thyself be approved (lines 34-5). Compared with the poem to Wotton there is an increase of agentiveness, awareness of agency, and the realisation of what are possible processes which men may carry out to reach a desired state. This increase in the poet's awareness of what social interaction and change could be about is accompanied by signs of a decrease in emphasis on the linguistic forms of interaction, as though a progress in understanding the causes of action leads to a progress from talk to action.

Of course, the stoic stance is classically one which the alienated intellectual may assume. We are interested to note—beyond the versions of self revealed—the uncertainty with which Donne holds this stance, an uncertainty which, as our analysis reveals, is based on his wish for incorporation (the plea for friendship, the interactional forms) and an insufficient understanding of social processes. The latter may be a direct consequence of the fact that he was not, as we have pointed out, committed to an ideologically based critique of his society.

In conclusion we turn briefly to a poem written in the period of the patroness poems discussed above. In 1610 Donne addressed 'Man is a lumpe' to Sir Edward Herbert, the son of one of his patronesses. The shifts in Donne's approach to the self, which had taken place over the preceding ten years in his drastically changed circumstances of renewed 'exile', are clear. They link up with the attitudes to self we discussed in relation to his patronage poems. This poem, written to a friend, fellow poet, and fellow philosopher, shows much of the obsession with negativity and annihilation (social and metaphysical) so marked in the patroness poems. The possibility of a virtuous and unequivocally valuable inner core, held out to Wotton and Woodward earlier, is now much further removed as he offers a traditional, compound platonic-Christian image of man composed of destructive and warring beasts which can only be controlled by equally destructive energies directed against the self, and a vision of a Christian God viciously indifferent to the fate of his creatures. Despite some surface suggestions that man may act autonomously to transcend internal wars and external social relations, in fact we get a version of the self and of society which is extremely close to that we described in the contemporary poems. Man in general only acts reflectively—given that 'the beasts' and 'nature' are his *own* beasts and his *own* nature. And though his 'businesse is, to rectifie/Nature, to what she was' (lines 33-4), we note that immediately Donne shows that this is not what man does, for 'wee'are led awry'. In all this Donne seemingly presents the friend as a means of overcoming the viciousness of man's existence. However, the last few lines of the poem undercut any such reading decisively:

> You have dwelt upon
> All worthy bookes, and now are such an one.
> Actions are authors, and of those in you
> Your friends finde every day a mart of new.
> (lines 47-50)

The friend produces, every day, actions, which are authors, which are books. And every day there is a market of these actions/authors/books. The principle of commodification is applied to the actions of the friend/patron; his friends, the real authors, may buy and may plagiarise. If the friends are poets in need of patronage they buy the already written texts; so the book or poem which Donne writes to the friend is not in fact written by Donne the poet, but by the friend/patron. Here the friend acts analogously to the patroness/creator, for while she creates the poet and with him his future actions and values, the friend in appropriating the very labour of the poet creates him as poet. The reality, as Donne presents it, is that the friend negates the actions of the poet and thereby the poet. The implications of this stance are if anything an even more savage comment by Donne on his society, where even those whom he calls his friends and lovers reduce him to powerlessness and inferiority. Here the friend is like the creator of the patroness poems; despite the negative view which Donne presents of this friendship, he needs it, either to be created, or to be written into the social world which he views so critically.

3

Vexatious Contraries: A Reading of Donne's Poetry

DAVID AERS and GUNTHER KRESS

Oh, to vex me, contraryes meet in one
>   Donne, *Holy Sonnets*, XIX, line 1

He ruin'd mee, and I am re-begot
Of absence, darknesse, death; things which are not.
>   Donne, 'A Nocturnall', lines 17–18

In February 1602 (modern calendar) Donne wrote: 'And though perchance you intend not utter destruction, yet the way through which I fall towards it is so headlong, that, being thus pushed, I shall soon be at bottom.' His words were neither addressed to God nor to a lover, but to Sir George More, the wrathful father of the woman Donne had dared to marry without obtaining the patriarchal consent he knew would not be given. He wrote from the Fleet prison, now sure that Sir George was determined to ruin his promising career. A few days later he appealed to his employer, Lord Keeper Sir Thomas Egerton in 'most poor and most penitent' vein, confessing that, 'The sickness of which I died is that I began in your Lordship's house this love'—a judgment on his love-marriage he reiterated long afterwards to his friend Sir Henry Wotton: 'I must confess that I died ten years ago.' Donne was freed from prison to live with the woman he loved but his social superiors ensured that his secular career was destroyed.[1] He viewed the prospect of unemployment as a living death, and even when it became clear that he and his increasing family would never go homeless or hungry this attitude did not change.

The letters of this period at Mitcham are most obviously pertinent to the patronage poems we discussed in the last chapter, but we think they are also relevant to the poems we shall now consider. We wish to keep in mind a letter written to Sir Henry Goodyer from Mitcham, and we quote the bulk of it here:

Every Tuesday I make account that I turn a great hour-glass, and consider that a week's life is run out since I writ. But if I ask myself what I have done in the last watch, or would do in the next, I can say nothing; if I say that I have passed it without hurting any, so may the spider in my window . . . I would not that death should take me asleep. I would not have him merely seize me, and only declare me to be dead, but win me and overcome me. When I must shipwreck, I would do it in a sea where mine impotency might have some excuse; not in a sullen weedy lake, where I could not find so much as excercise for my swimming. Therefore I would fain do something, but that I cannot tell what is no wonder. For to choose is to do; but to be no part of any body is to be nothing. At most the greatest persons are but great wens and excrescences; men of wit and delightful conversation but as moles for ornament, except they be so incorporated into the body of the world that they contribute something to the sustentation of the whole. This I made account that I begun early, when I understood the study of our laws; but was diverted by the worst voluptuousness, which is an hydroptic, immoderate desire of human learning and languages—beautiful ornaments to great fortunes; but mine needed an occupation, and a course which I thought I entered well into when I submitted myself to such a service, as I thought might employ those poor advantages which I had. And there I stumbled too, yet I would try again; for to this hour I am nothing, or so little, that I am scarce subject and argument good enough for one of mine own letters; yet I fear, that doth not ever proceed from a good root, that I am so well content to be less, that is dead. You, sir, are far enough from these descents, your virtue keeps you secure, and your natural disposition to mirth will preserve you; but lose none of these holds, a slip is often as dangerous as a bruise, and though you cannot fall to my lowness, yet in a much less distraction you may meet my sadness; for he is no safer which falls from an high tower into the leads, than he which falls from thence to the ground; make therefore to yourself some mark, and go towards it alegrement. Though I be in such a planetary and erratic fortune that I can do nothing constantly, yet you may find some constancy in my constant advising you to it.

(Letters, pp. 190–92)[2]

The state of mind so movingly disclosed here is often expressed by Donne in the years following his marriage and before he accepted preferment in the state church. There is an overriding despair at being 'nothing', being unable to act, being unable to exercise his immense energies and abilities in the social world. This letter illustrates how he experienced exclusion from a secular career as virtual annihilation and saw it as the consequence of his intense love for a woman and his marriage to her against patriarchal wishes. In his misery Donne reveals a set of attitudes which have had a long history in Western culture: the man perceives his masculine identity as inextricably bound up with his activity in the 'man's' world of public career structures and work; the home, the children, the tasks of maintaining and developing the marital relationship itself, all these become 'women's' work and 'female' identity. So that although Donne has material sufficiency, is able to read, write and be with the woman he married for love (an unusual enough achievement in his world), and with their 'gamesome children' (*Letters*, I.215), he often experiences all this as 'nothing' and himself as 'nothing'.

Furthermore it is well to recall Donne's previous experiences of being a kind of 'nothing'. Born into a Roman Catholic family he had *started* from an excluded position at a time when Catholics were literally classified as social nothings and ran a real risk of being killed by the state—his own family contained its record of English martyrs for the old faith. Donne himself described his ancestry in the 'Advertisement to the Reader', which prefaces his *Pseudo-Martyr* (1610), as 'such a stock and race, as, I believe, no family, (which is not of far larger extent, and greater branches,) hath endured and suffered more in their persons and fortunes for obeying the Teachers of Roman Doctrine'. He confessed that the time he had spent wrestling with his inherited faith 'not only retarded my fortune, but also bred some scandal, and endangered my spiritual reputation'.[3] Having rejected the family's religious traditions and obtained patronage and a promising place in the establishment Donne, as we have outlined, once again found himself totally excluded, a martyr in a different cause: for marriage grounded in love rather than in conventional social calculations.

The poet's experience was thus so far from achieving fulfilment and established self-identity through love, so far from creating an alternative community to the one from which he had been expelled (by Sir George More and the Lord Keeper), that he felt he had actually become 'no part of any body'. And that, he insisted, 'is to be nothing'. He so often experienced the woman he loved in this way because identity for him depended on being 'incorporated into the body of the world', and he unquestioningly assumed this to be the world of the Lord Keeper Egerton, of Lucy Countess of Bedford, in fact of the dominant social groups with powers of patronage. Outside these groups and dutiful service to them, Donne felt annihilated—'I am nothing'. As we saw in the last chapter, he was not one of those alienated intellectuals who were able to construct and inhabit a coherent oppositional ideology. In a letter of spring 1608 he noted his claims to be 'nothing' (again contrasted with those who were incorporated in the upper social world) and suggested that even these claims might be far too ambitious. For he argued that although self-annihilation may 'seem humbleness, yet it is a work of as much almightiness to bring a thing to nothing as from nothing'; so he (temporarily) renounced the effort as surpassing his crippled powers (*Letters*, I.181). Yet despite this metaphysical modesty Donne continued to express himself despairingly as 'nothing' in both prose and verse, for he consistently perceived his self-identity in relation to his social curcumstances and the upper class establishment in which he so desperately sought incorporation. Some of the consequences of this we studied in the last chapter, and we believe the same matrix of pressures is very relevant to some of his greatest love poetry in ways which have been rather overlooked. Donne did indeed feel that love had ruined him, that he was 're-begot/Of absence, darknesse, death; things which are not' ('A Nocturnall upon S. Lucies day'), and he wrote in earnest when he told Wotton in 1612, 'I died ten years ago'.

We will begin our discussion of some of Donne's finest love poems by considering one of the most celebrated and antholo-gised, 'The good-morrow'. The poet seems to lead us into a

completely different world from the one we have just been
observing, that so hauntingly realised in 'A Nocturnall'.⁴ Here we
seem to encounter joyful and confident mutuality:

> I Wonder by my troth, what thou, and I
> Did, till we lov'd? were we not wean'd till then?
> But suck'd on countrey pleasures, childishly?
> Or snorted we in the seaven sleepers den?
> T'was so; But this, all pleasures fancies bee.   5
> If ever any beauty I did see,
> Which I desir'd, and got, t'was but a dreame of thee.
>
> And now good morrow to our waking soules,
> Which watch not one another out of feare;
> For love, all love of other sights controules,   10
> And makes one little roome, an every where.
> Let sea-discoverers to new worlds have gone,
> Let Maps to other, worlds on worlds have showne,
> Let us possesse one world, each hath one, and is one.
>
> My face in thine eye, thine in mind appeares   15
> And true plaine hearts doe in the faces rest,
> Where can we finde two better hemispheares
> Without sharpe North, without declining West?
> What ever dyes, was not mixt equally;
> If our two loves be one, or thou and I   20
> Love so alike, that none doe slacken, none can die.

We can quite understand the straightforward enthusiasm with
which countless readers have responded to this poem, a poem by
one who is 'obviously a living poet in the most important sense:
and it is not any eccentricity of defiant audacity that makes the
effect here so immediate, but rather an irresistible rightness'.
Thus F. R. Leavis.⁵ Yet there are features which call for more
attention that Leavis habitually offered to the language of poets
he was 'revaluating' and which have been insufficiently noticed
by more recent literary critics.

The exuberant opening five lines bind together speaker and
addressee ('I' and 'thou') into a united 'we' for whom the
intensity of the present has reduced the past to an absurd and
comic memory. The present love and unity apparently obliterates
the lovers' history, turning it to dream and fancy. But the poet's
conviction about the present and the achieved unity is not quite
so complete, and in the last two lines of the first stanza he shifts

his perspective. The 'we' is now replaced by the speaker's 'I' as he jauntily (and/or teasingly?) brings some of his own past more into the foreground. These lines reflect a traditional version of male sexual identity in which the woman is treated as an objectified abstraction ('beauty') to be viewed and possessed ('I did see . . . desir'd and got') by the egotistic and manipulatively unemotional male. By introducing the predatory and impersonal 'got' (similarly used in 'Love's Alchymie', line 3) the speaker exhibits his contempt for the women who may have involved themselves with him, focusing attention on this aspect of his past even while he vauntingly gestures at transforming it into a flattering reference to his present partner—'t'was but a dreame of thee'. The last thing such a conventional male has habitually done is to meditate honestly on what his feelings would be if the woman who professes to love him gratuitously chose to express this love in terms of her previous sexual *gots*, assuring him that these other males were merely *dreams* of himself. Such lack of self-reflexivity is not surprising and still does not bother many readers (one recalls Leavis's confident assertion that all is 'irresistible rightness' in this poem): for in the traditional culture of male discourse (oral and literary) the woman has been treated as an object whose purpose is to bolster and gratify the male ego.[6] Even though the male actually needs and depends on the woman's love (or at least her devoted services) his 'masculinity' has conventionally been invested in an assertion of emotional autonomy and independence, an assertion which is riddled with bad faith and double-think.

The next stanza seems to back away from such issues as it opens with reaffirmation of a present and mutual awakening (line 8). Readers do not usually feel any troublesome undercurrents here. Yet there are at least some in the second and third stanzas and Donne acknowledges this by choosing to define the lovers' achieved state through the combination of negations, conditionals and references towards the environment that their relationship allegedly transcends. He states that the lovers 'watch *not* one another out of fear', and the negation here is significant because it presents their feelings only in terms of what the (male) speaker claims they do *not* feel. The negated feelings must be strong and immediate to govern the terms in which the lovers represent their glad day. (We also considered the role of negations in the previous chapter, pages 38–40). And indeed this acknowledgment of troubling undercurrents seems sufficiently motivated by the ostentatious assertiveness of the last two lines of the first stanza discussed in the preceding paragraph. In fact we may now note how such male egotism, in all its conventional sexual jauntiness, is a product of anxiety as well as being an attempt to exploit the woman's own anxiety. In vaunting his easy and irresponsible mastery over other members of her sex, reminding her of his range of choice and alternatives, the man deliberately threatens and tries to overcome the woman. But the very need for such assertiveness may well suggest a sense of insecurity about his own desirability and worth in the eyes of the person he addresses. It is certainly likely that, in a relationship with such mixed springs of feeling, 'feare' will need especial exorcism. The next line (line 10) invites similar comment since in the claim that 'love, all love of other sights controules' we are again returned to the first stanza where the speaker reminded the woman about the other 'beauty I did see . . . and got': line 10 acknowledges that such 'love of other sights' continues, a genuine centrifugal force, but claims that 'love' (the present mutual love) now 'controules' it. Here the poet's seemingly confident generalisation about 'love' is misleading because what it actually manifests is a wish for fixity, a wish for a love that will control the infinite possibilities and contingencies in his seeking, desiring and disturbingly fluid being.[7]

Similarly with the next lines which claim that 'love . . . makes one little roome, an every where'. The intensity of love may well be alchemical and able to create a new heaven and a new earth for lovers. But this magical power of love apparently depends on the couple being alone, as Donne also indicated in the use of negation and those allusions to the social world that must be excluded which we discussed earlier. (If the poem was indeed written, like the related poems 'The Canonization' and 'The Sunne Rising', after Donne's marriage, he already had come to lament the way 'one little roome', with its circumambient universe of powerful employers, patrons and patriarchs, could all too easily resist the magic forces of love and the poetic imagination.) In the movement outwards from the 'little roome' Donne dismisses the milieu as he attempts to escape all conflicts and processes of individual and collective history, transforming the lovers' situation into a contrastingly timeless and autonomous totality. Here we may think of the 'Nocturnall' where Donne envisaged the socially alienated lovers precariously creating an alternative 'whole world' (lines 23–6):

> Oft a flood
> Have wee two wept, and so
> Drownd the whole world, us two; oft did we grow
> To be two Chaosses, when we did show
> Care to ought else . . .

Here the exclusive world of the lovers is presented as most fragile, reduced to chaos by either partner showing care to 'ought else', to the very world whose existence they wish to deny as a non-entity. The attempt to construct this 'whole world' and its final dissolution only increases the completeness of the poet's alienation and his sense of annihilation so brilliantly and systematically invoked.[8] The destruction of the attempted alternative world is not enacted in 'The Good-Morrow', but the analogies in the states to which the lovers' aspire are evident enough.

Nevertheless, the conclusion of stanza two of 'The Good-Morrow' claims more than an *attempt* to create an alternative world. It claims a present and achieved state: 'each hath one ['world'], and *is* one'. Similarly, the opening of the last stanza provides an image of fixity and certainty, of 'rest' in which appearance is no longer ambiguous but a quite problematic revelation of truth:

> My face in thine eye, thine in mine appeares,
> And true plaine hearts doe in the faces rest,

This is certainly far from the mobility and instability so memorably expressed in 'The Second Anniversary' (lines 391–400):

> . . . that she, and that thou,
> Which did begin to love, are neither now;
> You are both fluid, chang'd since yesterday;
> Next day reapires, (but ill) last dayes decay.
> Nor are, (although the river keepe the name)
> Yesterdaies waters, and to daies the same.
> So flowes her face, and thine eyes, neither now
> That Saint, nor Pilgrime, which your loving vow
> Concern'd, remaines: but whil'st you thinke you bee
> Constant, you'are hourely in inconstancie.

In fact this seems to be just the vision Donne wished to exclude from 'The Good-Morrow'. The world of process and contingency must be expelled by the kind of controlling love he imagines in the central stanza of the poem. But he does not sustain this imaginative confidence. He indicates the directions of his anxieties by once more expressing his love in terms of the state of affairs it is supposed to have superseded—the 'sharpe North', the 'declining West' and all those compounded things that dissolve and die. On top of this, by phrasing lines 17–18 as a question he raises the possibility that we *can* find two better hemispheres, that there may be a real question here rather than a merely rhetorical one. (Perhaps too these lines subtly play on the fears used in lines 6–7, and 9?) Likewise the emphatically *conditional* form of the last two lines ('*If* . . .') completes the undercutting of the central desire the poem has embodied, namely the desire for a state where the speaker's obtrusively assertive ego would be submerged in a totally secure unification with another being.[9] This union was postulated as one which could provide an alternative world, an autonomous Utopian anti-world freed from social and historical processes with all their complex antagonisms and contingencies. It is central to the poem's greatness that it manifests the linguistic subtlety and imaginative power *both* to express this Utopia *and* to subvert it, placing it finally as an admirable but doomed attempt to create a transcendental oasis within an alien world. Donne's poem evokes the way we bear the world with us into our retreats and into our most secret harbours, for these themselves are partly moulded and shaped by that from which we seek to escape.

In 'The Canonization', definitely written after his marriage (the first stanza refers to a period when James was king), Donne focused a dramatic meditation on problems of the relation between Eros and civilisation. As we have sought to convey, he was intimately familiar with such problems, and this depth of experience is drawn on in 'The Canonization':

> For Godsake hold your tongue, and let me love,
>> Or chide my palsie, or my gout,
> My five gray haires, or ruin'd fortune flout,
>> With wealth your state, your minde with Arts improve,
>>> Take you a course, get you a place,
>>> Observe his honour, or his grace,

5

Or the Kings reall, or his stamped face
  Contemplate, what you will, approve,
  So you will let me love.

Alas, alas who's injur'd by my love?   10
  What merchants ships have my sighs drown'd?
Who saies my teares have overflow'd his ground?
  When did my colds a forward spring remove?
    When did the heats which my veines fill
    Add one more to the plaguie Bill?   15
Soldiers finde warres, and Lawyers finde out still
  Litigious men, which quarrels move
  Though she and I do love.

Call us what you will, wee are made such by love;
  Call her one, mee another flye,   20
We'are Tapers too, and at our owne cost die,
  And wee in us finde the' Eagle and the Dove.
    The Phoenix ridle hath more wit
    By us, we two being one, are it.
So to one neutrall thing both sexes fit,   25
  Wee dye and rise the same, and prove
  Mysterious by this love.

Wee can dye by it, if not live by love,
  And if unfit for tombes and hearse
Our legend bee, it will be fit for verse;   30
  And if no peece of Chronicle wee prove,
    We'll build in sonnets pretty roomes;
    As well a well wrought urne becomes
The greatest ashes, as halfe-acre tombes,
  And by these hymnes, all shall approve   35
  Us Canoniz'd for Love:

And thus invoke us; You whom reverend love
  Made one another's hermitage;
You, to whom love was peace, that now is rage;
  Who did the whole worlds soule contract, and drove   40
    Into the glasses of your eyes
    (So made such mirrors, and such spies,
That they did all to you epitomize,)
  Countries, Townes, Courts: Beg from above
  A patterne of your love!   45

The first two stanzas support the poet's opening demand that he
be left alone to love. They point out, and dismiss, dominant

practices in the world as Donne envisages it (economic, legal, militaristic, courtly). He brusquely mentions his 'ruin'd fortune' as something his audience, immersed in the world, will 'flout' as much as they will 'chide' his physical maladies. (We recall his 'sickness' and 'gout' in *Letters*, I.195, as well as the experiences surrounding his marriage and the quest for patronage in the poems discussed in the preceding chapter.) Love, the last word of the first and last line of every stanza, is under attack from the world to whom the poem is addressed, and Donne's initial strategy is to insist that 'Though she and I do love' the habitual practices of society are not threatened. As if to stress this, 'love' is first introduced as a non-transactive verb (line 9) in a world of most busy activity, and the address is directed to a person or group which seems to have the power of preventing the speaker from loving ('*let* me love . . . So you will *let* me love'). The poet argues that love is a purely privatised relationship which, although a real alternative to the social world, is utterly harmless, a-social and a-political.

While this may have become the 'common sense' of a much later period in our culture, the overall movement and emphasis of the poem discloses quite clearly that the speaker is having to assert the position against prevalent assumptions in a milieu where it will definitely be contradicted. We will discuss this movement in due course, but it is already foreshadowed in the second stanza. The five questions (lines 9–15) are of course ones which overtly demand the answers 'No-one', 'None', 'No-one' 'Never', and 'Never'. However, the very need to formulate these statements as questions before an antagonistic audience suggests that the poet is registering his awareness of those who would indeed attribute a rather different role to 'love' and answer the questions in an appropriately different manner. 'Alas, alas, who's injur'd by my love?' Both Donne and we ourselves can easily remember how Sir George More had felt himself severely injured by the poet's love, how John felt his love had injured Ann (e.g. *Letters*, I.215) and how he felt he too had been mortally injured by committing himself to love (*Letters*, I.100–16, and the letters from Mitcham mentioned earlier). Making 'my love' a nominal entity (line 10) he constructs a syntax in which his love is potentially a transacting agent which could feature in a sentence such as 'my love injured you' and demands that questions concerning the lovers' *interaction* with other people at least be put.

So when the last line of the second stanza returns to the non-transactive form of the first stanza ('she and I do love') we can now see how this is an integral part of his attempt to re-state the autonomy of his loving and her loving. Interestingly enough the form he selects does not even present the lovers themselves as interacting, but rather, as it were, in parallel: 'she does love' and 'I do love', *not* 'I love her' or 'she loves me'. Nevertheless, the syntax and questions of the second stanza have implied just how delusive the non-transactive form is likely to be in the matters Donne is considering, and these suggestions are thoroughtly well founded.

Stanza three expresses the positive aspect of their relationship, emblematised in the Phoenix which is placed in the middle line of the middle stanza, the formal centre of the whole poem. Before we encounter that emblem, however, Donne again notes the hostile judgments of his worldly audience (lines 19–20) and initially seems to concede the case—'wee are made such by love'. He seems to accept the destructive nature of love in his culture together with one of the most conventional stereotypes of love— namely love as an irrational and external force which dehumanises its victims (lines 19–21), a stereotype in which Eros is presented as a danger to established customs, social order and all civilised life.[10] Nevertheless, he does try to limit the implications of this view by asserting that only the lovers themselves are affected. He thus re-emphasises the autonomous nature of their relationship, claiming an utter self-sufficiency which seals them off from the social environment (lines 20–1).

In doing so he shifts away from the adverse value judgments implicit in (lecherous) Fly and Taper (here an emblem of self-consuming, destructive passion) to the Favourable Eagle, Dove and finally Phoenix, the unique mystical bird which often served as an emblem for Christ in his resurrectionary power. The Phoenix represents the core of the speaker's vision of 'us', the lovers. Unlike the Taper, the Phoenix rises from its ashes in a self-sustaining and infinite cycle of existence, a self-perpetuating universe. Here, as most readers of Donne notice, we meet the aspiration voiced in 'The Good-Morrow', 'The Sunne Rising', 'A Valediction: of Weeping' and 'A Nocturnall', the aspiration to establish a timeless self in a relationship which completely excludes society and history. Although they seem involved in action ('Wee dye and rise') the verbs of the stanza are all in the present tense and this enhances the sense of mysterious changelessness now attributed to their relationship—'Wee dye and rise the same'.[11] (It is probably worth remembering how, in traditional Christian doctrine of the resurrection, human beings would not rise the 'same' but transformed and with glorified bodies. A basic text is St Paul, I Corinthians 15, and in a sermon on Psalm 90.14 Donne himself makes some interesting comparisons between humans and angels in stressing the change involved here: '[the redeemed] shall be better than Angels in the next world, for they shall be glorifying spirits, as the Angels are, but they shall also be glorified bodies, which the Angels shall never be'.)[12] The mystery of a static present in an absolutely unified world is the mystery of this love which apparently fuses human sex and the speaker's metaphysical longings, the positive aspects of the love emblematised in the Phoenix.

Yet we must seriously qualify this account of 'the positive aspects'. Even if the lovers had managed to encapsulate themselves from the hostile culture, the poetry reveals how the 'cost', to use the poet's own turn of phrase, would undoubtedly be disastrous. The infinite potential of human love, together with the resonant language of resurrection, has been narrowed down to the intense but isolated sexual experience of orgasm referred to in the common pun on 'dye'. The important psychological and social issues that lie behind the punning fusion of sexual climax and death are certainly relevant to Donne's poem but here they are not explored and the poet rests content with the gesture. Furthermore, in appropriating the Phoenix emblem to describe their love, the speaker has transformed himself and the woman from animate human beings to inanimate things: 'we two being one, are *it*./ So to one *neutrall thing* both sexes *fit*'. The rhyme 'it'—'fit' is a neat reflection of this collapse, and even deprives the sexual act of any human direction and choice, let alone affection and personal warmth. The 'positive' mystery in which the speaker tried to establish himself turns out to be a sadly dehumanised and inanimate 'fit'. This is part of the revenge taken by the poet's culture on those who in their mutual love decide to challenge its established order of values, status and power. The lover bravely tries to transform his alienation and punishment into a glorious and transcendent triumph, but the particulars of the poetry disclose the grave 'cost' to both himself and the relationship. Once more Donne's poetry reveals how the most intimate areas of being and those we call public, or more external, interact in a living continuum. As Donne's own life and letters showed, the alienation he himself endured had no such 'mysterious' supersession, whatever the heart's desire. It seems to us that when he was reflecting on a recent sickness in the magnificent *Devotions* (1624) Donne drew on a web of experience very relevant to our present discussion. The fifth meditation is on his horror of solitude. He treats this horror as fully human and inevitable since man is unequivocally a *social*, gregarious being and God has even organised the cosmos on social principles. Indeed,

> God himself would admit a figure of society, as there is a plurality of persons in God; and all his external actions testify a love of society, and communion. In heaven there are orders of angels, and armies of martyrs, and in that house many mansions; in earth, families, cities, churches, colleges all plural things . . . there is no phoenix; nothing singular, nothing alone.

In *An Anatomie of the World* (1611) he treated the kind of individualism he believed a mark of his period with distaste, again using the Phoenix image:

> every man alone thinkes he hath got
> To be a Phoenix, and that then can bee
> None of that kinde, of which he is, but hee.
> (lines 216–18)

In the *Devotions* he notes the possibility of 'a plurality of worlds' and treats the exaltation of hermit-like solitude as 'a disease of the mind', crying out, 'woe unto me if I be alone'. So we are well prepared to grasp the full force and centrality in one of his most famous statements (too often taken without attention to its contexts) when later (during the seventeenth meditation), he writes:

> No man is an island, entire of itself; every man is a piece of the continent, a part of the main. If a clod be washed away by the sea, Europe is the less, as well as if a promontory were, as well as if a

manor of thy friend's or of thine own were: any man's death diminishes me, because I am involved in mankind, and therefore never send to know for whom the bell tolls; it tolls for thee.

The passionate intensity with which he knows 'how impotent a piece of the world is any man alone' connects plainly enough with the sense of annihilation we illustrated earlier in the letters from Mitcham.[13] There is, Donne knew, no human phoenix.

Given this texture of experience and the serious qualifications to the lovers' 'positive' aspirations which we have just traced in the third stanza we are not surprised when the fourth stanza of 'The Canonization' deftly turns the sexual pun on 'dye' towards a literal statement about the death to which he feels such love is leading. (We remember 'The sickness of which I died . . . this love', *Letters*, I. 114). He ruefully acknowledges that what they have done is enact a Utopian ideal in an alien society, create a *legend* fit for *verse* but not for practical embodiment in the contemporary milieu. For this they have been made to pay the penalty (lines 28–30): 'Wee can dye by it, if not live by love'.

The poet then glances at the hierarchy of aesthetic form in his culture and notes how even here the lovers are officially downgraded. We recall that when Donne celebrated Elizabeth Drury and the ideas she embodied for him, he had to counter a possible argument that even a long poem may not have been the appropriate form as she was 'matter fit for Chronicle, not verse' ('An Anatomie', lines 455–62). True enough, Donne embraces this downgrading and promises that if this is the case, then 'We'll build in sonnets pretty roomes', just as in 'The Good-Morrow' he had celebrated 'one little roome'. Simultaneously he uses the levelling destructiveness of death to mock the preservation of social stratification in death, favoured by the possessing classes with their 'half-acre tombes', and opens the last strategy in which the alternative values the lovers have tried to embody may be celebrated: 'all [all society including hostile addressee, offended patriarchs and employers? or just all those lovers who challenge social custom?] shall approve/Us *Canoniz'd* for Love'. But in taking up this traditional religious language of love (complete with its saints and martyrs) the speaker no longer tries to reverse the movement from stanza three to four. This strategy no longer makes *any* claims about the viability of love such as theirs as an autonomous realm within an alien society, nor does it attempt to present the lovers as achieving any phoenix-like independence and resurrection. Having abandoned such mythologising efforts to transcend their alienation he now turns his attention to the religion of love in which he has tried to live and where he and his partner will by hymned.

The last stanza is of course no longer in the speaker's own voice but is his report of the hymn in which future worshippers of 'love' will invoke the couple whose attempt and inability to survive in society has been followed through the poem. Donne fastens on how religious cults tend to falsify the realities of their saints' lives). The worshippers claim that the lovers *did* create an alternative world, *did* manage to be 'one another's hermitage', *did* create 'peace', and *did* manage to make one little room an everywhere, magically including all that may be desirable and valuable (in all senses) in the very social world which has expelled them—'Countries, Townes, Courts'. They assert that the Utopian venture was triumphant and without pain and 'cost' to its participants. But Donne's own poem has actually disclosed a very different and far more complex state of affairs, as we have seen. In diverse ways it has revealed the overwhelming power of the social world and the disastrous loss of community imposed on the lovers, forces which proved quite resistant to both magic and the more brusque appeals with which the poem begins. As in other poems we have analysed, we thus find an attempt to establish a version of identity and value which is utterly independent of the current social world and the market world of patronage, where the speaker is downgraded and disvalued. Yet, as in the 'darke texts' we examined, the poet has actually disclosed the pervasive effects of the alien world even in the most intimate and seemingly alternative spheres of existence. The poet who married Ann More and wrote the Mitcham letters understood far more about alleged hermitages than the well-intentioned but facile admirers he depicts in the final stanza. They seem to have forgotten that by the 'patterne' of love figured in the text the speaker explored how the couple could actually 'not live'. The saints' worshippers (neo-papists indeed) unwittingly beg for a martyrdom whose significance and experience they have quite mistaken.

There is a further irony in this delicately critical last stanza. Donne knew full well that the religion of love with its vocabulary grounded in medieval courtly literature, Petrarchism and eclectic Renaissance neoplatonism, was a literature avidly consumed by those who had place and status in the world which excluded him, an elite who sacrificed nothing for love but ensured that it was carefully controlled in the interests of property, patriarchy and family.[14] His own poem, obviously placed in deliberate relation to this literary tradition, concludes with a final glance at an important contradiction. The dominant social groups had generated a model of fulfilled human love involving mind and body, celebrated in much upper-class literature, and yet simultaneously made it virtually impossible to enact this admirable human ideal. This contradiction was one Donne knew intimately, with a profoundly inward knowledge, probably only available to its victims. In 'The Canonization' he certainly explored it dramatically, with great imaginative power and a linguistic precision essential to the theme's complexity. It is a fitting product for someone so well equipped to meditate on the painful attempt to create a relationship, founded in love, with an antagonistic social environment, and the terrible 'cost' to self-identity which might have to be borne: Love was a supreme positive, but Love in this society also 'ruin'd mee, and I am rebegot/Of absence, darkenesse, death; things which are not.' (A Nocturnall).[15]

We will now briefly consider the effects of Donne's transference of his love from a woman to God in his poetic images of the self. He himself was fully aware of the overt continuities that so many literary critics have noticed between his 'secular' and 'religious' writing. For instance we may take the following sonnet:

> Oh, to vex me, contraryes meet in one:
> Inconstancy unnaturally hath begott
> A constant habit; that when I would not
> I change in vowes, and in devotione.
> As humorous is my contritione   5
> As my prophane Love, and as soone forgott:
> As ridlingly distemper'd, cold and hott,
> As praying, as mute; as infinite, as none.
> I durst not view heaven yesterday; and to day
> In prayers, and flattering speaches I court God: 10
> To morrow I quake with true feare of his rod.
> So my devout fitts come and go away

Like a fantastique Ague: save that here
Those are my best dayes, when I shake with feare.
(*Holy Sonnets*, XIX)

Besides Donne's own preoccupations with the continuities we have just mentioned, there is one striking feature on which the poet does not explicitly focus, although it is quite as pervasive in the 'divine' poems as the 'profane'. This is the marked absence of organic process from the version of the self. Self is imaged as an unpredictable succession of emotions which replace one another at random, giving no sense of an organic identity immersed in a temporal process. (In this Donne's vision is quite strikingly unlike Shakespeare's in the latter's sonnet sequence.) The succession of states is experienced as frighteningly arbitrary and Donne can find no use for the kind of calvinistic framework for introspective analysis so powerfully deployed by Fulke Greville, any more than he can for those of the older religion he renounced.[16] The very first line of the sonnet evokes this as the speaker envisages himself as a *place* where a-historical 'contraryes' suddenly happen to appear and 'meet'. At no point in the poem does Donne assume, let alone articulate, an ideologically coherent diagnosis of his states (again unlike Greville).[17] He confesses that although those states traditionally regarded as positive (fear of God was allegedly the beginning of wisdom) do seem to him his 'best dayes', nevertheless they too are experienced as quite arbitrary 'fitts', as the product of 'a fantastique Ague'. He can thus never hope to draw them into a sphere of critical discourse and comprehension as the prelude to an attempted exercise, however 'fallen', of the will—'when I would not / I change in vowes and in devotione. / . . . ridlingly distemper'd'.

The other facet of this experience is a longing for a self fixed in one timeless state. This longing matches the dreams of lovers' transcendent and static union encountered in the *Songs and Sonnets*. This too is a version of self quite lacking any sense of process and any sustained account of dramatisation of the psychological and theological processes by which the speaker hopes to attain it. Instead Donne's hope is an idiosyncratic and violently assertive demand to be raped, overwhelmed and drowned—to be deprived in fact of all vestiges of the responsibility that might be part of a version of self which attributed some powers of conscious agency to the individual, however 'fallen':

> You which beyond that heaven which was most high   5
> Have found new sphears, and of new lands can write,
> Powre new seas in mine eyes, that so I might
> Drowne my world with my weeping earnestly,
> Or wash it, if it must be drown'd no more:
> But oh it must be burnt! alas the fire   10
> Of lust and envie have burnt it heretofore,
> And made it fouler; Let their flames retire,
> And burne me o Lord, with a fiery zeale
> Of thee and thy house, which doth in eating heale.
> . . .

>   (*Holy Sonnets*, V, XIV)
> Except you'enthrall mee, never shall be free,

God is perceived as a terrorising and brutal force uninterested in personhood or individual nuances and developments of awareness and love in his creatures. Donne begs this power to fix his identity in the most absolute way, to 'imprison' him, to make him a slave, thus virtually renouncing the fundamental idea of Christian Liberty so important in the history of Protestant thought. The sexual experiences that Donne uses to express his relationship with God (actual and hoped for) are explicitly linked (as in Sonnet XIX) with his 'prophane Love'. They are, to say the least, desperate, contradictory ones, fusing massive self-assertiveness with self-annihilation (also discussed in a letter quoted above, p.50) in a profoundly anguished and insecure manner. To him, in these sonnets, the only way he can now escape the 'fitts' that compose his life is by an act of divine power which totally subjugates him and obliterates his individual responsibility—a very different matter from the re-creating divine initiative designed to sponsor and enable human freedom, explored and celebrated by Milton in *Paradise Lost, Christian Doctrine* and elsewhere.[18]

Of course the very violence and repetitiveness of Donne's imperatives directed at God's overpowering force are a sign of the intensely world-centred orientation of the self, however 'ridlingly distemper'd' and miserable. The 'contraryes' here are perfectly intelligible and we find them present in various forms through the letters we referred to, patronage poems and some of the greatest achievements of the *Songs and Sonnets*. As we have indicated in this and the previous chapter, Donne consistently expressed utterly worldly, courtly and careerist aims right up to the time of his preferment in the Church of England. These ambitions were so emphatic that when frustrated they could lead to chronic dejection (e.g. *Letters,* I.191, 215) or the quite unprincipled selling of himself which he tried to effect with the corrupt Lord Viscount of Rochester in one of the most unsavoury businesses conducted at James's court. Yet we have also seen an alternative response to the frustration of his ambitions. Namely, an intense wish for detachment from this world, the substitution of a realm in which his 'true' merit would be justly valued and the society that rejected him be completely transcended. So we found him simultaneously torn by the wish to affirm and negate the social world whose acclaim he so desperately sought. These 'contraryes' were matched in his feelings towards God and the self-images that emerge in his *Holy Sonnets*. He is often terrified of the supernatural power he invokes and worships, yet believes his salvation depends on his total enslavement to this power ('imprison mee') as the only way his uncontrollable 'fitts' could be terminated. The problem here which he fails to face is absolutely vital. Since the stability he craves apparently entails the annihilation of will and intellect there seems to be no identity to whom the achieved stability could be attributed. Nor is there even any specifiable moral commitment or framework to this coveted state. Furthermore there are explicitly theological problems lurking here, for orthodox Christians have never accepted anything remotely resembling the Buddhist notion of Nirvana, or the Brahman-Atman of the Hindus, and Donne seems to have no intention whatsoever of challenging orthodox doctrine. The issues are relevant enough and raised by the text, but Donne ignores them. The feelings directing the movement of the poems seem to be a mixture of resentful rejection of God and longing for God's decisive intervention in his life, of fear and desire to be overwhelmed. It is not surprising that the language in which he addresses God, in 'flattering speaches I court God', is closer to the language he uses to patrons than to his 'prophane Love' (*Holy Sonnets,* XIX). For example: 'bid me either hope for this business in your Lordships hand or else pursue my first purpose or abandon all; for as I cannot live without your favour, so I cannot die without your leave; because even by dying I should steal from you one who is by his own devotions and your purchase your Lordship's most humble and thankful servant'. The purchase is not the one effected by Christ, and the addressee is not God; in fact it is addressed to the Viscount of Rochester, an especially depraved lord but, according to the future Dean of St Paul's, one of those whom God 'hath made stewards of His benefits upon earth' (see *Letters*, II. 22–9, 42).

We believe there is one outstanding sonnet which evokes a version of self and a stance towards God which are not at all characteristic of Donne's religious poetry in the period with which we are mainly concerned. Because we reckon it in many ways an exception to his habitual outlook this most impressive and self-aware of poems should be mentioned. It is written after the death of the earthly lover who was his wife, and is numbered XVII in Grierson's edition.

> Since she whom I lov'd hath payd her last debt
> To Nature, and to hers, and my good is dead,
> And her Soule early into heaven ravished,
> Wholly on heavenly things my mind is sett.
> Here the admyring her my mind did whett   5
> To seek thee God; so streames do shew their head;
> But though I have found thee, and thou my thirst hast fed,
> A holy thirsty dropsy melts meè yett.
> But why should I begg more Love, when as thou
> Dost wooe my soule for hers; offring all thine: 10
> And dost not only feare least I allow
> My Love to Saints and Angels things divine,
> But in thy tender jealosy dost doubt
> Least the World, Fleshe, yea Devill putt thee out.

The opening quatrain is centred on the dead woman he loved and it presents God as Donne's rival, the one who has 'ravished' her away from him. The word 'early' (line 3) contributes delicately to the sense of the untimely and unjust action of God. When Donne, punning on 'Wholly' claims that 'since' (used in both temporal and causal sense) the woman is dead his mind is set on 'heavenly things', he is exploiting the vocabulary shared between religion and earthly love (as in 'The Canonization') to equivocate about his new orientation. Indeed, as most readers notice, the woman herself is now one of the 'heavenly things' on whom Donne may legitimately set his mind, and whether he will do so in a manner that has traditionally been thought appropriate to orthodox asexual Christian heavens remains a deliberately open issue. The two lines which follow (lines 5–6) will strike a reader of the patronage poems and the letters as themselves wittily equivocal. His love of Ann did indeed 'whett' his mind to seek God, but only very indirectly and very reluctantly. For his love of her had terminated his secular career and he did all he could, as we have seen, to try and get back into service with very earthly masters. Only in the frustration of these efforts was he pushed toward God's service, finally achieving the coveted incorporation into the society of the world's possessing groups by accepting royal patronage in the state church.

From here he moves to the stunningly candid confession of God's inadequacy (lines 7 ff.). Acknowledging that he has 'found God' and God has now offered '*all*' his love (an extremely rare feeling about God in the 'divine' poems), Donne makes his own need for more (or probably other) love fully explicit. With most unusual self assurance he calmly presents the deity as the fearful one in their relationship, anxiously wooing the unfulfilled human soul. Moreover, the poet does not deny that God has very good cause to fear and he certainly does not retract anything he has said about the dissatisfaction he feels with God now that he has found the deity but lost his own wife, 'she whom I lov'd'. The honesty, self-awareness and complex precision of the poem are fine achievements—literary, psychological and intellectual. Perhaps it is reasonable to speculate that the calm assurance and frankness of the poem are connected with the fact that by the time Donne wrote this sonnet (Ann died in 1617) he was well on the path to incorporation in the social world of the establishment. With his change of circumstances it must have become possible to shed many of the anxieties, the wretched sense of isolation and the crippling frustration of energies which had dogged his life for so long. But whatever the cause, Sonnet XVII projects a different self-image from the others. The self moves in time as a choosing agent and is the subject of transactive verbs deploying a range of tenses and exhibiting the kind of continuity in change which contrasts so strikingly with the unpredictable bursts of emotion and the wish for total self-annihilation reflected in other poems.

We conclude our consideration of Donne by looking at one last divine poem, written after his incorporation into the elite of the state church, yet a very different performance to Sonnet XVII. 'A Hymne to Christ, at the Author's last going into Germany' was apparently written in 1619 when Donne served the Lord Doncaster on a European mission. In the first stanza he establishes his confidence in God and his knowledge of God (a conviction also found in Sonnet XVII)—'through that maske I know those eyes'. He then recounts his own attitude as he is about to 'embarke':

> I sacrifice this Iland unto thee,
> And all who I lov'd there, and who lov'd mee;
> When I have put our seas twixt them and mee,
> Put thou thy sea betwixt my sinnes and thee.
>
> (lines 9–12)

Commentators do not always seem ready to acknowledge what Donne is saying here. His approach is actually that of a Moloch-worshipper, Moloch being the deity devoted to consuming human beings sacrificed by his followers. Christians traditionally have at least claimed to pursue an ideal in which they should sacrifice themselves and worldly ambitions in the consciously chosen response to God's call and in love of their fellow human beings. But instead of this Donne says he sacrifices *others*—England and 'all' the human beings who have loved him and whom he has loved. Leaving England with his aristocratic leader he actually sets up a rather remarkable model of current relationships: *myself* (i.e., *Donne*): all I loved and who loved me:: *God:* my sins. All the people Donne had loving relationships with in the past are indiscriminately aligned with his sins, and there is no inkling of love towards any human being. Yet the sacred texts of his professed religion abound in instructions to cultivate such love: 'he that loveth not his brother whom he hath seen, how can he love God whom he hath not seen? And this commandment have we from him, That he who loveth God love his brother also' (I John 4: 20–1; see too I John 4: 7–12, I Corinthians 13 and, of course, the many sayings of Jesus himself on love of other, e.g. John 13:34). There is little of love in Donne's stance here.

Leaving this important feature aside, we also note that although there seems no more anxiety on the speaker's part than in Sonnet XVII, something else has also been lost. There is now no

sense of that subtle continuity in the self so well established in the
sonnet, nor any sense that in such continuity the self may have to
discriminate between kinds of love which are finally different but
have very much in common. Furthermore the poet gives no
attention to the ways in which the self must, willy-nilly, engage
with the world even if this involves pain and rejection. For it is
only by engagement that identity will be achieved, although one
that is always evolving, in process and at risk, something the
author of the passages we quoted from the *Devotions* knew well
enough. Yet in this poem Donne actually claims a *total* rupture
with his past and a retreat from a social world into an isolation far
more complete than the one he so loathed in his years at Mitcham
or described so eloquently and distastefully in his *Devotions*. The
irony here would be that having achieved the incorporation he so
longed for, Donne now enacts a deliberate, absolute, even cruelly
vindictive withdrawal—on his own terms and, at last, under the
control of his free will. There does indeed seem to us to be
something of this irony and savagery in the lines we have been
discussing, whatever Donne's conscious intentions may or may
not have been. However, when we focus on the extravagance of
the poet's claim ('I sacrifice this Iland unto thee') and the actual
occasion on which it was made (Donne about to 'embarke' as an
upper-class priest on a state mission), we cannot miss the bad
faith in this posture and its sadly strained distortion of his present
practice and commitments. He was no longer in circumstances
which could possibly allow him to claim that he was annihilating
the social world and/or totally withdrawing himself. Of course,
he *does* claim this, and the poetry we have just been describing
reveals the lack of charity and impoverished, simplified version of
the self that accompanies such bad faith in this text.

But if this is so, there are still features familiar enough from a
reading of other poems by Donne such as those we have
discussed. He still wishes to eliminate process, change and
development from the self, reminding us just how exceptional
was Sonnet XVII, and prompting the suggestion that the self-
image and overall movement of that sonnet proved too open-
ended, too risky for even an established Donne to live with:

> Nor thou nor thy religion dost controule,
> The amorousnesse of an harmonious Soule,
> But thou would'st have that love they selfe: As thou

Art jealous, Lord, so I am jealous now,   20
Thou lov'st not, till from loving more, thou free
My soule: Who ever gives, takes libertie:
   O, if thou car'st not whom I love
    Alas, thou lov'st not mee.

Seale then this bill of my Divorce to All,   25
On whom those fainter beames of love did fall;
Marry those loves, which in youth scattered bee
On Fame, Wit, Hopes (false mistresses) to thee.
Churches are best for Prayer, that have least light:
To see God only, I goe out of sight: 30
   And to scape stormy dayes, I chuse
    An Everlasting night.

(lines 17–32)

After the unattractive combination of lovelessness and utter
self-absorbtion we commented on above, the reader may well be
relieved to find the poet now seeming to rectify that impression
by writing of spiritual 'amorousnesse'. But while stanza three
does indeed open with the assertion that God does not control the
Christian's 'amorousnesse' this is immediately qualified. First the
freedom is limited to 'harmonious' souls, and this is hardly an
epithet one would use of Donne's soul (any more than he himself
habitually did). It is then still more drastically limited in the
following, complicated lines (19–24). These show that the freedom of love is actually the most coercive *restraint*. It is the
freedom (actually *restraint*) to love only God (in contrast to the
delicately multi-faceted vision of Sonnet XVII), and, perhaps yet
more strikingly, the freedom (actually *restraint*) not only from
loving more than God, but even from loving God more (lines
21–2). The significance of this statement for us is that it reveals
how absolutely Donne wished to eliminate the risks bound up
with open-ended processes of human development and choice.
Even though the subject was the potentially infinite love of the
Christian in and for his God, 'th'Eternall root/Of true *love*'
(lines 15–16), the poet wished to fix the relationship into a state
from which all process was banished. As in *Holy Sonnets,* XIV
(and other 'divine' poems) he wants the termination of all choice,
history and process. He is thus obliged to present human freedom
and Christian liberty as the total *loss* of liberty. The lines are
almost an oblique attack on God for ever having given man the

liberty essential to all moral activity and human responsibility—
'Thou lov'st not, till from loving more, thou free / My soule: Who
ever gives, takes libertie'. It is certainly relevant to remember
here how in *Holy Sonnets*, XIV, Donne insisted that he never
could be 'free' unless God imprisoned, enslaved and ravished
him. This version of freedom is a desperate flight from the
God-given Christian liberty which Milton was soon to celebrate
and struggle for in his writing and his life, yet it is one that recurs
in Donne's poetry.

The last stanza at last acknowledges certain continuities
between other objects of love and Donne's present quest for God.
Although there is absolutely no statement of reciprocal *relationship,* since Donne envisages himself as a weak sun beaming on
sundry recipients, this is far more promising than the line taken in
the poem's second stanza. It could lead to a genuinely self-reflexive exploration of how he was now indeed marrying very earthly
'Fame, Wit, Hopes' and service of God in a well-paid and
thoroughly respectable career among the elite of the state
church—a career which placed him in social circumstances in
keeping with his earlier secular aims. But he develops no such
explorations of the self and its continuities. Instead he repeats the
assertion of the second stanza, claiming that he has actually
chosen to 'goe out of sight' (line 30), a most strange phrase to
apply to himself at this stage of his life and work. The eloquent,
histrionic preacher and poet we admire was actually attaining the
public office and recognition he had always craved for, and the
very last thing he now intended was to 'goe out of sight'. The
'stormy dayes' he really chooses to escape seem to us more
properly perceived as those such as he had experienced in the
Mitcham period (often felt as a kind of hell by Donne) and
expressed in some of the writing we have examined in this and the
previous chapter. Far from choosing 'An Everlasting Night' in
this life, and in London, he had found that the way to establish his
self identity was exactly the one he had always wanted—
incorporation in the establishment. The life of an alienated
intellectual was not one Donne could embrace. Quite lacking any
oppositional ideology or coherently stable version of the self
(with its change and continuity), such a life was, in fact, one he
could never even tolerate.

4

The Language of Social Order: Individual, Society and Historical Process in *King Lear*

DAVID AERS and GUNTHER KRESS

> 'Who is it that can tell me who I am?'
> (*King Lear*, I. 4. 238)

In chapter 2 we noted Donne's ambivalent attitude to the 'established' society, to which he sought access. He saw clearly that access and membership bore no relation to intrinsic merit, but depended rather on 'use', on value derived by one individual from another within the contingencies of a market-oriented society. Donne, starting from an excluded position, was nevertheless prepared to put aside his misgivings about such values and seek access to that society no matter what the cost. The critical stance which he adopted in his poetry was thus a means of accounting to himself for his excluded position, rather than a fundamental critique of the society to which he sought admission. His critiques contain no suggestion of reform or revolution: provided only that he could be a member, he was content to leave society as it was, and accommodate himself to its demands and values.

There are some surprising overlaps between Donne, and Edmund in *King Lear*. Edmund is presented to us as someone who is excluded from the court, geographically and socially. The 'sojourn' from which he has briefly returned is a metaphor of his exclusion from court, an exclusion based on the accident of his birth, as, in a different sense, was Donne's. Edmund actively seeks to gain the place to which he feels himself fully entitled. The terms in which he articulates his position contain striking parallels to Donne's lines addressed to the Countess of Bedford. Here is Edmund:

Edmund   Wherefore should I
Stand in the plague of custom, and permit
The curiosity of nations to deprive me,
For that I am some twelve or fourteen moonshines
Lag of a brother? Why bastard? Wherefore base?
When my dimensions are as well compact,
My mind as generous, and my shape as true.

(I. 2. 2-8)

In our reading of Donne we have encountered the attack on convention and on values derived from convention, the reference to 'real' values beyond those sanctioned by the 'curiosity of nations', and, perhaps, in the way he opposed refined/unrefined, a form of Edmund's play on 'base'. Edmund, like Donne, is neither a reformer nor a revolutionary. However, his contempt for the society in which he seeks to establish himself is thorough, quite unlike Donne's ambivalent attitude. Edmund, unlike Donne, is plagued neither by feelings of self-negation nor by the wish for annihilation, which can, in Donne's case, only be alleviated by admission to the social group from which he is excluded. Edmund needs no alchemist to bring him into social existence, he will thrive by his own 'invention', and he grows and prospers with assistance from no-one. His personal position is buttressed by an ideology, and his analysis of the established society is founded on that alternative ideology: it is, as has been pointed out, that of the new breed of individualist men whose ideological position Hobbes was to articulate in *Leviathan*.[1]

King Lear is contemporaneous with Donne's Mitcham period, and provides an exploration of the society of which Donne and Shakespeare were both members. The terms in which that exploration was conducted were, as our initial comparison of Donne's views and those given by Shakespeare to Edmund suggest, at least in part the same. However, Shakespeare, in contrast to Donne, gives an account of how individuals find themselves to be as they are, he exemplifies the social construction of individuals. He examines the forces which form individuals, and the action of individuals, against the backdrop of the modes of action which a given society regards as legitimate. In the play a large number of individuals act outside the recognised modes. Lear is outraged at Cordelia's refusal to act as expected; significantly, no-one suggests that Lear's outrage was unjustified. Kent's argument with Lear is not over how Cordelia ought to have behaved, but that there may be other explanations for her failure to behave as expected. And while both the Fool (in I. 4) and Regan (in I. 1. 293–4) consider that Lear acted foolishly in his response to Cordelia, it is his action beyond the expected and recognised modes which they both, with their different motives, condemn. Albany is outraged by his wife's and sister-in-law's actions: 'Tigers, not daughters, what have you performed?' he shouts at Goneril (IV. 2. 40); she does not dispute that the action was beyond the bounds of the socially and conventionally acceptable, her defence is expediency. In *King Lear* new modes of behaving are thus actually being implemented, but Shakespeare shows the characters as more acted on than acting. The actions in which they are caught up stem from the momentum of a society which is in a process of change. They are forced to act in response to this momentum, and in so acting they establish new modes of conduct and behaviour. And, significantly, many of the characters undergo change. Indeed, *King Lear,* its society and its characters, are all marked by process, and with process, by history. The society we see at the end of the play is different to that we saw at the beginning. Certain modes of action have ceased to be possible.

Shakespeare explores the possible forms with which the society provides its members for evolving their identity, their relationships and practices. In *King Lear* language reflects and indicates these concerns in an astonishingly precise manner. Hence we have used detailed analysis of language to describe Shakespeare's examination of these topics. In this, our approach is based not only on an intuitive assumption that the form of language and its meaning stand in a determinate relation to each other, but on a general theory of language which holds that ideological systems are coded accurately in systems of linguistic features which, as a whole, go to make up texts. A speaker's choice of a given linguistic form always arises out of the ideological system which is relevant and operative for him at that point. Once a linguistic form is uttered it assumes a seeming reality, even for the speaker , so that the ideology appears in reified terms to the speaker and hearer, a second nature, which in time becomes the perceived and effective nature for speaker and hearer alike. This mechanism is involved in the construction of individuality and in the process of transmission and diffusion of social values. And it is this process which allows us to infer a speaker's values from the linguistic forms he uses.[2]

The play opens with a seemingly bland introduction of two noble, but secondary characters, at court. However, even within the first few lines, the problem of the definition of the individual is touched on, and foreshadowed. In the initial exchange between Gloucester and Kent we are shown two contrasting models of self: Gloucester, who is inclined to see himself in terms of the ascribed status of a hierarchically ordered society, and Kent, who presents himself as an individual who is not dependent on the status he holds in that society:

Kent	I thought the King had more affected the
	Duke of Albany than Cornwall.
Glou.	It did always seem so to us;

(I. 1. 1-3)

Gloucester's use of the plural pronoun form 'us', signals his wish to present himself as a member of the power-elite.[3] Kent by contrast, uses the first person singular form about himself—'I'. Shakespeare has at once, within the first brief utterance of each character, drawn a fundamental distinction between the two earls. Putting it schematically, within the society of *King Lear*, individuality may be defined and expressed in one of two distinct modes. Either an individual realises himself through socially given characteristics, apprehended by him as what is conventionally acceptable, hence accepted and internalised as 'natural' without any examination; or else the individual takes a critical stance towards the categories of the social world and attempts to express his individuality in a way which, while inevitably social, is not passively dependent on external and imposed definitions of socially appropriate identity and values. While the bare outline of such a schema does not do justice to the manifold nuanced ways in which different characters do realise and express their individuality, it allows us to perceive a point Shakespeare is making here about Kent and Gloucester, and about this society in general. Kent and Gloucester are equals socially, both are earls, and they are products of the one society. We are made aware that some choice remains, at least the choice between the models which one society offers.

Edmund's appearance on the scene forces Gloucester to confess to past behaviour which is not in keeping with the role he would wish to maintain: his admission of getting a wench with child, begetting a 'whoreson', forces him to relinquish the grand 'we' and use the personal 'I' instead:

Kent   Is not this your son, my Lord?
Glou.   His breeding, Sir, hath been at my charge:
        I have so often blushed to acknowledge him,
        that now I am braz'd to't.

(I. 1. 8–10)

Self-perception is shown to be contingent on situation. Although this opening appears as no more than a very minor by-play within the grander, more riveting theme which unfolds itself in the opening scene, Shakespeare is meticulous in his development of it. Here we have the merest hint of what Kent and Gloucester might be about, and what models they have chosen for themselves. Within the space of ten lines Gloucester has presented himself in two ways: as the status-conscious earl, and then, of necessity, as the wenching old man. Kent has remained unchanging.

Throughout the play the use of personal pronouns is a precise indicator of self-assessment and assessment of others by the characters. Lear's use of the royal 'we' of himself contrasts with the slighting 'thou' to Goneril and Regan. His use of the honorific 'you' to Cordelia serves to highlight the distinction he had drawn between her and her sisters; and it accentuates his abrupt switch to 'thou' when she refuses to accede to his demands. Similarly, Kent maintains the respectful use of 'you' to Lear, until the latter shows his unfitness to receive it:

Kent	be Kent unmannerly
	When Lear is mad. What wouldst thou do, old man?
	(I. 1. 145-6)

The two forms of the pronoun represent two fundamentally opposed modes of perceiving and representing the self. In these categories the multifaceted human being, with all his diverse potentialities, is fixed into the given social moulds, and individual identity becomes confined to the conventionally appropriate social form. If the human being, for whatever reasons, begins to resist such a process, he will probably experience the tension as some kind of alienation from his habitual social life. In the text we are discussing, the singular form of pronoun presents the person as an individuated being defined by specific personal qualities. The plural form presents the person as defined in terms of categories given by the social structures and the individual's position within them; self becomes a purely social concept. The different modes of perception indicated by the two forms of pronoun are certainly bound up with the existing social organisation and reflect important aspects of the individual's perception of relations between self and world. Hence it is Edmund, the most individualistic of the characters in the play, who by his social position as an outsider, by his virtual exclusion from the society of Lear's court, is least affected by its laws and conventions, who recognises and asserts that man is not governed by the stars, and is prepared to accept responsibility and acknowledge agency for his own actions. And it is Gloucester, perhaps the character most locked in the hierarchical order of his society, who does not see himself as an actor, and who assigns responsibility to an external, non-human, fixed hierarchy, to the planetary influences. Edmund's and Gloucester's language indicate how they perceive actions and their own possibilities of action.

Glou.	These late eclipses in the sun and moon
	portend no good to us: . . . yet Nature finds
	itself scourg'd by the sequent effects.
	Love cools, friendship falls off, brothers
	divide: in cities mutinies; in countries
	discord; . . . the King falls from bias of nature
	(I. 2. 107–16)

In this speech Gloucester either ascribes causes for actions to external agencies: 'these late eclipses in the sun and moon portend no good to us'; or he describes actions and events as simply happening: 'Love cools, friendship falls off, . . .'; that is, without discernible cause, or without the action of human agents, love 'just' cools, friendship 'just' falls off. Or else, actions just are: 'in cities mutinies; in countries discord'. The meaning of this syntax is a summary of Gloucester's ideological position at this time: to deny responsibility or ascribe it outside the human world, to refuse to look for or acknowledge the sources of human action, and to reify actions and treat them as unchanging attributes of social entities. However, Gloucester has an alternative syntax and ideology available:

Glou.   Find out this villain, Edmund; it shall lose thee
         nothing: do it carefully.
         (I. 2. 120–1)

Here he commands Edmund to act, and exhorts him to exercise full control in his actions. (Not: Attend the finding out of this villainy, Edmund). In the following concluding lines Gloucester reverts to the former syntax:

Glou.   And the noble and true-hearted Kent banish'd! his offence
         honesty! 'Tis strange.

                    (I. 2. 121–2)

Edmund brands Gloucester's attitudes as the 'excellent foppery of the world'. His soliloquy at the opening of Scene 2 shows a fundamentally different perception of the world:

Edmund   Thou, Nature, art my goddess; to thy law
          My services are bound. Wherefore should I
          Stand in the plague of custom, and permit
          The curiosity of nations to deprive me,
          For that I am some twelve or fourteen moonshines
          Lag of a brother? Why bastard? Wherefore base?
          When my dimensions are as well compact,
          My mind as generous, and my shape as true,
          As honest madam's issue? Why brand they us
          With base? with baseness? bastardy? base,
          base?
          Who in the lusty stealth of nature take
          More composition and fierce quality
          Than doth, within a dull, stale, tired bed,
          Go to th' creating a whole tribe of fops,

> Got 'tween asleep and wake? Well then,
> Legitimate Edgar, I must have your land:
> Our father's love is to the bastard Edmund
> As to th' legitimate. Fine word, "legitimate"!
> Well, my legitimate, if this letter speed,
> And my invention thrive, Edmund the base
> Shall top th' legitimate—: I grow, I prosper;
> Now, gods, stand up for bastards!
>
> (I. 2. 1–22)

The causes of actions and events which affect Edmund are clearly stated: The curiosity of nations deprives me, they brand us with base. The agents who are responsible for social conditions are known and named, and the effect of their actions indicated. And Edmund is equally clear that the remedy for his exclusion, far from being mystically bound up with lineage and inherited nature, is economic—'I must have your land'. The 'comparison' of base, baseness, bastardy shows Edmund's awareness of the source of abstract concepts: they derive from actions performed by human agents. He is not gulled by the reifications with which his society confronts him. He describes his eventual success in equally clear causal terms; he himself is responsible: 'Edmund shall top th' legitimate'. So when Edmund uses the non-transactive form 'I grow, I prosper' we know that these actions happen because Edmund intends to make them happen. And only then, only under those conditions, which *he* has made, does he invoke the 'gods', ironically—for he makes his own success. Of course, if self is defined in terms of status, and status exists as part of the social order quite apart from the individual's abilities, then the individual indeed merely fills a pre-existent position, without the ability to act, without the possibility or the need to claim responsibility for the actions which he carries out.

In contrast, the syntactic forms which Gloucester uses in the extract above related systematically to his use of pronouns, as discussed earlier. These are all part of the one ideological system which finds clear articulation in the language. The plural form of the pronoun, which defines the person in terms of the status he holds in society, and which distances the social *persona* from self is a part of the same ideological/linguistic system which uses agentless forms and forms with deleted agents. The impulse which seeks to define identity in terms of a position in a static hierarchical system is the same impulse which talks about actions and .events in reified terms. Edmund's use of the first person pronoun is similarly part of one ideological/linguistic system, a part of which will be his use of agentive syntactic forms, proclaiming his own responsibility or indicating the kind of causes involved in an event. And just as Gloucester is content to derive his self-definition from what he assumes or at least desperately hopes is a static social system, so the syntax he uses is marked by static forms: 'in cities (there *are*) mutinies', 'in countries (there *is*) discord', where the stative verb *to be* is used; or forms where actions performed by human agents are presented as noun/objects—'machinations', 'treachery', 'disorders'. Edmund relies on action initiated and performed by himself, and the syntax of his language is consequently a relatively more active syntax. These tendencies in the use of language are marked enough and consistent enough to allow us to speak of two distinct languages: one, a static and reified language, which belongs to the upper class ideology appropriate to a stable feudal society;[4] the other, a less formal, process-oriented language, which belongs to the ideology of the self-reliant individual, responsible for his own destiny. It is important to realise that these are tendencies. Shakespeare shows us not only a society composed of contradictory forces and individuals influenced by contradictory forces, he also shows a society in process, and individuals in the midst of a process, of change. Hence we are not likely to find—what would in fact amount to caricatures—characters who fully illustrate only one of the ideologies and languages. Nevertheless, some characters do at times come close to such positions, for instance Lear in his rage at Kent:

Lear   Hear me, recreant!
On thine allegiance, hear me!
That thou has sought to make us break our vows,
Which we durst never yet, and with strain'd pride
To come betwixt our sentence and our power,
Which nor our nature nor our place can bear,
                                              (I. 1. 166–71)

Lear uses the formal, alienated pronouns *we, our,* to refer to himself, and the contemptuous *thou, thine* to Kent. He talks about his actions in the reified nominal form: 'vows', 'sentence', and presents them as his attributes or possessions: '*our* vows', '*our* sentence', '*our* power', '*our* nature', '*our* place', '*our* potency', etc. Lear has gone further than Gloucester. Not only does he take his definition of self from his social place, he presents his self as constituted by the attributes which he lists. He exists as the sum-total of 'our power, our sentence, our dominion, our potency,' and his raging at Kent is due to the fact that in challenging one of Lear's actions, Kent has indeed challenged the very identity of Lear. The obverse of such a self-definition is that the human individual has become completely absorbed in the set of social abstractions and has ceased to exist, except in these fragmentations. Of course the irony of Lear's predicament is that he is annihilating himself when he relinquishes his claim to these abstractions. For Lear the rest of his life is a journey to re-establish an identity. When he finds it towards the end of the play the language he speaks is totally purged of these forms:

Lear   Where have I been? Where am I? Fair daylight?
I am mightily abus'd, I should e'en die with pity
To see another thus. I know not what to say.
I will not swear these are my hands; let's see;
I feel this pin prick. Would I were assured
Of my condition!

(IV. 7. 52–7)

Lear's changing perceptions of self do of course depend on and are a response to his changing social condition: he has contributed to the collapse of his social position, and with this he is inevitably rejected by the new ruling elite. Shakespeare exhibits changing individual identity and social identity in dialectical unity.

However, *King Lear* is not about a simple dichotomy between the two modes of perceiving self. As we have shown, a character may assume either position at different times; as does Gloucester even in the first few lines when his pomposity has been undercut by Kent's allusion to Edmund's birth; as does Kent when he loses faith in Lear's ability to act reasonably, and indeed, as do several characters as they undergo change during the play. Lear lapses from the formal mode of speech in this opening scene when he loses his temper, first with Cordelia, then with Kent, and last with

France. For these characters therefore, a shift from their normal mode of interrelation and self-perception arises as the result of some unsettling, undercutting experience, from a loss of control. For Lear, Kent and Gloucester alike, albeit in different ways, relations directly as one human being to another human being are proscribed by the social laws which govern their actions. 'Loss of control' has, for them, an ambiguous meaning; on the one hand they lose control of a situation in terms of the forms of conduct which they know they ought to be following, on the other hand, the social conventions lose their control over the characters they are meant to govern. Direct human relations, and immediate perceptions of self as an individual, are possible only in conditions of stress, which cause the characters to move unwittingly and unwillingly out of their habitual forms of perception. This extremely painful process entails loss of control, tension and the subversion of existing conventions. This may be an indication of the insecurity and uncertainty about the depth to which the traditionally dominant value system reaches even for those characters who are the firmest adherents to the received mode of social organisation and the conventions arising from it.

Edmund has no allegiance to this system. As someone who is outside the system he cannot, even if he would, define self in terms of status, for he has none. Perhaps more precisely, the status he has is an ambiguous one: as an aristocratic bastard he is much superior to an Oswald, or a servant, though he has no settled status within the court-hierarchy. This ambiguity is documented by Lawrence Stone:

> in the sixteenth century, husbands felt free to take lower-class mistresses and to beget bastards without any sense of shame and any attempt at concealment. The children of these unions were frequently mentioned in wills and open provision was made for their upkeep and education. In the early seventeenth century, however, the public attitude towards these liaisons temporarily altered under Puritan pressure, and they became much more secretive. Bastards largely disappear from aristocratic wills, and far greater discretion seems to have been exercised in the degree of public recognition afforded to a mistress.[5]

The only pronoun Edmund uses in referring to himself, is the first person singular; though in referring to others he changes between 'you' and 'thou' as the situation warrants. Even when he has been made Earl of Gloucester, he continues to refer to himself in the same fashion. He is 'self-made', so this makes sense. He has assumed responsibility for his actions from the beginning, hence he need not see his achieved status as an alienating state. In the society of *King Lear* Edmund represents a force which owes no loyalty to the traditional order, indeed he sees through the ideology supporting the traditional order and recognises it as vacuous. He is prepared to use the existing order: he aims to get what he regards as his, due to him by virtue of his own 'nature', and if it will be his within the terms of the existing social order then Edmund is prepared to operate within that order, using it for his purposes. In itself his is not a revolutionary position—that is, no specific alternative form of social order is implied in his actions. However, the tendency is clearly subversive of the traditional value system. So we find Edmund using the language of the traditional system in order to manipulate it or individuals within it for his own ends. In this he is not alone. Goneril and Regan are, like Edmund, prepared to manipulate the existing social order, to achieve their aims. They have no commitment to the traditional upper class ideology, and while they have not articulated their own ideology as clearly as Edmund, and are quite content to leave the social forms as they are, their actions are as subversive of the social order as Edmund's.[6]

The society of *King Lear* is unstable. On the one hand there are the proponents of the old order. For them personality is constituted in terms of status; even those who, like Kent, are able to separate individual self from social self, derive their social relationships, their obligations and loyalties, in short all of their social actions, from the existing social order. Yet even for them this system is unstable. On the other hand there is Edmund who owes no allegiance at all to this system, but is prepared to manipulate it for his own gain; or those who, like Goneril and Regan (or Oswald) receive their awards as a result of being members of the system, without commitment to any of its values, and who are prepared to exploit it cynically for their own ends. Paradoxically, the instability also derives from those characters who have a single-minded commitment to the old values. Cor-

delia's unyielding adherence to some of the forms of the old order
contributes to this instability:

Cor.   I love your Majesty
                   According to my bond; no more nor less.
                                          (I. 1. 92–3)
Cor.   Good my Lord,
          You have begot me, bred me, lov'd me; I
          Return those duties back as are right fit,
          Obey you, love you, and most honour you.

                                          (I. 1. 95–8)

Her equally fierce determination to uphold the values of the
society in their purest form leads her to transgress against one
fundamental requirement within the traditional system, that of
obedience.

Cor.   Unhappy that I am, I cannot heave
            My heart into my mouth:

Here she is asserting that where words have been totally cor-
rupted, it is impossible to use them to describe reality, so that
silence is the only option. The kind of conservatism which
Cordelia exhibits here, which takes the traditional ideology so
literally, with such relentless commitment, may become a subversive force in itself. And, as we have noted, the refusal to speak is
a rebellion against one plank in the received ideology—the
patriarchal and hierarchical authorities have been challenged by
Cordelia. No doubt Cordelia's action is based on a careful
weighing of the contradictory demands of aspects of the traditional ideology. Her kind of individualistic affirmation of the
'platonic' values drives her into a negation of the hierarchical
loyalties which she might otherwise affirm. In a similar fashion,
the servant who kills Cornwall, acts out of a belief in the older
values:

First Servant   Hold your hand my Lord.
          I have serv'd you ever since I was a child,
          But better service have I never done you
          Than now to bid you hold

                                          (III. 7. 72–5)

Such a belief—in the realities of the older values, and actions carried out on the basis of them—is subversive in a society that supports the forms, but not the meanings. In that context a literal belief in the values constitutes a challenge to the existing order. The servant is, of course, no revolutionary with a specific programme. However, he is very much a revolutionary in relation to the new emerging order represented by Edmund, Goneril, Regan, the Captain. To that new order the servant's conservatism poses a real threat—indeed he kills the new-style king![7] Regan may perceive the ideological as well as the direct physical threat when she says 'A servant stand up thus!' The kind of employee needed by Regan and the order which she represents is illustrated by Edmund's 'captain' in Act V. 3. 26–40. The exchange between the two exemplifies the new ethos in action. Edmund appeals to no personal loyalties, traditional values or fixed obligations. Instead he accepts social mobility and market relations as the reality within which 'employment' is bestowed: men's labour and obedience is to be *bought* for particular services, and men who sell their labours to an employer in this way, and wish for continued 'employment' from him, will be 'as the time is', in the current employer's definition. All consideration of human ends, of moral or social values, is dissolved as the employee accepts a highly abstract definition of 'man's work', one which is appropriate to the new social organisation and relationships. Like Oswald, Goneril's steward, this employee accepts that obedience and employment must take place within an impersonal, pragmatic market nexus. He embraces the alienation of his labour-powers, the alienation of his moral being and personal relationships in the pursuit of 'man's work' in the newer social order which Shakespeare portrays through Edmund and his allies.

Cordelia recognises that in the society of *King Lear* the relation between meaning and symbol has broken down; the servant does not, and wishes to protect his master Cornwall from carrying out an action which he feels Cornwall would not wish to commit. Lear, like the servant, is unaware of the meaninglessness of symbols in his world:

Lear   Only we shall retain
            The name and all th' addition to a king; the sway,
            Revenue, execution of the rest,

> Beloved sons, be yours: which to confirm,
> This coronet part between you.
>
> (I. 1. 135–9)

His delusion is that the symbols carry their meaning in themselves, rather than being expressions of referents in the real world. Hence he believes that he can dispose of the referents (his lands, etc.) and retain 'the name and all th' addition to a king', not realising that there is no name and there are no additions once the material and social basis of the King's power has disappeared. This is of course what the Fool realises only too well and with evident anguish (I. 4. 167–71; I. 5; II. 4. 46–55) As the link between meaning and form has been severed Cordelia is unable to say anything, to 'heave her heart into her mouth'. If words have no constant relation to meanings it is impossible to express what one feels. Hence the only statement she can make is in terms of the conventions of the traditional system. She characterises her father's actions and her own in terms of rights and duties. Lear discharged the duties of begetting, breeding, and loving her, and she discharges hers in turn, in loving and honouring Lear. Indeed it is questionable whether anything in Cordelia's past experience or any past action on her father's part prepared her for anything other than the discharging of duties. There is no indication that Lear's relation with his daughters had been other than on a formal plane. When Goneril and Regan superciliously berate Cordelia for her conduct they articulate clearly the terms in which they had seen the demand:

Regan   Prescribe not us our *duty*
> (I. 1. 275)
Gon.   You have *obedience* scanted
> (I. 1. 278)

Clearly it was the daughters' duty to utter rote expressions of 'love'. Regan's shock at Cordelia's behaviour may even be real; it seems to be the same shock that she displays at the peasant's 'standing-up'. It may well be that she firmly holds that obedience must not be scanted—unless it serves her to do so. Goneril's charge also pinpoints Cordelia's error: it is not that she scanted her father, but obedience. Goneril, Regan and no doubt Cordelia too, saw Lear in terms of abstractions which constituted the monarch, and hence for him and for the daughters, constituted the father. As we mentioned above, Lear's faulty understanding of symbols may have led him to believe that a demand for love—expressed in imperatives—could call forth the expression of real love.

Lear   *Tell* me, my daughters,
             (Since now we will divest us both of rule,
             Interest of territory, cares of state)
             Which of you shall we say doth love us most?
             That we our largest bounty may extend
             Where nature doth with merit challenge. Goneril,
             Our eldest-born, *speak* first.
                                               (I. 1. 48–54)

The heavy irony of this demand, in which Lear even switches from the pronouns 'me', 'my', appropriate to a father speaking to his daughters, to the formal, power-laden pronouns 'we', 'us', seems to have gone unnoticed by everyone except Cordelia. In fact, the nature of life at Lear's court may be judged not just by the kind of demand Lear makes, but by the form in which he makes it. It seems unlikely that anyone who commands love, in these terms, was capable of a loving parent-child relationship.[8] Lear had of course made his decision about the value of his children's love beforehand: the map which he has handed to him has the new partitions of the kingdom already marked in. Life at Lear's court prior to this event may also be judged from the language employed by Lear in dismissing Cordelia.

Lear   Here I disclaim all my paternal care
        Propinquity and property of blood,
        And as a stranger to my heart and me
        Hold thee from this for ever
                                (I. 1. 113–16)

Even though he uses the pronoun *I* (he has lost control) the syntax appropriately describes the manner in which he sees this event. Not as 'I cease to care about you', which would indicate a direct relationship between the father and the daughter, but as a relation between himself and an abstraction 'my paternal care'—which Lear treats, syntactically, as yet another attribute possessed by, but separate from him. The social world exists for

Lear in a system of reified entities; as we have pointed out, this extends to Lear's perception of himself and of his relations even with his children. In speaking to Kent, he says

Lear   That thou has sought to make us break our vows,
           Which we durst never yet, and with strain'd pride
           To come betwixt our sentence and our power
           Which nor our nature nor our place can bear.

                                          (I. 1. 168–73)

Here the relation between individual and social self is totally externalised. The nouns 'vows', 'sentence', 'power', stand in a determinate relation to the sentences *I vow, I sentence you, I have power/am powerful*. In these sentence forms Lear is the actor who initiates and is responsible for the process expressed by the verb. In the nominalisation the processes have become abstract reified states, conditions, objects, to which Lear stands in a relation of possession. Lear conceives of these as being beyond his own influence so that he has become the pawn of his own abstractions. If we relate this to our earlier comments about alienation of self from self, we can see that this is the same phenomenon in an extreme form. Though the symbols may be losing their potency in the social world of *King Lear,* they have not yet lost their potency for Lear.

It is important to acknowledge that a less alienated form of language is available to members of the court. The choice, as we have shown, is between the formal, powerful language, which refers itself to the existing static hierarchy, and the less formal language which does not assert power and refers itself to the individual. In the choice between a full sentence form and its nominalised equivalent (for instance the difference between a judge saying *I sentence you* and *my sentence*) the former mentions the individual, who appears as the subject/actor in the sentence, whose responsibility for the control of the action is acknowledged; the latter form, the nominalisation, omits mention of the individual as actor (though the individual may appear as *possessor*). Just as members of Lear's court may use the singular or the plural pronoun to refer to self, so they may use the sentence-syntax, or the nominal syntax. Cordelia, in answering Lear, uses the sentence syntax, without the burden of the nominalisations and reifications of Lear's language.

Cor.   You have begot me, bred me, lov'd me: I
         Return those duties back as are right fit,
         Obey you, love you, and most honour you.

                                              (I. 1. 96–8)

Cordelia might have been made to speak in the nominalised, alienated syntax, using *begetting, breeding, love, obedience, honour,* etc. Her language is not wholly free of such abstract forms; even in the few lines that follow those above she uses *my plight, my care.* But in doing this Shakespeare is making an important point: no-one can fully escape the dominant modes of thinking and speaking in his or her society. The ideological position which any one individual holds is likely to be a specific amalgam of the ideological models which are current and available in a given society. As language encodes these ideologies, the language spoken by any one individual will, similarly, be a mix of the available linguistic forms. These amalgams and mixes are not unmotivated or amorphous, for individuals make selections which are guided by their own social contingencies and psychological needs. Shakespeare is being highly realistic, not inconsistent.

   In fact, Shakespeare has distributed his characters into roughly three groups: 1. those whose perceptions are formed within the alienated formal language: Lear, Gloucester, to some extent Kent; 2. those who move easily out of and into the two forms of language: Goneril, Regan, Edmund; and 3. those who, like Cordelia, and the Fool, seem to stand initially within the direct personal, individual language. For the first group, the move to the informal, personal, individual language involves the destruction of their former self, a painful process of disintegration and reconstitution. For the second group, the use of the formal language is a mere device, and hence nothing of any personal cost is involved. Their ideology is clearly articulated by their use of the direct, personal language. The third group is more problematic: the Fool dies, and so we do not know what psychological effect Shakespeare thought his experiences would have had on him. The Fool does not change his language during the part of the play where we meet him. And though he seemingly takes a detached view of events, his anguish is evident. Above all we may note that he himself does not take the advice which he offers to Kent: 'Let go thy hold when a great wheel runs down a hill, lest it break thy neck with following' (II. 4. 71–3). In the conflict between understanding and practice, between his penetrating grasp of social change and his emotional resistance to accommodation with a new order, we may perhaps see the figuration of one type of the alienated intellectual we have met in earlier chapters. The manifestation of critical insight in the traditional forms of wise-folly, inspired-madness, is shown to be the result of insight without any possibility of its being realised in social practice. Cordelia however, survives long enough for us to note a change in her language: when we meet her again she is in command of the French army, she is the queen, and her language has become regal. She uses the plural pronoun of herself:

Cor.   A century send forth;
        Search every acre in the high-grown field;
        And bring him to *our* eye
                        (IV. 4. 6–9)

and she uses the abstractions and nominalisations which characterise the formal language:

Cor.   *our preparation* stands
        In *expectation* of them. O dear father!
        It is thy business that I go about;
        Therefore great France
        My mourning and importun'd tears hath pitied.
        No *blown ambition* doth our arms incite,
        But love, dear love, and *our ag'd father's right.*
                        (IV. 4. 22–8)

From this we might infer that Cordelia's movement, psychologically, has been in the opposite direction to her father's—that is, having gained power she has assumed the linguistic forms of power and the perceptions of self which these entail. However, it seems that Shakespeare is making a different point, for in her relations with those characters who are important to her, Kent and Lear, she uses the direct, personal language.

Cor.   O *thou* good Kent! How shall *I* live and work
        To match *thy* goodness?
                        (IV. 7. 1–2)

Cor.   And wast *thou* fain, poor father
            To hovel *thee* with swine and rogues forlorn,
            In short and musty straw?

                                      (IV. 7. 38–40)

The point Shakespeare seems to be making is that it is possible to
fulfil the duties and obligations entailed in the role of the
powerful, and yet maintain personal, human relations with other
human beings. It seems that Shakespeare is positively asserting
this point, for in Kent's form of address to Cordelia, and in
Cordelia's to her waking father, these two use the polite *you*.

Cor.   O *thou* good Kent
Kent   My boon I make it that *you* know me not

                                      (IV. 7. 1, 10)

Here, decorum is observed, and those who deserve it are paid
due deference. Shakespeare is momentarily showing how the old
society might have been in its ideal form, and suggesting that it
would be a desirable state to achieve. The form here has its
'ideal', full meaning. Similarly with Cordelia to Lear:

Cor.   How does my royal Lord? How fares your Majesty?

                                      (IV. 7. 44)

Shakespeare is not attacking the traditional language and the
inherited social form as such, but is attacking its debased version,
where it has lost value and significance, and is used merely as a
cynical device by those who hold a quite different ideology.
However, it is important to point out one condition which
accompanies the use of this language, even in its ideal form.
Cordelia, as the queen, is able to use the intimate *thou* to Kent,
suspending any assertion of her power and authority. Kent
cannot reciprocate the intimate form of address, he uses the
formal *you*. There is thus an inevitably skewed relationship,
where the powerful may attempt to deny their power, but the
(relatively) less powerful must always acknowledge the fact of
power. It is not clear whether Cordelia is aware of this unbridge-
able gulf; though at the beginning of the play she stood on the
other side of this same chasm when her royal father attempted to
elicit a statement of genuine love from her—unaware on his part
of the fundamental impossibility of the enterprise.

Of course, Lear and Cordelia are killed, and there is a strong implication that Kent intends to commit suicide. Hence those who have learned to operate with full perception, those who might be able to wield power and yet maintain human relationships, cannot survive in this society. Nor indeed do the proponents of the new ideology. Left on the stage are Edgar and Albany. Albany's actions throughout the play have not given any indication of either the ability or the willingness to act positively, or indeed of any inclination or ability to change. Goneril's contemptuous dismissal of him from the very beginning of the play seems entirely appropriate. Albany's language is that of the agonised humanistic moralist, beating his breast in anguish at the lamentable state of the world. In depicting Albany, and in leaving him alive on the stage at the end, Shakespeare may have been exploring one possible critical response to the new world. Albany's preferred modal adjective is *may:*

Albany   Well, you may fear too far
                              (I. 4. 338)
Albany   How far your eyes may pierce I cannot tell:
                    Striving to better, oft we mar what's well
                                      (I. 4. 355–6)

His discourse consists largely of pious platitudes, as in the lines above, or in the following lines:

Albany   Well, well; th' event
                              (I. 4. 358)
Albany   Wisdom and goodness to the vile seem vile;
                    Filths savour but themselves
                                      (IV. 2. 38–9)

His preferred utterance form is the rhetorical question, and the outraged, indignant exclamation:

Albany   What have you done?
                    Tigers, not daughters, what have you perform'd?
                                      (IV. 2. 39–40)
Albany   Could my brother suffer you to do it?
                              (IV. 2. 44)

'Fitness' however, prevents him from acting in opposition to the evil which he sees:

Albany   Were't my fitness
To let these hands obey my blood,
They are apt enough to dislocate and tear
Thy flesh and bones; how'er thou art a fiend,
A woman's shape doth shield thee.

                                        (IV. 2. 63–7)

Moralistic attitudes are separated from practice, and Goneril's
retort—'Marry, your manhood—mew!'—is very much to the
point. It is typical of Shakespeare's profound grasp of psychological and social tendencies that he next shows us Albany as one of
the generals fighting against Cordelia and Lear: the man who
represents educated, privatised benevolence joins action on the
side of Goneril, Regan and Edmund, the side where current
power resides—in spite of the fact that this is a group which
Albany has characterised as 'barbarous' (IV. 2. 43). However
much he attempts to distance himself from his role in this battle,
he lends his respectable moral and religious face to the evil cause,
thereby giving it much needed respectability. Edmund is fully
aware of Albany's position:

Edmund   Now then, we'll use
His countenance for the battle; which being done,
Let her who would be rid of him devise
His speedy taking off.

                                        (V. 2. 62–5)

Albany's strategy of sheltering behind decorum, the 'done thing',
is clear enough, and explicit in his lines, 63–7. However, we also
note the linguistic forms which speak of the alienated individual,
who regards his powers as having been usurped by the reified
abstractions of his psychological and social world. Thus the
ruling category (and potent actor) in his world is 'my fitness'; and
the urgings of his 'blood' are not permitted by his 'fitness' to act.
Even so, 'fitness', 'hands' and 'blood' seem curiously dissociated
from Albany himself, as though the individual existed as a
collection of disparate entities, with nowhere an integrating self.
Indeed the will of this person comes from outside, from the social
category 'fitness'. This is not to say that Albany is not 'sincere' in

what he feels. The point is that he is caught between the conventional imperatives, and the urgings of his 'blood', which include ties to his wife, to his land, and to his foolishly irrelevant nationalism. Hence we can believe him even when he says:

Albany   Where I could not be honest
I never yet was valiant: for this business
It touches us, as France invades our land,
Not bolds the King, with others, whom, I fear,
Most just and heavy causes make oppose.
                              (V. 1. 23–7)

These lines sum up Albany: again 'fitness' prevents him from exercising valour in an unjust cause; while he ought to be defending his country against the invaders, he can see the justice of their cause, though in fact he does eventually fight a victorious battle against them. Edmund's caustic 'Sir, you speak nobly.' is an entirely appropriate reply, but speaking nobly is an empty exercise for people in this society—noble speech has no content.

Edgar is somewhat more difficult to assess. As with Albany, or the servant, Shakespeare uses Edgar to explore the possibilities which critical resistance to the new world might take. He has experienced life at the extreme ends of the social scale. His compassion is undeniable; his experience has exposed him to human suffering at its most extreme. He is a 'noble' human being. Yet his response to Edmund in Act five is conducted totally within the conventions of the traditional social order, in terms of both his language and the form of ritualised knightly combat (for example, V. 3. 107–50 and 165–74). As Tom he speaks a less formal language in his soliloquies and asides than the other 'high' characters at the beginning of the play:

Edgar   Yet better thus, and known to the contemn'd
Than, still contemn'd and flatter'd to be worst.
                              (IV. 1. 1–2)

or to his father

Edgar   Give me thy arm:
Poor Tom shall lead thee.
                              (IV. 1. 78–9)

But he finds the language of poor Tom difficult to sustain.

> *Edgar*   Why, then your other senses grow imperfect
>   By your eyes anguish
>
>   (IV. 4. 5–6)

This is the typical 'court language', where abstractions are the potent agents. Gloucester immediately recognises this and comments on it.

> *Glou.*   Methinks thy voice is alter'd, and thou speak'st
>   In better phrase and matter than thou didst.
>
>   (IV. 6. 8–9)

This language is, in the end, Edgar's preferred language: he slips into it 'naturally'; it is the language in which he thinks. Edgar's case illustrates the difficulty of getting beyond the determining and shaping influences of the prevalent modes of thought. Those characters who do, pay for the escape with their lives.

As we have attempted to show, neither of the two survivors, Albany and Edgar, has achieved knowledge of self or society. Albany's moral convictions no doubt remain, both high-flown and unconvincing. There is no suggestion that he would act differently were the circumstances of the play renewed. Edgar has experienced life fully; yet he lapses into convention and ritual, and his concluding speech is platitudinous. Yet Albany is left as the figure with authority, and we must ask what Shakespeare may have meant by doing this. Is it that Shakespeare felt a nostalgia for the traditional social order he presented both critically and as one in the process of disintegration? Our brief discussion of Cordelia as Queen and of the feudal servant's fine and basic decency lends support to such an interpretation. Possibly Shakespeare wished to endorse Edgar's platitudes? Perhaps he did, yet he also wrote the last two lines of the play to convey a wholly negative effect. He offers absolutely no sign that Albany or Edgar are capable of reversing the historical processes he has shown dissolving the old social order and the individual identities of its leaders. The play, after all, disclosed the old order as generating its own supersession, not overwhelmed by some external contingency. In our view, the tension here comes from Shakespeare's inability to imagine any real alternative beyond the disintegrating traditional order and the utterly destructive individualism which emerges from it. The bafflement and despair in this simultaneous affirmation and negation of a lost 'past' are fully understandable in the historical moment of the play, and would certainly have struck answering sympathies in contemporaries such as Donne.

5

Mine Eyes Dazzle: False Consciousness In Webster's Plays

BOB HODGE

There is a widespread myth that the audience of Elizabethan drama, Shakespeare's audience, transcended class boundaries. Jacobean drama, the same myth has it, degenerated when the organic unity of the Elizabethan audience was destroyed by the development of the private theatres. Here is Harbage, whose scholarly work on the size and composition of Elizabethan audiences has done much to give a basis for the myth:

> Shakespeare's audience was an audience of the many. It was com-
> posed of human beings like ourselves, with craftsmen and shop-
> keepers predominating, but with the gentry and nobility well repre-
> sented, the selective principle consisting simply of possession by each
> spectator of some spiritual vitality, some trace of the contemplative
> mind—in a word susceptibility to the appeal of dramatic art.[1]

In fact there was another selective principle at work, which would have excluded over half the population from attending plays, by Shakespeare or anyone else. The earliest attempt at a comprehensive estimate we have of the makeup of English society as a whole was written by Gregory King in 1696.[2] It gives a picture of English society that is likely to be true, in outline at least, for the early seventeenth century as well. In King's estimate, the total population was 5,500,250. He divides these

100

into two large categories, those who 'increase the wealth of the kingdom', and those who 'decrease' it. This is a quaint way of distinguishing between those whose income was greater than their expenditure, and those who could not make ends meet. Those who 'decreased' the wealth of the kingdom weren't particularly extravagant. Their average expense per head was only £3.38 a year, or 6 pence a week (£3 7s. 6d a year: 1s 3½d a week). Their problem was an income of only £3.15 a year, or 5 pence a week (£3 3s a year: 1s. a week). At the top of the table of those who increased the wealth of the country were what King calls 'temporal Lords'. The expenses for the family of one of these temporal Lords were £70 per head a year, twenty times more than for the 'decreasers'. This still left the family of such a lord with £10 per head a year surplus, which is three times the total income of the spendthrifts below the poverty line. This group of indigent people included 2,825,000 out of the total population, slightly over half. They would have been unlikely to go to any theatre, in King's or in Shakespeare's time.

The position of the poorer members of the community was almost certainly worse in Shakespeare's London. Price inflation was rampant through most of the sixteenth century. Wages also rose, but not nearly so steeply. The urban working populace were especially hard-hit. Rural workers often had a small patch of land whose produce could eke out their wages. Urban workers had to live on what their wages could buy in the market. Phelps-Brown and Hopkins carried out a study of the wages of building workers over a seven-century span, relating the wages to the cost of a standard 'shopping basket' of basic necessities of food and clothing.[3] They took 1451-75, a period of stable prices, as their base. By 1610, prices were five times higher. The purchasing power of wages, however, had dropped to 40 per cent, or two fifths of its value. Phelps-Brown and Hopkins take their figures up to 1954. The *real* wage value of building workers in this year was five times what it had been for their Jacobean ancestors in 1610. Games with figures can be misleading, of course, but on all accounts the impression given by these figures corresponds to the situation of many workers in Jacobean society. They must have been living very close to the bread line. There would have been little left over for the luxury of going to the theatre, even if they had possessed large amounts of what Harbage calls 'spiritual vitality'. In King's scheme, there is a large group of people just above the break-even point, including shopkeepers, tradesmen and artisans, whose income per head averaged £10 or less a year. If we assume that these people could not have afforded to go regularly to plays, we have 80 per cent of the populace who can't normally be included in 'Shakespeare's audience'. Harbage's 'many', who are 'human beings like ourselves', were perhaps only 20 per cent of the whole. This is roughly the same percentage of the populace in England today who study English at 'O' and 'A' level, where Shakespeare is likely to be a set text. The analogy is intriguingly close. Perhaps nothing much has changed in three and a half centuries.

But Harbage's case about developments in the Jacobean theatre is essentially correct. The public theatres charged 1 pence, 2 pence and 3 pence a head. They undoubtedly drew their audiences from a wider spectrum of the populace than did the private theatres, where the cheapest seats cost 6 pence, and better seats cost 12 pence and upwards. The two kinds of theatre developed different kinds of repertoire and styles, as dramatists tried to reflect the interests and values of the different kinds of audience. The split no doubt reflected the fissure that was developing in society at large, which was to lead to a revolutionary confrontation within three decades. The drama witnesses to a growing class consciousness, a growing sense of allegiance to a class. The class antagonism was expressed and simplified by exclusions, the rich and powerful withdrawing into the closed world of the private theatre, leaving the public theatres to the lesser citizens.

This whole development seems prophetic of later events. But it is important to point out that once the sense of class conflict has been expressed in this way, through a split in the audience, it is less likely to be expressed or explored directly in the drama itself. A class consciousness is of its nature partial. It involves an ability to grasp the whole of society and to see that its sense of the whole is one-sided and distorted. Elizabethan and Jacobean drama show how this can affect works produced in a class context. Elizabethan drama was class drama. The interests and experience of three quarters of the population were not available to provide it with subjects or problems. But writers like Shakespeare and Marlowe were at least able to focus directly and powerfully on the division between the ruling classes, or more precisely, on the challenge for hegemony that was then taking place, even if they were unable to see the full context of this struggle, or the role that could be played by those who were excluded.

Jacobean dramatists were working within much narrower limits. In the rest of this essay I will be looking at one dramatist, John Webster, in order to explore in greater detail the consequences of this situation for the artist. Webster is of course a minor figure, probably less intelligent than either Jonson or Middleton at least among his more immediate contemporaries. The quality of his work is notoriously uneven. He shows a bewildering mixture of insight and naïvety, manifest control and apparent incompetence. It is precisely this mixture that makes him an interesting and significant figure. His problems and confusions have a representative status. They also obscure the nature of his real if limited achievement.

A sense of class conflict can be seen in various parts of Webster's life and work. Webster himself was born into the middle of the middle classes. He was a freeman of the Merchant Taylors company from birth, he claimed late in his career.[4] But his career as a dramatist shows some degree of ambivalence. His early plays, written in collaboration with dramatists like Dekker, were directed unmistakeably at a city audience. But *The White Devil* of 1612, his first independent play and one of the two works on which his reputation is largely based, shows signs of dissatisfaction with the values of city drama, though it opened at the Red Bull, one of the public theatres. *The Duchess of Malfi*, of 1613-14, his other major work, is even more equivocally placed. It apparently played with success before both kinds of audience. It has the elevated style and aristocratic cast typical of plays for the private theatres, though in this play as in all Webster's productions Webster's language is notoriously mixed in levels, ranging from high poetic to the vigorously colloquial with bewildering rapidity. But *The Devil's Law-Case*, written about 5 years after his success with *The Duchess*, returns closer to the language and situations of city drama again.

Webster's prefaces to these three plays, the only ones which survive that can be wholly attributed to him, show a marked ambivalence of tone that seems to come from uncertainty or insecurity about his class position. In the preface to *The White*

Devil he exclaims disgustedly against the 'ignorant asses' who attended the first performance at 'that Playhouse': however fine a play may be, '*O dura messorum ilia,* the breath that comes from the uncapable multitude, is able to poison it'. These 'ignorant asses' in fact were mostly members of his own class. The 'multitude' exists only as an image for his rejection of his origins. But towards George Harding, Baron Berkeley, the dedicatee of *The Duchess,* he adopts a more equivocal stance, a prickly and assertive parody of Jonsonian independence. There has been no preliminary personal contact, he begins, yet he protests, 'I do not altogether looke up at your *Title:* The ancient's *Nobility,* being but a rellique of time past, and the truest *Honor* indeede beeing for a man to conferre Honor on himselfe'. 'Altogether' has a highly problematic force in this dedication. It suggests only a slight witholding of total reverence for a noble title, yet the rest of the sentence professes total indifference for the basis of such claims. George Harding, 13th Lord Berkeley since the writ of 1295, had an ancient title, but the only honour he conferred on himself was to act as patron to Robert Burton, author of *Anatomy of Melancholy.* But Webster had died by then. *The Devil's Law-Case* has a double dedication, one to the 'Juditious Reader' (not to be confused with the 'windy Plebs', he insists,) the other to 'the right worthie, and all-accomplisht Gentleman, Sir Thomas Finch, Knight Baronet'. His independence of this knight is even less gracious. 'I present this humbly to kisse your hands, and to find your allowance. Nor doe I much doubt it, knowing the greatest of the *Caesars* have cheerefully entertain'd lesse Poems than this: and had I thought it unworthy, I had not enquired after so worthy a Patronage.' Here the humility of 'kisse your hands' changes to total confidence in the worth of his poem, which then seems to guarantee Finch's worth, not vice versa. The comparison with the 'greatest of the *Caesars*' does not elevate Finch, it only devalues the literary judgment of Caesars. Finch, it seems, is lucky to have such a good poet around who has chosen to honour him. The only 'worth' left for Finch's patronage to exhibit is its cash value. 'Allowance' could mean 'income' in Jacobean English. The admirable Delio uses the word in this sense in *The Duchess,* II. 4. 80. If it had the same meaning here, Webster would be presenting the patron-poet relationship in a particularly unpleasant form, degrading and resentful servility on the one side, mere economic power on the other.

The three plays themselves seem, superficially at least, to be concerned with class conflict and its resolution. The action of all three starts from an alliance that goes across class boundaries. Even at this level there are some interesting differences to see over Webster's career. In both *The White Devil* and *The Duchess of Malfi* there is a marriage which precipitates the conflict. In *The White Devil* the non-aristocratic Vittoria marries Duke Brachiano. In *The Duchess,* the aristocratic Duchess marries her steward, Antonio. In both plays, there is ducal opposition to the match. Duke Francisco and Cardinal Monticelso, church and state, oppose Brachiano and Vittoria. The Duchess of Malfi's brothers, Duke Ferdinand and the Cardinal, oppose her match. This opposition is successful in both plays, and the central couples both die. But there is one important difference. In *The White Devil,* Vittoria's whole family dies, and Duke Francisco and the Cardinal (now Pope) have absolute control. Giovanni, who closes the play, is the son of Brachiano by his first wife, Francisco's sister the noble Isabella. It is a total victory for the aristocracy. In *The Duchess* Duke Ferdinand and the Cardinal both die, and it is the noble house of Arragon which is eliminated. More significant, the son of Antonio and the Duchess amazingly survives the carnage to occupy the structural position held by Giovanni in .the previous play. For him to be there, the son of the Duchess by her previous, noble husband (mentioned III. 3. 28) is made to disappear, forgotten out of existence by Webster and the audience. This symbolic reconciliation of aristocrats and middle class has been achieved at some cost in terms of the plot.

The Devil's Law-Case is a different kind of play, a 'Tragecomaedy', so comparisons need to be tentative, but a similar pattern emerges. The city heiress Jolenta and the noble Contarino want to marry. The main opposition now comes from her middle-class brother, the merchant Romelio, but only because he wants her to marry the richer, equally noble Ercole, Knight of Malta—which she finally does, leaving the noble Contarino for her mother. The triumph of the bourgeoisie here is total, though in this play the nobility does not exist as an opposing class, just as a source of malleable and decorative mates.

A consistent picture emerges from all this, of a strong but ambivalent kind of attraction towards the hereditary nobility, temporarily obscuring a stronger, more basic allegiance to the middle classes from which he came. However, this ambivalence towards the ruling class is largely located in four characters, Romelio in *The Devil's Law-Case*, Bosola and Antonio in *The Duchess* and Flamineo in *The White Devil*. In fact the sense of class conflict in the plays is largely the creation of these characters. Without their commentary, the action of the plays would not be seen in terms of class or status. The plays are essentially city drama, involving ordinary (i.e. bourgeois) characters whose conflicts have nothing to do with supposed class differences. In *The White Devil* for instance, the Cardinal doesn't like Vittoria, but there is a strong sexual undercurrent in his hostility, and Duke Francisco had good reasons for disliking Brachiano's match, since Brachiano had murdered Francisco's sister to make it possible. Ferdinand in *The Duchess* is the only main protagonist who is concerned about class or status, but his incestuous obsession with his sister's purity is a stronger motive than his concern for Antonio's lowly status. It is as though the dramatist had conceived his plays from two totally unrelated points of view. The Webster of the prefaces, uneasily concerned with his own status, created these discontented, class-conscious characters with his aspiring left hand, while his solidly bourgeois right hand wrote the plays themselves.

Romelio in *The Devil's Law-Case*, for instance, claims that he despises titles, using words very close to Webster's preface to Harding:

What tell you me of Gentrie? It is nought else
But a superstitious relique of time past
                              (I. 1. 40–1)

But in the first act of the play he refers obsessively to Contarino and Ercole as 'My Lord', the only character to do so. Single-handedly he establishes their noble status. Antonio and Bosola in *The Duchess* similarly are Webster's main means of establishing the noble status of the Duchess. They see the issues in class terms. Since the action is incomprehensible in these terms, they never find their way through to effective action. They are articulate and intelligent observers who are constantly mistaken: brilliant studies of a kind of ideological confusion which Webster no doubt knew at first hand.

Antonio's speech which opens the play seems intended to introduce the norms that will govern the subsequent action. He gives a version of the Elizabethan order, a hierarchical structure which attaches primary importance to the ruler as a source of good and evil in the state:

> A Prince's Court
> Is like a common Fountaine, whence should flow
> Pure silver-droppes in generall . . .
>
> (I. 1. 12)

But the action of the play itself does not proceed in these terms. There are no national repercussions from the Duchess's tragedy. All the deaths stay in the family, except for Bosola's. So does the corruption. No-one is infected by ducal example to marry their servant or murder their sister. The conception of society invoked is so irrelevant to the action of the play that it could not begin to be normative.

But this is not a convincing version of this particular commonplace. 'Common' has slightly disturbing implications of egalitarianism. 'Silver-droppes' is close to cliché, but if it has any force at all it sees the state as a source of wealth not health. Webster, or Antonio, clearly has no vital sense of the state as an organic community.

Three lines later Antonio slots a new element into the hierarchical structure:

> And what is't makes this blessed government,
> But a most provident Councell, who dare freely
> Informe him the corruption of the times?
>
> (I. 1. 17)

The virtue that previously seemed to diffuse down from above, via the ruler, now arrives by another channel, 'a most provident Councell', consisting of persons like Antonio himself. But immediately after this Bosola enters, another informer of 'the corruption of the times' to courtly persons. Antonio, however, dismisses him as 'The onely Court-Gall', because his motives are suspect:

    Indeede he rayles at those things which he wants
                        (I. 1.26)

In this speech Antonio's respect for a traditional hierarchical
order co-exists with his belief in the unqualified importance of the
'councellor' class to which he himself belongs, though he repudiates the next member of that class he sees. He can see through
Bosola, but apparently lacks an equivalent insight into himself.
Webster's characterisation of Antonio proceeds unerringly in
these terms in the play that follows. Such a man might well be
paralysed by self-doubts if a real Duchess were to choose him as
her husband, as Antonio is when the Duchess proposes to him.
Antonio is often regarded as a disappointingly grey figure.
Certainly he is dull, in spite of the skills and graces Webster tries
to equip him with by report, but that is what he is, an anxious
middle-aged accountant whose accommodation to his position in
life has become too important to be abandoned. He remains
rigorously honest, a stickler for ceremony even when the Duchess commands the contrary. When the crisis comes he hardly
resists: his energies have been turned against himself too long,
and he almost wills his end.
    Bosola is an interesting complementary study of this kind of
character. His role in society and in the action of the play is more
peripheral than Antonio's. For most of the play he is a spy for
Duke Ferdinand in the household of the Duchess of Malfi, where
he spends most of his time parading an extreme form of cynicism.
After Ferdinand discovers his sister's marriage to Antonio,
Bosola becomes her jailor, torturer and finally executioner. After
the murder of the Duchess, Duke Ferdinand immediately disowns
him, and Bosola has an attack of remorse. He tries to make
amends by killing the two evil brothers, but first he accidentally
kills Antonio. He finishes up on the side of virtue, having seemed
at the beginning to be committed to a life of evil, but this switch is
foreshadowed in the beginning, in Antonio's acute observation:
'He rails at those things which he wants.'
    His attitude to rulers is more strongly ambivalent than An-
tonio's, but he is more dependent as well as more hostile. He is a
main source in the play for organic images of society. Images of
this kind were used by ideologues of the establishment to give the
sanction of Nature to the existing social order, but Bosola does

not use them quite in the conventional way. For instance, on one
occasion he uses the metaphor of trees for Ferdinand and the
Cardinal.

> He, and his brother, are like Plum-Trees (that grow crooked over
> standing pooles) they are rich, and ore-laden with fruite, but none but
> Crowes, Pyes, and Caterpillars feede on them: Could I be one of their
> flattering Panders, I would hang on their ears like a horse-leach, till I
> were full, and then droppe off: I pray leave me.

(I. 1.50)

Clearly he doesn't see nature as a beneficent, regenerative order,
in which all parts contribute to the health and welfare of the
whole. Bosola's state of nature is like Hobbes's, where everything
preys on what it can. But there is still some respect for a
hierarchical order surviving in Bosola's use of this imagery. The
hostility towards the brothers is clear, but Bosola's strongest
contempt is reserved for people like himself, parasites on the
court. The plum trees, in spite of growing crooked, seem to
produce healthy and edible fruit. His images for parasites show
him accepting hierarchical categorisations of nature, according to
which crows and pyes are self-evidently lowly and despicable
creatures. Ferdinand brings out the underlying system later in the
play, when he contrasts 'Crowes, Dawes, and Starlings that
flocke together' with noble and solitary Eagles like himself.
Bosola basically accepts differences of rank as natural, and he is
more disgusted with himself than with the noble brothers.

  Bosola in fact would really have liked to have been a faithful
servant, bound to his master by natural ties. Even his early
cynicism expresses itself most characteristically in the form of an
exaggerated willingness to serve his master. When Ferdinand
says he has employment for him, and offers him gold, Bosola asks
'Whose throat must I cut?' (I. 1. 226)). He is eager to do the
worst, long before Ferdinand has any such task for him. After
Ferdinand has finally rejected him, he complains, with some
truth, that he

> rather sought
> To appear a true servant, than an honest man

(IV. 2. 358)

At this point he sees that he made a mistake in trying to escape
from the role of an 'honest man' (essentially the same role as

Antonio's 'provident Councellor') into the alternative 'truth' of a
neo-feudal identification with the cause of his master. He is not
completely amoral, like Edmund in *Lear*: he is more like the
captain, who will do what he is told, so long as it is 'man's work'.
But Bosola, like others of his type in Webster, never really
understands his situation. Although he recognises his real kinship
with Antonio, he kills him: 'In a mist, I know not how'. He does
kill the aristocratic brothers who had exploited him, but he sees
himself as revenging the noble, virtuous Duchess as well as
himself. He dies isolated on all sides, yet still essentially dependent.

Characters of this kind in Webster do not understand the society
they live in, but they are understood as social types. Their
consciousness matches their attributed position. But the rest of
the society of the plays is not conceived in the same terms. The
impression that Webster has created a full image of a stratified
society collapses under closer examination. The lower classes of
course are mere cyphers, and Webster's nobility turns out to be
the bourgeoisie in fancy dress. The split between ostensible social
class and forms of consciousness can be seen especially clearly in
the last play, *The Devil's Law-Case*. Contarino there is described
as noble before he enters:

> There lives not a compleater Gentleman
> In Italy, nor of a more ancient house
> (I. 1. 38–9)

His opening words indicate that his source of wealth is land. Yet
almost immediately after this, Romelio urges the merits of travel,
and Contarino replies:

> Yet I have heard
> Of divers, that in passing the Alpes,
> Have but exchang'd their vertues at deare rate
> For other vices
> (I. 1. 63–6)

After only seven lines Contarino has forgotten he is meant to be
an Italian nobleman, and speaks as a sturdy English citizen, on
the right (i. e. English) side of the Alps. The image he uses now to
describe the process of corruption comes from commerce. It is

not a well-chosen image. A simple moralist would suppose that to change virtues into vices was the definition of depravity. 'At deare rate' ought to be redundant. It is apparently meant to reinforce the conventional moral, making moral corruption a kind of bad bargain, as though that were more evidently wrong than vice itself. In fact if the image is attended to closely it exactly inverts the moral sentiment. In its terms travel is bad business, as far as morality is concerned, only because the rate of exchange is unfavourable: if English virtues earned enough Italian vices, travel would be worth while. Contarino could have been a study of a type of moral confusion of a specifically bourgeois kind, where virtues and vices are treated as commodities, and moral propositions are transposed into inappropriate mercantile terms with bizarre results. But there is no sign that Webster has noticed this.

Contarino also sees human relationships as mediated through imagery drawn from mercantile activity. He wants to marry Jolenta but has not revealed his intentions till now, he explains to Romelio:

> I would not publish to the world,
> Nor have it whispered, scarce, what wealthy Voyage
> I went about, till I had got the Myne
> In mine owne possession

> (I. 1. 95–8)

The heiress Jolenta is frankly seen as a 'Myne', a source of wealth, and the pun on 'mine' seems to establish a kind of natural connection between possession and exploitation. Immediately after this, Contarino tries to win over Leonora, Jolenta's mother, who in fact loves him herself. There follows a long passage of double-talk. He refers to Jolenta as her mother's 'picture', which he says he wants to possess. She thinks he means herself, her own likeness. The result is a misunderstanding, but this arises only because they have mistaken the other's currency. The depersonalising process itself seems to be accepted by everyone as entirely natural. Leonora clearly sees the financial aspect of the exchange, and offers Contarino a large advance, realising the nature of Contarino's interest in her self/picture. She makes no mistake here. Contarino exclaims, as soon as she has gone: 'What a Treasury have I pearch't!' (I. 1. 185). Leonora is a kind of 'myne' too, to be 'pearch't', penetrated. But Webster does not make any judgment on this attitude. Romelio suffers large losses later in the play, which reduces Jolenta's financial value, but Contarino is not deflected from his love, which we must therefore suppose is a genuine feeling. Although he finally marries Leonora not Jolenta, neither is richer than the other, so the change cannot be attributed to his avarice. So though we see him using images of this kind for the two women, we also have to accept that he is capable of sincere love and a humanly adequate relationship.

Something like this is also true of a more generally admired Webster character, the Duchess of Malfi. She uses of herself the same image that Contarino used of Jolenta, when revealing her love to Antonio:

So, now the ground's broake,
You may discover what a wealthy Mine,
I make you Lord of

(I. 1. 492)

'Mine' may be a pun here, too. Certainly she is simply offering herself as something to be exploited. The 'ground' that is 'broake' is the barrier that has prevented communication, but it is also herself, and the verb recalls the kind of action of 'pearch't'. In the later play it is Contarino who thinks of women and relationships in this way, but here it is the Duchess who says of herself the words a Contarino would write for his ideal of womanhood. Earlier, in an exchange with Ferdinand, she had seen herself as a diamond, in an argument for frequent remarriages:

Diamonds are of most value,
They say, that past through most Jewellers hands

(I. 1. 330)

Ferdinand retorts:

Whores, by that rule, are precious.

This ought to be decisive, but it is Ferdinand who says it. Webster is so clear that Ferdinand is nasty-minded that he does not seem aware that he is also correct.

These dramatic devices, including the diamond metaphor, recall Marlowe's *Jew*. Webster may simply have lifted them from there: he was a notorious borrower. But Marlowe's use of them showed a profound critical grasp of social and psychological fact. He understood how these attitudes grow out of relations of production in the society at large, and what disastrous effects they have on primary feelings and relationships. Webster in contrast seems totally uncritical. His characters' self-images directly reflect bourgeois ideology. They happily think of themselves and others in its terms, as though there was no other way to see things. His women especially find it natural to talk of themselves as commodities. Webster is a sexist, in spite of his justified reputation as a champion among Jacobean dramatists for the woman's point of view.

Webster's Duchess is the great positive of the play—his single convincingly positive creation, some would say. So it is well to be aware of the conglomerate nature of this figure whom Webster so unequivocally admires. Her servant, Cariola, gives the judgment on her which seems closest to Webster's own:

> Whether the spirit of greatness, or of woman
> Raigne most in her, I know not, but it shewes.
> A fearful madness. I owe her much of pitty
>
> (I. 1. 576)

She is meant to display the 'spirit of greatness' and of 'woman' in nearly equal proportions. But the 'greatness' or nobility is indicated through external attributes, mainly the title of Duchess. The 'spirit of woman' is conveyed by giving her recognisable characteristics of a city wife. As such, she is a convincing if limited creation. Although in exchanges with Ferdinand and Antonio she talks of herself as a mere commodity, she is basically unaffected by such conceptions. She comes across most strongly as a simple, good-natured woman with an uncomplicated capacity for domestic affection. Her first words in the second act come from this centre:

> Your arme Antonio, do I not grow fat?
> I am exceeding short-winded
>
> (II. 1. 110)

There is a real positive here. She shows an unpretentious wholeness of response that relegates the tiara back to the props room, seeing herself not as a mobile diamond mine but as a pregnant woman who relies affectionately on her husband.

Yet this kind of positive is not grand enough for the part Webster requires her to play in the tragedy as a whole. Webster is a snob. Her status is important to give her death dignity, to leave the final effect one of tragedy not pathos. When she has been imprisoned by her brother, Bosola is sent to try to drive her mad. 'Who am I?' she asks at one point, seeming to raise great problems of personal identity. Bosola responds with a jumble of images from the morbid side of conventional morality:

> Thou art a box of worm-seed, at best but a salvatory of green mummy. What's this flesh? A little crudded milk, a fantastical puff paste . . . etc.
>
> (IV. 2. 126–8)

The Duchess responds to all this with one of her most famous lines

> I am Duchess of Malfi still . . .

This has seemed, to many critics, to be a definitive solution to problems of identity (available only to members of the aristocracy). But in this scene, her great moment in the play, Webster also emphasises 'the spirit of woman' in her. Executioners enter 'with a coffin, cords, and a bell'. There is no mistaking their intentions. But as they drag Cariola, her servant away, the Duchess says pathetically:

> I pray-thee looke thou giv'st my little boy
> Some sirrop, for his cold . . .
> (IV. 2. 207)

This is the mother speaking, not the Duchess. But in this situation it ought to seem grotesquely inadequate as a response, a maternal reflex still operating after the mind has broken and lost all contact with reality. The children are about to be strangled, as is Cariola, their source of 'sirrop'. But the Duchess otherwise seems clear-headed and heroically resolved. So Webster here seems to be merely juxtaposing two uncritically held positives, what he might term the twin spirits of 'greatness' and 'woman', relying on the admiration called forth by the one to elevate the pity aroused by the other into a tragic effect. He can have things both ways like this only because the character is formed out of such imprecise and unexamined notions of both greatness and humanity.

But Webster could also be subtle and profound in his understanding and presentation of human relationships. One instance is his treatment of latent incest. He deals with this theme so subtly that until this century no-one seems to have noticed its existence in his works. But now it is generally accepted that the action of *The Duchess* at least is incomprehensible unless Ferdinand is understood to be in the grip of an incestuous passion which remains entirely unconscious.[5] Latently incestuous relationships proliferate in the other plays as well. What is especially interesting about this is not the relationship itself—Elizabethans knew well enough that brothers and sisters can be sexually attracted to each other—but its invisibility. No character in any of the plays seems aware of this motive, and the audience is encouraged to share the characters' bewilderment and misconceptions. The infra-plot, as it can be called, not only concerns unconscious motivation, it remains at that level for the audience.

The sensational nature of incest is perhaps a distraction, for it is only one aspect of a recurring relationship which is central to Webster's work. It is a world without fathers—Crispiano in *The Devil's Law-Case* is the first old man with a son in the three plays—a society in which brothers act as fathers to sisters whom they love as wives. The impulse takes a curious form in the plotting of *The Devil's Law-Case*; Romelio acting as father forbids Jolenta's marriage to Contarino, apparently on prudential grounds. But later, when Romelio has made another girl pregnant—Jolenta's 'play-fellowe', Angiolla (V. 1. 2)—he persuades his sister to own the child, and to name its father as Ercole, the husband he chose for her who is now presumed dead. That is, Jolenta is to 'have' his child, with Angiolla the proxy mother and Ercole the proxy husband. She certainly misleads Ercole into thinking along these lines when he asks her to say who was the real father of the child:

> Shee writes backe, that the same she goes withall,
> Was begot by her brother

> (V. 2. 35)

Contarino, to whom Ercole repeats this, makes the inevitable inference: 'O most incestious villain!'

Contarino's behaviour in this play is also odd, particularly his switch from daughter to mother at the end of the play. This certainly seems sudden, but there are a few preparatory hints of motives that would explain the change. Immediately after Ercole has revealed to him what he believes is the scandalous truth about Jolenta, the disguised Contarino exclaims in disgust:

> *Cont.* I will no more thinke of her
> *Erc.* Of whom?
> *Cont.* Of my mother—I was thinking of my mother
> (V. 2. 45)

Ostensibly he is preserving his disguise, concealing his thought of Jolenta, but perhaps his wooing of Jolenta concealed his wooing of her (his?) mother, in which case the ambiguity of the picture— exchange with Leonora—was not such a misunderstanding after all. There would, of course, be no warrant for this speculation on such slight grounds, except for the twist at the end, where he does in fact marry the mother.

The relationship is explored more directly in *The White Devil*. Flamineo and Vittoria clearly have an odd brother-sister relationship, but Flamineo's relationship with Marcello, his 'good' brother, is also interesting from this point of view. The bad brother kills the good brother (just as Ferdinand stabs the Cardinal, and analogously Bosola kills Antonio and Romelio imagines he has killed Contarino). All these deaths are gratuitous in terms of the plot. Flamineo, for instance, had seemed a cool villain up to this point. A trivial quarrel then rouses him to an action that does not help his cause in the least, on the contrary making him highly vulnerable. Significantly, it is Marcello's arrogation of the father's role that Flamineo finds intolerable. Flamineo's mother disapproves of his affair with Zanche the Moor, Vittoria's maid and confidante. Flamineo is suspected of having honourable intentions towards the lady. She is undoubtedly not a good match, but Flamineo claims not to be especially interested, and Zanche herself immediately reveals that her ambitions lie elsewhere. There was no reason to be agitated about the matter. But Marcello takes his mother's side, and Flamineo reacts violently;

> You're a boy, a foole,
> Be guardian to your hound; I am of age
> (V. 1. 189)

He then runs Marcello through in his mother's presence: and Marcello dies in her arms.

The relationship clearly has Oedipal roots (Marcello once explicitly compares himself and his brother to 'the two slaughtered sons of Oedipus', V. 1. 198). Ferdinand threatens the Duchess with a phallic dagger in their opening confrontation, with the revealing comment:

> You are my sister,
> This was my Father's poyniard: doe you see,
> I'll be loth to see't looke rusty, 'cause 'twas his.
> (I. 1. 369)

The sister/mother usually generates hostility as well as love by her rejection of the brother/son. When Flamineo's mother rejects him ('O that I nere had borne thee:' I. 2. 326), he wishes that his mother had been a courtesan, so that he would have had 'a plurality of fathers'. Incestuous oedipal feelings might readily express themselves as a kind of radicalism, exactly the kind that Bosola and Flamineo show. Such radicalism would be rootless, based neither on real understanding of society nor any wish to change it. It would express a purely personal ambivalence, directed against a 'society' which exists only as an image for something else. If this is the case, these characters show an extreme form of false consciousness, one which Webster seems to share; an inability to distinguish private images from the realities of social fact.

However, there is one kind of relationship which Webster explores with a strong sense of social fact. Arranged marriages were normal among both the nobility and the bourgeoisie, transactions carried out by parents in the interests of wealth, power or status.[6] (George Harding, the dedicatee of *The Duchess,* was one example among many from the aristocracy. In 1615, aged 13, he went through a marriage ceremony with a 9 year-old girl, Elizabeth, who brought some modern riches to buttress Harding's 'ancient nobility'. Elizabeth went back to her family for several years, after the wedding contract had been signed.) Webster's plays are concerned with the response of both partners, especially the woman, to such loveless and constrained unions. The unacceptability of this kind of marriage is typically the starting point of the action, a prime motive for his main protagonists. All the plays begin with a woman about to marry. In every case, the strongest motive seems to be a wilful resistance to an imposed union, rather than an overmastering positive love. *The Devil's Law-Case* is the clearest, and simplest, example. Jolenta refuses Ercole, the husband her brother Romelio arranged for her, apparently out of mere wilfulness. She shows this by accepting Ercole at the end, which serves as a tacit justification of the system, implying that she, and other reluctant brides, would be well advised to marry whoever they're told to in the first place. The Duchess of Malfi resists the non-union imposed on her by her brothers with more spirit and fire than goes into her love for Antonio. We are meant of course to believe that she genuinely loves the man of her choice, but the positive attraction never seems exactly irresistible.

The White Devil explores a more complex set of relationships of this kind. The marriage Vittoria recoils from, which her family (Marcello and Cornelia) and the church, in the person of the Cardinal, strive to maintain, is evidently a disgusting and sterile union. Her husband Camillo is old and impotent ('I do not well remember, I protest / When I last lay with her,' I. 2). Brachiano's marriage with Isabella is a more subtly perverse relationship. Isabella has usually been seen as a pious cypher in this play. However, the attitudes that lie behind her first extended speech are not unequivocally virtuous:

> all my wrongs
> Are freely pardoned, and I do not doubt
> As men to try the precious Unicornes horne
> Make of the powder a preservative Circle
> And in it put a Spider, so these armes
> Shall charme his poyson, force it to obeying
> And keepe him chaste from an infected straying
> (I. 1. 12)

By 'all my wrongs' she means wrongs done *to* her, not by her, but the form of words seems to attribute them to herself. This may seem a perverse misreading, but it is exactly the misreading Brachiano makes when she says that 'Devotion' (meaning affection for Brachiano) brought her to Rome.

> Devotion?
> Is your soule charg'd with any grievous sinne?

Isabella replies 'Tis burdened with too many', implicitly accepting his interpretation: and later on she will take the blame for his cruel act of divorce on herself. This may all be long-suffering Piety, not a pathological state, but the image of her arms as a 'preservative Circle' in which a spider is put—as a test—has other implications, of a fastidious revulsion from her husband and his sexuality.

> You are welcome to these longing armes,
> As I to you a Virgine
>
> (II. 1. 165)

she protests, meaning of course that he is as welcome to her as she was to him when she was a virgin, but the way she puts this odd analogy seems to preserve her virginity, as though she only welcomes him insofar as she is a virgin, which she is not. She dies kissing his poisoned picture, an apt image for her relationship with her spider-husband.

Brachiano blames the match on the Duke of Florence's pressure, which he fiercely resents:

> Your brother the great Duke . . .
> (Now all the hellish furies take his soule)
> First made this match
>
> (II. 1. 190–2)

He feels reduced by the political marriage. The affair with Vittoria is a kind of rebellion, a way of discovering himself, though to do so he puts himself under obligation to a less potent brother, Flamineo.

The Brachiano-Vittoria relationship is not a particularly satisfactory one. Webster is clearer about what is wrong with the relationships that society has imposed than about what a fully healthy and mature love would look like. At bottom he has a simple faith in freedom of choice, and he does not examine closely its consequences for human relationships. Yet this belief provides the basis for an extremely subtle and penetrating critique of the consequences of unfreedom, and the Brachiano-Vittoria relationship is presented honestly for what it is, with no attempt to give it extrinsic value through pathos or sentimentality, as sometimes happens with the Duchess and Antonio. Where Webster fails, in comparison with Shakespeare or Marlowe for instance, is in his sense of the larger whole and its effects on individual relationships. Marlowe and Shakespeare see how the failure of relationships derives from a system where the conditions of the market prevail, and human powers and affections are treated as commodities. Webster represents both features of his society, but doesn't connect them. Some of his best marriages— the Duchess and Antonio for instance—are a free union between two commodities.

'False consciousness' is not a clear term, but that is as it should be. The processes of false consciousness are far from simple, including all the innumerable ways in which social experience is refracted and distorted by a class standpoint.

> The division of society into classes makes of man a being all divided up into bits. The man who exploits other men becomes incapable of seeing society in its totality, incapable of feeling the interests of society as his own interests. In a word, he ceases to be a social being in general. Corresponding to the divided and limiting character of his existence and social practice there is a type of consciousness that is also divided and limited—his class consciousness.[7]

The example of Webster shows the complexity of this process; how far it is from being a matter of straightforward determinism as he mixes isolated insights and lack of general grasp, unfocused critique and naïve acceptance of the values of his class. What is most revealing is his failure to understand what most concerned him. The Bosola-Flamineo figure, for instance, is clearly an examination of an aspect of his own situation, but the figure is set into a social context which would make it impossible for him or the audience to understand this character, or the options open to him.

Webster's failure here can be generalised, as a failure to understand the coming role of his own class. Within three decades of Webster's major works, there was to be a civil war, something like a 'bourgeois' revolution. Webster's plays give no premonition of this great event: it doesn't exist even as a possibility. Bosola or Flamineo would be the closest to being agents of such a revolution, but their complicity with the ruling class is total, and there is nothing within the world of the play from which they could draw strength. This is not a matter of demanding that an artist be a prophet. Marlowe and Shakespeare, writing two decades earlier, were better prophets only because the alignments that led to the civil war, the preconditions for that struggle, were contemporary facts, which they made the material of their plays. That struggle briefly entered a revolutionary phase when the element that the great dramatists ignored, people from the lower classes, was enlisted in the battle. But for Webster the struggle did not seem possible, or necessary. The experience of a single class determined the limits of his world. Yet the action of his plays grows out of his intermittent sense of the inadequacies of that world. They constitute his uncomprehending attempt to redress its imbalances. Flamineo gives the closest Webster himself got to an understanding of his situation, and the reasons why the attempt was doomed.

No, at myself I will begin and end.
While we look up to heaven we confound
Knowledge with knowledge. O, I am in a mist!

6

'Rational Burning': Milton on Sex and Marriage

DAVID AERS and BOB HODGE

The immediate, natural and necessary relationship of human being to human being is the relationship of man to woman. In this natural relationship of the sexes, man's relationship to nature is immediately his relationship to man, and his relationship to man is immediately his relationship to nature, his own natural function. Thus, in this relationship is sensuously revealed and reduced to an observable fact how far for man his essence has become nature or nature has become man's human essence. Thus, from this relationship the whole cultural level of man can be judged.

(Karl Marx, "Private Property and Communism", *Economic and Philosophic Manuscripts of 1844*, tr.D. McLellan, Blackwell 1971, 147)

Milton, as is well-known, lived before the days of Women's Liberation and we have many modern critics and scholars grateful for the fact. They teach us that Milton's most repressive attitudes towards women are so basic to 'the seventeenth-century mind' as to be beyond criticism. We must accept them, we are told, with an earnest appeal to our historical sense, if we are ever to appreciate the Great Work in the context of its age. And there is a civilising reward for making this imaginative leap. If only we can accept the initial premise that women are naturally inferior and subordinate to men we will inhabit a magnificently coherent and yet generous, human and moral universe. Every time we read the Great Work we will be chastened and purged of our inadequate 'modern' responses: our 'historicism' will be part of our moral education. Or so we are promised by critics of the neo-Christian tradition.[1]

Regrettably this whole line of criticism rests on quite unsound 'historical' and interpretative bases. As for the latter, claims for the coherence of the universe depicted by orthodoxy have been somewhat undermined by Empson's stimulating and exuberant *Milton's God*, in which he also argues that *Paradise Lost* would be morally repulsive if it had the kind of coherence attributed to it by the neo-Christian critics. But such critics have proved impervious to criticism: Patrides, Halkett and others proceed as though Empson had not written. It would be naïve to suppose that these critics would abandon their pieties merely because someone had demonstrated their incoherence: indeed, accepting incoherence itself can become a criterion of orthodox faith, as the much used word 'paradox' suggests. Their appeal to history, however, is also distorted and inadequate. They write as though there was no revolution in the seventeenth century and no radical challenges to the orthodox pieties they champion. Yet Milton himself was seen as a 'libertine' by such orthodox contemporaries as Clement Walker and Prynne, while, as Christopher Hill has reminded us, Ranters like Coppe were as much his contemporaries as the Presbyterian Baxter or the chaste Cambridge Platonists. Too many academic critics have presented a homogenised Milton and a homogenised seventeenth century, resolving all tensions, blind to all contradictions and dissidence in Milton or his society. They are certainly not inspired by any disinterested regard for the truth or historical fact, so sadly and reluctantly we must suspect them of ideological motivation. It is our purpose to penetrate some of the ideological mists that have accrued round 'the Poet-blind, yet bold'. Milton's position, in fact, was neither constant nor consistent. His attitudes to women and sex entailed contradictions which he never fully resolved. Yet there is a development over his lifetime, from the prose tracts on divorce to *Paradise Lost*, and this development constitutes a critique of the neo-Christian appropriation of Milton. He did not collapse back into orthodox pieties in his great poem, as has been claimed: on the contrary, *Paradise Lost* shows how far he was able to go in his heroic and radical struggle towards a more adequate view of sexuality and the relationship between women and men. From this struggle, indeed, 'the whole cultural level' of Milton and his social group can be judged. And of his critics.

In thinking about sex and marriage Milton had to deal with two aspects of what Marx called alienation:[2] estrangement of man from his species and from himself. It is in these terms that we need to see both the dominant seventeenth-century ideology governing relations between the sexes, and Milton's complicity and struggle with that ideology.

Neo-Christian critics are of course right that Milton's views grow out of the dominant puritan tradition. These critics do not usually juxtapose this tradition with an account of the actual position of women in seventeenth-century society, but that is not here in dispute—discriminated against legally, economically and socially, there is no doubt that they made up an oppressed class. There were differing degrees of servitude, and certainly there were hopeful signs of change, which we must not overlook and underestimate;[3] but none of these factors challenges the basic fact of massive repression at all levels of society.

But there were a number of contradictions in the position of a middle-class wife, which was inevitably registered in the dominant ideology. She was both of the class and not of it: a bourgeois but a woman, united to her husband by class, separated and subordinated by sex. She was exploited by her husband yet entrusted with the management of the household, servants and children, perpetrator of the ideology yet a victim of it. So the ideology had to present a basically exploitationary relationship as a mutually beneficial one, while also reinforcing masculine consciousness of its conviction that the right to rule was the male's. 'The husband must so unite Authority and Love, that neither of them may be omitted or concealed, but both be exercised and maintained', wrote Baxter, one of the more humane of puritan divines, anxious that men should not 'omit or conceal' the real differences in authority, the difference between ruler and ruled.[4] 'Love', we see, is something to be 'exercised and maintained', not felt. Yet the same ideology had to mediate the wife's equivocal status as ruled and ruler, wife and lover.

The ensuing contradictions can be seen in a representative

treatise, John Dod and Robert Cleaver's *A Godly Form of Household Government*. They begin by showing the family in explicitly political terms: 'An household is as it were a little commonwealth, by the good government whereof, God's glory may be advanced.'[5] They then analyse the primary relationship as follows:

There are two sorts in every perfect family:
1. The governors,
2. Those that must be ruled.

In this basic scheme, the wife is one of the governors, though not absolutely. The governors, they say, 'are, first, the *chief governor*, which is the *Husband*, secondly, a *fellow-helper*, which is the wife' (p.7). This seems to present the wife as ruler rather than ruled, subordinate only to her husband, a near-equal belonging to the same class. But when Dod and Cleaver reach the section on the duties of the wife they are almost exclusively concerned with her subordination to her husband:

> So then the principal duty of the wife is, first to be subject to her husband, Ephes. 5:22, Coloss. 3:18, 1 Pet. 3:1,2. To be chaste and shamefast modest and silent godly and discreet. To keep herself at home for the good government of her family, and not to stay abroad without just cause.
>
> (p. 175)

Three texts buttress the announcement of her subjection. A whole section of the book reinforces it. The second 'duty' repetitiously insists on her submissive behaviour. The third seems as anxious that she should be bound to the home as that she should manage the household efficiently. So much for the near-equality of status of this 'governor'.

A similar contradiction undercuts the ideology of love and companionship. Dod and Cleaver's definition of matrimony is 'a lawful knot and unto God an acceptable yoking and joining together of one man and one woman, with the good consent of them both; to the end that they may dwell together in friendship and honesty, one helping and comforting the other' (p. 85). Which one helps which? we might ask. But the ideal of marriage seems blandly benign here. 'Good consent' and 'friendship' and comfort (though interestingly, not love) are part of the very definition of marriage, an image of a humane and rich social relationship.

But when Dod and Cleaver come round to advising a husband how to pick this companion of his most intimate hours, his comfort and friend, they give a useful rule of thumb. 'As the echo answereth but one word for many, which are spoken to her; so a Maid's answer should be in a word' (p. 94). A lifetime of richly mutual conversations stretches out in prospect.[6] But some husbands do not see the advantages of a loving marriage early enough. Dod and Cleaver present its real and substantial attractions winningly:

> And if we have regard unto commodity and profit, there is nothing that giveth so much as doth a good wife, no not horses, oxen, servants or farms: for a man's wife is the fellow and comforter of all care and thoughts, and doth more faithful and true service unto him than either maid-servant or man-servant, which do serve man for fear, or else for wages: but thy wife will be led only by love and therefore she doth everything better than all other.
>
> (pp. 145–6)

The preacher is certain that a middle-class husband will have due regard for 'commodity and profit', and will see the usefulness of 'love'.[7]

The Hallers' comment on Milton's relation to this tradition is just, as far as it goes: 'though Milton voiced the accepted tenets of Puritan doctrine, he did not draw back as the preachers had done from its extreme implications'.[8] Milton did indeed have the habit, sometimes unfortunate in an ideologue insofar as his own social group is concerned, of taking basic premises of the ideology very seriously, so that its inherent contradictions began to obtrude, its moral bromides turning into calls for action. But his idiosyncratic development of the ideology had its roots in a state of mind that was probably typical of his class. He came at this ideology as its victim. Shocked by his traumatic experience of marriage into realising the destructive nature of the conventional bourgeois sexual ethic, he struggled to find in marriage the complete solution to the psychic consequences of middle class individualism: isolation, fragmentation of personality, crippling frustration, and hence despair.[9]

Protestantism could provide ideological support for the economic individualism basic to the middle-class view of man, and Weber has some interesting comments on the doctrinal basis:

The Father in heaven of the New Testament, so human and understanding, who rejoices over the repentance of a sinner as a woman
over the lost piece of silver she has found, is gone. His place has been
taken by a transcendental being, beyond the reach of human understanding, who with His quite incomprehensible decrees has decided
the fate of every individual and regulated the tiniest details of the
cosmos from eternity. God's grace is, since His decrees cannot
change, as impossible for those to whom He has granted it to lose as it
is unattainable for those to whom He has denied it.
In its extreme inhumanity this doctrine must above all have had one
consequence for the life of a generation which surrendered to its
magnificent consistency. That was a feeling of the unprecedented
inner loneliness of the single individual. In what was for man of the age
of the Reformation the most important thing in life, his eternal
salvation, he was forced to follow his path alone to meet a destiny
which had been decreed for him from eternity. No one could help him.
No priest, for the chosen one can understand the word of God only in
his own heart. No sacraments, for though the sacraments had been
ordained by God for the increase of His glory, and must hence be
scrupulously observed, they are not a means to the attainment of
grace, but only the subjective *externa subsidia* of faith. No Church, for
though it was held that *extra ecclesiam nulla salus* in the sense that
whoever kept away from the true Church could never belong to God's
chosen band, nevertheless the membership of the external Church
included the doomed. They should belong to it and be subjected to its
discipline, not in order thus to attain salvation, that is impossible, but
because, for the glory of God, they too must be forced to obey His
commandments. Finally, even no God. For even Christ had died only
for the elect, for whose benefit God had decreed His martyrdom from
eternity.[10]

Milton specifically invokes marriage as the divinely ordained cure
for 'loneliness', what Weber calls the 'unprecedented inner
loneliness' of protestant and bourgeois man.[11] 'Loneliness'
redefined in this way becomes an immensely important and
multiple loss of connections: alienation in its many related forms.
However, in his prose works, Milton was never able to relate this
experience of alienation to repressive social relationships.[12] So
although he made new demands on the marriage relationship and
weakened the repressive forms of the basic ideology in this area,
he did not bring himself to renounce an exploitationary relationship which he as a male benefited from in seventeenth-century

society (as his descendants of male gender in the twentieth century continue to benefit).

Milton's thinking on marriage was precipitated by his own marriage to Mary Powell and her prompt departure in 1642. At the age of 33 he had hastily renounced all his previous dedication to chastity and with equal speed had himself been renounced. The divorce tracts grew out of this double experience, and express two potentially opposite cases: Milton's high claims for marriage and his urgent need for divorce. The particular circumstances in which he argued the case also contributed dramatically to his education. He faced the problem, nearly fatal to his enterprise, that God's word did not say what he wanted it to. He had to wrest the Bible violently to suit his case, and this drew him towards a version of the radical Protestant position that scripture was only clearly understood by the illuminated individual spirit, the saint. As he pressed on with his case he evolved the tacit principle that the clearest of God's commands might mean the exact opposite of what it said. So when Christ said, 'What therefore God hath joined together, let no man put asunder', he should be understood to mean, 'let the husband put asunder if he is dissatisfied'. Milton did not assert this blatantly: the argument he used was that God could not have done the joining in the first place if the man was dissatisfied. So the man becomes the sole judge of what God intended.[13] The procedure effectively leads to the creation of an alternative deity, whose relation to his apparent commands is accessible only to the higher reason of the saints. This whole debate certainly radicalised Milton's theology and brought him closer to extreme individualistic ethics.

Another important factor shaping his thinking in these tracts was his simultaneous immersion in political controversy. He was in mid-career as an ideologue for Parliament. He was specifically aware of a connection between power relations in the family and the state (the connection was of course a commonplace), as he pointed out in the dedication of *The Doctrine and Discipline of Divorce* (1644 edition) addressed to Parliament:[14]

> Advise ye well, supreme Senate, if charity be thus excluded and expulsed, how ye will defend the untainted honour of your own actions and proceedings. He who marries, intends as little to conspire

his own ruin, as he that swears allegiance: and as a whole people is in proportion to an ill government, so is one man to an ill marriage. If they against any authority, Covenant, or Statute, may by the sovereign edict of charity, save not only their lives, but honest liberties from unworthy bondage, as well may he against any private Covenant, which he never entered to his mischief, redeem himself from insupportable disturbances to honest peace and just contentment.

(CPW II. 229)

Here the Parliamentarians' ideologue is using the basic premises of their ideology against them. But what Milton says here about Parliament is surely even truer of himself. If he was 'sincere' in devotion to justice and individual liberty, he should be equally tender of the rights of women. In fact we shall see that he is intermittently and uneasily aware of this consequence. Nevertheless, this paragraph does show graphically how ideology can be manipulated and absorb contradictions, even when the ideologue is actually engaged in pointing out the consequences and potential contradictions of a position to his masters. The analogy is lop-sided in favour of males. As the 'whole people' are to government, so a 'man' is to marriage. But surely, for Milton, it is a man who governs in marriage. The analogy would work more naturally, in keeping with his general account of marriage, if it went, 'people: government; wife: husband'. This would give the oppressed wife the full right Milton denies her, of rebellion against what she herself judges to be 'unworthy bondage'. The effect of Milton's use of bondage is to make women non-people, as the lower classes in general were in his version of the liberal ethic.[15]

The anti-feminist bias which various critics acclaim in *Paradise Lost* is present in *Doctrine and Discipline of Divorce*. But very rarely is it unqualified even there. In chapter fifteen of the first book, for instance, he argues against the view that 'divorce was permitted only for wives':

Palpably uxorious! Who can be ignorant that woman was created for man, and not man for woman; and that a husband may be injured as insufferably in marriage as a wife. What an injury is it after wedlock not to be beloved, what to be contended with in point of house-rule who shall be head, not for any parity of wisdom, for that were something reasonable, but out of a female pride.

(CPW II. 324)

The vehemence of this expostulation comes from that premise beloved of male chauvinists of all periods: 'woman was created for man, and not man for woman'. But the development of the rhetorical case is interesting. He only argues equality for suffering for the man, thus tacitly acknowledging that men can be insufferable too. The tone is surprisingly plaintive, like a post-Women's Liberation plea for consideration for the unfortunate male, an appeal from weakness, not strength. The parenthetical 'not for any parity of wisdom, for that were something reasonable', is also a dangerous concession. What if the woman, despite all the controls of a male-dominated society, is as intelligent as the man, has the 'parity of wisdom' that Milton does seem to demand for a valid marriage—or worse, what if she is more intelligent? Milton is extremely vulnerable here, for the near-equality necessary for fit minds is liable to topple over into equality or even female superiority. The later *Tetrachordon* (1645) attempts to absorb these implications. For instance, discussing the key proposition, 'he not for her but she for him', he makes this qualification:

> Nevertheless man is not to hold her as a servant, but receives her into a part of that empire which God proclaims him to, though not equally, yet largely, as his own image and glory: for it is no small glory to him, that a creature so like him should be made subject to him. Not but that particular exceptions may have place, if she exceed her husband in prudence and dexterity and he contentedly yield, for then a superior and more natural law comes in, that the wiser should govern the less wise, whether male or female.
>
> *(CPW* II. 589)

This qualification goes counter to his text, and has no text to support it. Its motivation comes from elsewhere, perhaps Milton's God-given insight into what God really meant. 'Man is not to hold her as a servant': why not, when wives are ordered to be 'subject to your husbands in everything'? Part of the reason is that she must participate in his rule, his 'empire', as we saw Dod and Cleaver trying to explain. Another reason is that the more equal she is the greater the 'glory'—'to him', Milton emphasises. To dominate 'a creature so like him' is much more satisfying than training a horse or kicking the dog around. But 'so like', he again uneasily recognises, that she might be superior in 'prudence and

dexterity', as well as in her domestic and reproductive speciali-
ties. The 'superior' law he invokes here to justify government by
females is the same law he and the fifth monarchists invoked to
justify the rule by a minority elite. Of course, as we can see in
the later *Ready and Easy Way* he made this 'law' less subversive
by accepting that this rational elite coincided with the property
owning elite who were in control.[16] And we are reminded that an
ideologue cannot be trusted to mean what he seems to be saying.
In the present case he gives with one hand and takes away with
the other. He establishes a connection, gratuitously it seems,
between the rights of women and the claims of the most radical
elements of the middle classes, the connection we saw he
suppressed in the earlier *Doctrine and Discipline*. Yet he also
includes an escape clause: 'and he contentedly yield'. So the man
remains the sole judge of who is the wiser, even when Milton
concedes his inferiority.

At one point in *Tetrachordon* Milton goes further than this.
'The wife also, as her subjection is terminated in the Lord, being
herself the redeemed of Christ, is not still bound to be the vassal
of him, who is the bond-slave of Satan'. (*CPW* II. 591) Here he
approaches the classic radical sectarian position, with its subversive implications for the traditional view of marriage, which Keith
Thomas has analysed well.[17] So Milton knew where the logic of
his position took him, at least once in his intellectual life.

The position argued in *Doctrine and Discipline of Divorce*,
however, was less liberal, and remained his basic position. The
man, he insists, can unilaterally decide to divorce his wife. She
has not the same freedom, nor is there any outside redress for
her:

> Another act of papal encroachment it was to pluck the power and
> arbitrement of divorce from the master of the family, into whose hands
> God and the law of nations had put it, and Christ so left it, preaching
> only to the conscience, and not authorising a judicial Court to toss
> about ahd divulge the unaccountable and secret reasons of disaffection
> between man and wife, as a thing most improperly answerable to any
> such kind of trial.

> (*CPW* II. 343)

This leaves the husband as judge, jury and accuser in his own
case, ruling with arbitrary power. No justification is offered here
for this large claim, beyond the negative pseudo-reason that since

'papal encroachment' took this power away it must be restored. His contention rests partly on a belief in male supremacy: 'For even the freedom and eminence of man's creation gives him to be a law in this matter to himself being the head of the other sex which was made for him: whom therefore though he ought not to injure, yet neither should he be forced to retain in his society to his own overthrow, nor to hear any judge therein above himself' (*CPW* II. 347). The other basic premise here is the extreme form of individualism we have already met, unrestrained by any claims of society, including that of his rejected marriage partner. He 'ought not to injure her', certainly, but he is to be sole judge in deciding whether he has or not.

On the role of law in all this Milton is merely sophistic:

> The law can only appoint the just and equal conditions of divorce, and is to look how it is an injury to the divorced, which in truth it can be none, as a mere separation; for if she consents, wherein has the law to right her? or consent not, then is it either just and so deserved, or if unjust, such in all likelihood was the divorcer, and to part from an unjust man is a happiness, and no injury to be lamented.
>
> (*CPW* II. 349)

Heads he wins, tails she loses. No talk of any economic settlement, no recognition of the grave problems of a divorced woman in seventeenth-century society. He is totally impervious to all social considerations, here and elsewhere. He hardly mentions children, for instance, as a possible complication, and in *Colasterion* he jeers at this objection from an anonymous critic:

> And for those weak supposes of Infants that would be left in their mother's belly, (which must needs be good news for Chambermaids, to bear a serving-man grown so provident for great bellies) and portions, and jointures likely to incur embezzlement hereby, the ancient civil law instructs us plentifully how to award . . .
>
> (*CPW* II. 734–5)

It seems from this that only chamber maids get pregnant, and only servants need be concerned. Does Milton suppose that procreation can be left to the lower classes? Or does he trust the scrupulous generosity of the middle-class male? The 'ancient civil Law' which was rejected in *Doctrine and Discipline* as a popish imposition is hastily and perfunctorily wheeled in again, to silence the objection.[18]

What we have here is a vivid example of a central illusion in bourgeois (and much Protestant) thought: the myth of individual autonomy, and the failure to grasp the truth that life and development of individuals depend unequivocally on social reciprocity, that the individual can only become a human individual through social relationships and is essentially a social individual. In Milton's case his version of individualism coexists with his intense loneliness, and felt need for human society.

His more orthodox contemporaries saw the marked individualism in his thought clearly enough, and knew where it led: to the anarchic experimentalism of the Ranters. Prynne made the connection explicitly as he comments on 'the late dangerous increase of many *Anabaptistical, Antinomian, Heretical, Atheistical opinions, as of the soul's mortality, divorce at pleasure etc.* lately broached, preached, printed in this famous City, which I hope our grand Council will speedily and carefully suppress'.[19] Milton indignantly repudiated Prynne's retitling of his work as *Divorce at Pleasure*. Prynne, Milton assumed, had failed to see how high-minded he really was. But Prynne was right about the tendencies of Milton's views on divorce, right about its affinities with Antinomian and extreme Protestant individualism (Milton certainly finished up a moralist and a heretic many times over); he was right too about the vulnerability of such individualism before well-organised forces of repression. The story of the preaching lace-woman, Mrs Attaway, shows how unorthodox contemporaries also interpreted Milton in Prynne's way. She left her husband for William Jenney and Jenney abandoned his wife and children to elope with the female preacher: she also recommended 'Master Milton's *Doctrine of Divorce*' to her audience, recognising the implications of Milton's version of Christian liberty, just as Prynne did.[20] As Christopher Hill also recognised, Milton shared something of the Ranter's faith in his own unerring illumination, and this illuminated reason led him to doctrines which had important areas in common: 'They say that for one man to be tied to one woman, or one woman to one man, is a fruit of the curse: but they say, we are freed from the curse: therefore it is our liberty to make use of whom we please.'[21] (The later Milton also endorsed polygamy, though characteristically less generously than this, since he limited it to men). For another example, here is Laurence Clarkson:

> This to me by Reason is confirmed, and by Scripture declared, *That to the pure all things are pure:* So that for my part I know nothing unclean to me, no more than it is of it self, and therefore what Act soever I do, is acted by that Magesty in me . . . So to conclude, the censures of Scriptures, Churches, Saints, and Devils, are no more to me than the cutting off of a Dog's neck.[22]

Clarkson is like Milton in believing that Scripture must be interpreted by reason and the individual's illuminated spirit: he is only more frank and vehement in dismissing any contrary authorities.

These extreme individualistic views were not truly radical in the fullest sense of 'going to the roots' of the issues, based on an awareness of the concrete relations of men in that society. So it is appropriate that the most intelligent and cool critique of such views comes from the communist Winstanley. His grasp of social realities and commitment to developing social liberty for the mass of people led him to see such individualistic autonomy as a delusion which was deeply irresponsible to the women and children concerned. His critique applies equally to Milton's views on divorce:

> The Ranting practice . . . breaks the peace in Families . . . separates those very friends, causing both sides to run into the sea of confusion, madness and destruction, to leave each other, to leave their Children, and to live in discontent . . . And the mother and child begotten in this manner is like to have the worst of it, for the man will be gone, and leave them; and regard them no more than other women, like a Bull begets a Calf, that never takes care neither for Cow nor Calf, after he hath had his pleasure. Therefore you women beware, for this ranting practice is not the restoring, but the destroying, power of the creation.[23]

He might have added, 'Beware of John Milton too.' The dominant ideology of marriage justified permanent repression of women, but at least it provided the repressed with *some* guarantees of whatever material protection was available.

On sexuality Milton's position changed considerably over his life, but at every stage there is a degree of tension and ambivalence all too rarely acknowledged. In the poetry he wrote before his marriage, the literary eroticism of his early sonnets (decently veiled in foreign tongues) gave way to the militant chastity of

Comus, threatened on all sides by sensuous and erotic energies. The *Apology Against a Pamphlet* (1642) has the famous critique of unchaste verses, and the self-portrait which attributes to himself 'a certain niceness of nature, an honest haughtiness and self-esteem either of what I was or what I might be (which let envy call pride) and lastly that modesty',[24] or self-righteous priggishness arguing very little self-knowledge at that age (thirty-three).

But that was before his marriages and his strenuous attempts to come to terms with the demands of his own sexuality. In contrast to the crude split between body and soul of his earlier work, in *Christian Doctrine* he asserts their total identity: '[man] is not double or separable: not, as is commonly thought, produced from and composed of two different and distinct elements, soul and body. On the contrary, the whole man is the soul, and soul the man: a body, in other words, or individual substance, animated, sensitive, and rational' (*CPW* VI. 318). In *Christian Doctrine* he holds to this belief through heresy after heresy. Certainly, in theory at least, he resolved the body-soul split. Two questions then arise. By what route did he come to this final position? And how deep did the resolution go, how totally did it modify the attitudes and values that governed his responses in human relations? To answer the second question we will go to *Paradise Lost,* not to any conjectural biography.

Even in the early *Doctrine and Discipline* Milton is capable at times of near Blakeian insights. Here he is invoking Parliament:

> The greatest burden in the world is superstition; not only of Ceremonies in the Church, but of imaginary and scarecrow sins at home. What greater weakening, what more subtle strategem against our Christian warfare, when besides the gross body of real transgressions to encounter; we shall be terrified by a vain and shadowy menacing of faults that are not: When things indifferent shall be set to over-front us, under the banners of sin, what wonder if we be routed, and by the Art of the Adversary, fall into the subjection of the worst and deadliest offences. The superstition of the Papist is, *touch not, taste not,* when *God* bids both: and ours is, *part not, separate not,* when God and charity both permits and commands.

> (*CPW* II, 228)

Superstition, mystery, prohibitions which sap energy, intelligence and the will to resist, leading to paralysed subjection, all seem recognised here and repudiated. The Urizenic 'touch not, taste not' has, it seems, been superseded. Milton appears an iconoclastic *and* affirmative revolutionary.

But the enemy here is the Papist, whose defeat is a thing of the past although it has left some vestiges in the Protestant 'part not, separate not'. Milton understands the repressive uses of religion by the papists, but does not yet extend this insight, as Winstanley and others did, to Protestant strategies. He claims that 'our' (i.e. Protestant) superstitition is 'part not, separate not'. Yet, as Weber noted, Protestant individualism tended to *separate:* man from friends, from priest, from church, and perhaps even from God. This brings out again the contradictory nature of Milton's enterprise. He is arguing for marriage as a cure for 'loneliness' and using this as the basic premise in his case for easier divorce. If he had not insisted on the one-sidedness of the relationship, if a woman could divorce her husband as easily as a man could divorce his wife under the Miltonic dispensation, then marriage would only intensify his loneliness and insecurity. (As Mary's rapid departure must have done). No friends, no priest, no church—and no reliable wife either, the last prop kicked away. Marriage is specifically the escape from individualism yet he cannot prevent himself from seeing it in destructively individualistic terms.

The affirmation of touch and taste, the easy transcendence of papist prohibitions, is a much more equivocal matter in practice than theory in the *Doctrine and Discipline*. He argued that the grounds for divorce should be extended to include non-physical aspects of marriage. (It is interesting that it was the despised papists, in spite of their 'touch not', who had included sexual incapacities as grounds for annulment). However, Milton does not only elevate the non-physical, he degrades the physical with intense images of disgust: 'when as the mind from whence must flow the acts of peace and love, a far more precious mixture than the quintessence of an excrement' (*CPW* II. 248). The image works against itself, for the reader's response to 'acts of peace and love' is coloured by the implicit comparison with the excremental quintessence: it is as if the 'acts of peace and love' themselves 'flow' like an excremental 'mixture' from a soul-penis. Milton's control of implication is uncertain, probably a sign of an unsuccessful attempt at sublimation.

There are similar revealing shifts in his glossing of St Paul's 'It is better to marry than to burn'. Papists and Protestants alike saw the sexual implications of 'burn' as relevant. Milton's interpretation is at least original and it is unlikely that even St Paul thought of it:

> that desire which God saw it was not good that man should be left alone to burn in; the desire and longing to put off an unkindly solitariness by uniting another body, but not without a fit soul to his in the cheerful society of wedlock. Which if it were so needful before the fall, when man was much more perfect in himself, how much more is it needful now against all the sorrows and casualties of this life to have an intimate and speaking help, a ready and reviving associate in marriage: whereof who misses by chancing on a mute and spiritless mate, remains more alone than before, and in a burning less to be contained than that which is fleshly and more to be considered; as being more deeply rooted even in the faultless innocence of nature.
>
> (*CPW* II. 251)

Really he equivocates with the traditional sexual interpretation of 'burn'. He starts with physical union, 'uniting another body', and has spiritual compatibility edge its way in ('not without'). As he continues, the place of sexuality is usurped by the intense focus on loneliness, isolation. The sense of need comes over strongly. Why is God not man's source of solace against 'all the sorrows and casualties of this life'? Weber might answer, 'No god'. The 'mute and spiritless mate' rejected so vehemently here is the perfect wife of Puritan ideology who answers only like an Echo, with one word. Immediately after this he acknowledges, in order to reject,

> that other burning, which is but as it were the venom of a lusty and over-bounding concoction, strict life and labour with the abatement of a full diet may keep that low and obedient enough: but this pure and more inbred desire of joining to itself in conjugal fellowship a fit conversing soul (which desire is properly called love) *is stronger than death* . . .
>
> (*CPW* II. 251)

Although it is 'venom' (so that papists were right to warn against taste and touch?) it is easy to control. The other burning is both much more intense, and more valuable. But in spite of this distinction, he has retained the same metaphor, and the same basic gloss to that metaphor. He realises that the higher burning is specifically erotic too, an urgent desire, not the wish for a chat. So although it would be logical to satisfy a mere burning for conversation by visiting intelligent male friends, by joining some platonic academy, Milton does not even consider that option:

> Lest therefore so noble a creature as man should be shut up incurably under a worse evil by an easy mistake . . . the aggrieved person shall do more manly to be extraordinary and singular in claiming the due right whereof he is frustrated, than to piece up his lost contentment by visiting the Stews, or stepping to his neighbours bed, which is the common shift in this misfortune, or else by suffering his useful life to waste away and be lost under a secret affliction of an unconscionable size to human strength.

> (*CPW* II. 247)

No mention of platonic academies here. One doesn't go to brothels ('the Stews') to cure 'loneliness'. The word becomes an obvious euphemism, though the sense of isolation remains part of the experience. The 'due right' Milton is talking of here is a man's right to a fully satisfactory sexual relationship (a woman's right is not, of course, contemplated). Paradoxically, his means of achieving this right involves being 'extraordinary and singular', isolated from the rest of society, rejecting all its constraining norms. The way out of the prison of egotistic individualism is through 'extraordinary' singularity, extreme individualism. The paradox is grounded in contradictions intrinsic to his (and his class's) individualism.[25]

In *Tetrachordon* Milton hides less behind a pose of high-mindedness. It did not take a Freud to see through the rationalising that was going on in his first stance. Prynne, we saw, renamed it 'Divorce at Pleasure', and Milton's anonymous critic in the *Answer* had been able to point out that the best cure for Milton's loneliness would have been a good friend. The answerer had paraphrased an argument to this effect by St Augustine, though without acknowledgement. In *Tetrachordon* Milton explicitly repudiates this view, assigning it to its source: '*Austin* contests that manly friendship in all other regards had been a more becoming solace for *Adam*, than to spend so many secret years in an empty world with one woman. But our Writers deservedly reject this crabbed opinion . . .' (*CPW* II. 596). He maintains that

Adam was essentially 'alone' until Eve was created. A host of angels as well-informed as Raphael would not have counted as company. Again, 'our Writers', the Protestant theologians, have effortlessly transcended the crabbed asceticism of the Papist past. By this stage Milton is more clear about his commitment to a reintegration of reason and feelings in a sexual relationship, and aware that mutuality, if not equality, was of the essence of such a relationship. How far had this theoretical insight advanced by the 1660s? How integrated was this theoretical awareness with attitudes that prevailed in social relations of practical life? It is time to turn to Milton's dramatic exploration of these concerns in *Paradise Lost*.

Here is Milton's Eve, when Adam is visited by an amiable top academic, Raphael, and is able to talk about the latest developments in astronomy. Eve goes off.

> Yet went she not, as not with such discourse
> Delighted, or not capable her ear
> Of what was high: such pleasure she reserved.
> Adam relating, she sole auditress;
> Her husband the relater she preferred
> Before the angel, and of him to ask
> Chose rather; he, she knew would intermix
> Grateful digressions, and solve high dispute
> With conjugal caresses, from his lip
> Not words alone pleased her.
> (*Paradise Lost* VIII. 48–57)[26]

This seems a vision of reason and feelings harmoniously reconciled. Adam's lips are a source of both kisses and words, erotic sensations and reasoning. His explanations would be part of an erotic game, but the erotic play would not invalidate or interfere with the rational argument. This is the point of the activity. But underlying some of the details remains a striking distrust of women and of sexual feelings. Milton carefully denies that Eve is unintelligent or uninterested, yet (as so many of our women students have pointed out to us) still gives the impression that she is both. Adam can be absorbed in scientific discussion, she cannot be. It is Eve who wants astronomy mingled with love, not Adam. And Eve being the inferior partner, such intermingling is by implication inferior. The motive for it comes from the weaker partner. It is only Adam who can 'solve high dispute' with conjugal caresses, or who is allowed to solve them that way— manipulating his partner sexually as and when he chooses, while not being manipulated in return. Beneath the affirmation of the unity of the pair, in the unity of body and soul, reason and feelings, lie unresolved tensions, unexorcised anxieties. The problem is that Milton's conscious mind affirmed the value of the body and its essentiality to human relationships, while he still deeply feared and resisted the dissolution of the ego. The tension appears in the poetry partly through slight uncertainties of tone—as in 'from his lip/ Not words alone pleased her'. Why veil a kiss in a coy negative? It is as though Eve/Milton is proud of having gone so far in overcoming her/his inhibitions.

The particular discussion into which this passage is set also bears obliquely on Eve's position. Adam's question is about hierarchies in heaven. Why is the 'sedentary earth . . . Served by more noble than herself'? (*Paradise Lost* VIII. 25ff.). Raphael's answer, given after Eve has left, is this:

> consider first, that great
> Or bright infers not excellence: the earth
> Though in comparison of heaven, so small
> Nor glistering, may of solid good contain
> More plenty than the sun that barren shines,
> Whose virtue on it self works no effect,
> But in the fruitful earth; there first received
> His beams, unactive else, their vigour find.
>
> (*Paradise Lost* VIII. 90–97)

The parallel with human sexuality is explicit: the earth as female, the sun as male. The lesson is clear too. The apparent excellence of the active male principle is illusory: without the earth it is barren, since its beams find their 'vigour' in the fruitful earth. In spite of its apparent greatness the sun exists for the earth. So man, in spite of doctrine to the contrary, exists for woman? It is just as well that Eve is not around to hear (though later we find she has been listening behind a bush: she was not so uninterested in Raphael's discourse, unaccompanied by 'conjugal caresses', after all). We are again presented with Milton's covert rejection of hierarchy, now in connection with the role of woman.

What Eve is described as doing makes a complex comment. She

> went forth among her fruits and flowers,
> To visit how they prospered, bud and bloom,
> Her nursery; they at her coming sprung
> And touched by her fair tendance gladlier grew.
> *(Paradise Lost* VIII. 44–7)

She functions here partly as gardener, but also unmistakably as sun, active principle of growth and hence a male force. As she leaves, Graces

> from about her shot darts of desire
> Into all eyes to wish her still in sight.
> *(Paradise Lost* VIII. 62–3)

Again images of masculine aggression (Cupid? Apollo?). Not only does Milton imply, through the earth-sun analogy, that the woman may be the superior being, he also, inconsistently, attributes male potency to her. (Perhaps the lines just quoted also relate *typologically* to Christ's aggression in VI. 844ff?[27]) Here she represents the transcendence of the conventional categories of male and female, and so momentarily we glimpse a supersession of initially opposed categories. But only glimpse. For it is only in types and images that Milton can allow Eve to achieve such a transcendence, not as human being, however unfallen.

In this section we have a microcosm of the poem as a whole: a timid doctrine of near-equality and partial integration of body and mind, undercut by a dramatisation which implies the opposite, glossed by a context which by way of analogy implies an extraordinarily radical concept of sexual relationships which manifestly does not prevail in Eden, in practice or in theory. Milton's sense of a conceivably perfect union, transcending the opposites of body and soul, male and female, is thus not directly represented in *Paradise Lost,* not dramatically created. In fact, he uses angelology to indicate schematically what it would involve. Here all his departures from orthodoxy are important and positive.[28] Angels, for instance, eat—in reality, not 'in mist, the common gloss of theologians' (V. 435–6). Raphael makes the point that angelic digestion will probably be the model for fulfilled man: 'time may come when men/With angels may participate'

(V. 493–4).[29] So there is a trans-paradisal condition envisaged which is as superior to paradise as paradise theoretically should be to the fallen world.

At the conclusion of his discussion on love, Raphael hints at what this might be like. Adam asks if the angels make love:

> To whom the angel with a smile that glowed
> Celestial rosy red, love's proper hue,
> Answered. Let it suffice thee that thou know'st
> Us happy, and without love no happiness.
> (*Paradise Lost* VIII. 618–21)

Again the tone is uncertain. Is Raphael embarrassed? Or is red the colour of passion kindling at the memory of angelic inter-course?[30] His answer is indirect but unequivocal, like an honest but inhibited parent refusing to put his/her child off with stories about birds or bees, but very uneasy nonetheless. Raphael continues:

> Whatever pure thou in the body enjoy'st
> (And pure thou wert created) we enjoy
> In eminence, and obstacle find none
> Of membrane, joint, or limb, exclusive bars:
> Easier than air with air, if spirits embrace,
> Total they mix . . .
> (*Paradise Lost* VIII. 622–7)

Behind this is a rejection of merely genital sexuality in favour of total orgasm, total union. Distinction of the sexes and associated contraries are superseded. And here it is important to register Milton's emphasis on the materiality of angels for this explicitly makes them and their experience an extension of human poten-tial, not a wholly other mode of existence. They become a way of expressing what it should be to be fully human, fully alive:

> All heart they live, all head, all eye, all ear,
> All intellect, all sense . . .
> (*Paradise Lost* VI. 350–51)

Angelic existence is a state of heightened sensuality, heightened feelings, coexisting with heightened intelligence. The angels represent a full spontaneous enjoyment, matter fully energised and humanised, a vision which was to be explored by Blake in *The Visions of the Daughters of Albion* and elsewhere.[31] It is a sad commentary on the evolution of western society that even for Milton angelology was his chief means of conceiving satisfactory sexual relations. All those he could otherwise imagine and represent were deeply flawed and contradictory.

It is now time to ask, where is the male chauvinist so beloved of the neo-Christian critics? How do we take those passages which have given them so much satisfaction? And what is the significance of the Fall? What happens to the unerring discrimination between pre-lapsarian and post-lapsarian love that was meant to shame us fallen readers?

The most famous, apparently the most unequivocal statement of the inequality of the sexes, is the introduction to Adam and Eve:

> Two of far nobler shape erect and tall,
> Godlike erect, with native honour clad
> In naked majesty seemed lords of all,
> And worthy seemed . . .
>> (*Paradise Lost* IV. 288–91)

This is how they appear to Satan; so 'seemed' presumably places the judgment inside his consciousness. His initial judgment sees their undistinguished pre-eminence over all other creatures, their 'empire'. Then distinctions are made:

>   though both
> Not equal, as their sex not equal seemed;
> For contemplation he and valour formed,
> For softness she and sweet attractive grace,
> He for God only, she for God in him:
> His fair large front and eye sublime declared
> Absolute rule . . .
>> (*Paradise Lost* IV. 295–301)

Does the 'seemed' continue, placing the judgment as Satan's? Or has Milton forgotten Satan and become immersed in repressive seventeenth-century orthodox ideology? If he has, he has been reduced to repeating the contradictions of that ideology we discussed above. 'Absolute rule' for instance: does Adam really have that? To the horror of the orthodox he does not claim it in the crucial exchange with Eve before the Fall. And in Eden all things are held in common (IV. 752), so what does 'Absolute rule' mean? Then one might wonder whether 'declared' (IV. 300) undercuts the whole speech on male rule since these signs may only 'declare' absolute rule to the fallen Satan, who does not know what Raphael told Adam, 'that great/Or bright infers not excellence' (VIII. 90–1). After all, Satan, an automatic respecter of visible hierarchies, landed on the Sun first and had to be told by Uriel that Eden was on earth.

However, it must be said that these doubts or equivocations are not dominant, and the passage basically supports a male supremicist reading. At a later stage it is easier to argue for Milton's conscious control. This is the debate on love between Adam and Raphael. Neo-Christian critics, unlike Milton, are so awed by authority that they assume the archangel must be right, or more right than Adam. So since Raphael argues a strict anti-feminist line, which Adam resists, Milton must endorse Raphael and be dramatising Adam's fatal propensities to uxuriousness.[32]

However, this debate is preceded by Adam's reported debate with God. (Or rather, with some one he takes to be God: strictly it is the Son, though he sounds like, and pretends to be, the Father: compare VII. 174–5 and VIII. 356–451: Adam is unaware of the distinction.)[33] This deity clearly has no satisfactory relationship with Adam, no meaningful friendship, in spite of Adam's later claims in his fallen and nostalgic despair (X. 720–5, XI. 315–17). And he seems to lie. For instance, he claims that he is 'alone from all eternity' (VIII. 405–6). If this is the Son he has never been alone, unless the company of the Father constitutes loneliness; and he has not existed from all eternity. If this is the Father, and strictly it isn't, he seems not to be satisfied with the near-equality of the Son, in spite of the exaltation of the Son in Books III and VI. Either way the existential abyss and confusion is striking. Furthermore, he 'seemed' (VIII. 376) to order Adam to live in solitude, whereas he actually wanted Adam to disagree with him—'Thus far to try thee, Adam, I was pleased' (VIII. 437). The conviction Adam clings to is that he needs an equal, clearly stated in these extremely important lines:

> Among unequals what society
> Can sort, what harmony or true delight?
> Which must be mutual, in proportion due
> Given and received . . .
>
> (*Paradise Lost* VIII. 383–6)

Here the unfallen Adam explicitly makes the equation Milton did not make in his prose works, the crucial equation between mutuality, equality and delight. This of course directly contradicts God's conception of man's ideal existence at VIII. 374–5, but it turns out that God *wanted* to be contradicted in precisely this way. And God, Milton would have us know, outranks Raphael. So the effect of placing the debate with God immediately before the debate with Raphael is two-fold. It gives divine sanction for Adam's view of marriage as a mutual relationship between equals; and it gives a precedent for God's official spokesman giving out an inadequate ethic in order to 'try' Adam, relying on Adam's man-centred ethic to prevail in argument.

The crucial debate between Adam and Raphael thus has a context which undercuts the authority of the angelic case. The traditional response to Adam's opening speech is given by Bush in his Oxford edition of Milton's poetry: 'Adam's speech, which contains the seeds of catastrophe to come, is made a subtle revelation of mixed feelings, both right and wrong.' Bush's comment on Adam's reply to Raphael is: 'Though Adam now expresses a corrected view, he has revealed his instinctive weakness.'[34] The 'revelation' may be subtle but for the neo-Christian critic and literary scholar the difference between right and wrong is unmistakable. Raphael gives the correct view: whenever Adam deviates from a coldly pragmatic egoism, he is to be condemned. Bush spells it out: 'neither intellectual pride nor human love should come between man and God—or man and his integrity'. The alternative gloss here, replacing Milton's God by integrity is itself revealing about the values Bush sees Milton as reinforcing.

Whatever the judgment, Adam's speech is certainly an account of his experience of difficulties with the orthodox sexist view. Eve's beauty was undoubtedly disturbing to his cool egoism:

> in all enjoyment else
> Superior and unmoved, here only weak
> Against the charm of beauty's powerful glance.
> (*Paradise Lost* VIII. 531–3)

In order to exorcise this (God-given) experience, he repeats the ideology of male supremacy:

> For well I understand in the prime end
> Of nature her the inferior, in the mind
> And inward faculties, which most
> excel
> > (*Paradise Lost* VIII. 540–42)

He then describes how inadequate this 'understanding' is:

> yet when I approach
> Her loveliness, so absolute she seems
> And in her self complete, so well to know
> Her own, that what she wills to do or say,
> Seems wisest, virtuousest, discreetest, best;
> > (*Paradise Lost* VIII. 546–50)

'Seems' is repeated twice here, matching the use of 'seemed' in the introduction to Adam and Eve which we discussed earlier. To Satan, Eve 'seemed' less than equal. To Adam she 'seems' evidently superior, 'absolute' (repeating Satan's word for Adam's own mode of rule—IV. 301). Adam here is strenuously trying to distinguish appearance from reality, or trying to discredit the reality of how he feels by the qualifying 'seems'. But there is nothing evidently wrong with these appearances. 'Absolute' is literally true of her; she has been 'freed from' *(absoluta)* him; and metaphorically this is untrue of her to the same extent as it is untrue of him: neither is a self-sufficient individual. (Robinson Crusoe, we recall, is a mythological figure embodying many of the classic illusions of middle-class individualism.)

Eve does indeed have a devastating effect on his earlier certainties:

> All higher knowledge in her presence falls
> Degraded, wisdom in discourse with her
> Looses discountenanced, and like folly shows

Again he asserts that his knowledge is (as in the dominant ideology) superior to hers, and threatened by conversation with her. His judgment on this is severe, acting through 'degraded', certainly a very harsh judgment on paradisal conversations. But the speech concludes like this:

> Authority and reason on her wait,
> As one intended first, not after made
> Occasionally; and to consummate all,

Greatness of mind and nobleness their seat
Build in her loveliest, and create an awe
About her, as a guard angelic placed.
           (*Paradise Lost* VIII. 554–9)

No more 'seems' here. He now repudiates his claim to 'higher knowledge' and to power over her. Nor is he grudging and resentful about it. His praise is unqualified: 'Greatness of mind and nobleness'. His response does *not* show him 'sunk in carnal pleasure' (VIII. 593) but is full of reverence, 'awe'. The basic premise that Eve was 'not after made/Occasionally' (VIII. 555–6) is not wrong in terms of the poem. God himself had said:

           I, ere thou spakest,
     Knew it not good for man to be alone
           (*Paradise Lost* VIII. 444–5)

For neo-Christians Adam's statement is an unsubtle revelation of wrong feeling. Certainly that is how Raphael reacts. With 'contracted brow' (VIII. 560) he condemns Adam's stance, and opposes it by a neoplatonic asceticism, marked by the disjunction between reason and feelings (so typical of 'the Christian tradition') and an insistence on the need for male domination.

At the centre of the kind of love recommended by Raphael is a simple egoism:

           weigh with her thyself;
     Then value: oft times nothing profits more
     Than self-esteem, grounded on just and right
     Well-managed
           (*Paradise Lost* VIII. 570–3)

Adam's trouble has been that he cannot get this crude weighing operation to come out right. It is certain that Milton would at one time have totally endorsed Raphael here; in the *Apology* of 1642 he referred to his own 'self-esteem either of what I was or what I might be (which let envy call pride)' (*CPW* I. 890). Did he never go beyond this? If he did not, must we nonetheless admire the doctrine? As even the younger Milton knew, there were those (whom he accused of envy) who called this pride. And, in fact, our discussion of this quest for marriage and woman, and of his dread of loneliness, has suggested how he did come to find this inflated individualism quite inadequate.

Raphael is contemptuous of what 'transports' Adam so, 'An outside' (VIII. 568), he sneers. This is a profoundly ungenerous response to Adam's celebration of Eve's loveliness, which troubled him precisely because it did not remain simple and external. The so-called love that Raphael advocates repudiates 'the sense of touch' (VIII. 579), equating it with the bestial, absolutely distinct from 'true love' (589). This too can be paralleled in Milton's prose, in his rejection of 'the mere motion of carnal lust, the mere goad of a sensitive desire' as a motive to be considered in marriage.

The 'corrected' Adam is only 'half abashed' and retracts nothing. When he says,

Though higher of the genial bed by far,
And with mysterious reverence I deem
(*Paradise Lost* VIII. 598–9)

he implicitly corrects Raphael. 'Higher' is ambiguous—higher than 'her outside' (596), or higher than Raphael deems, or both? In any case he is rejecting the sterile egoism of Raphael's kind of love, with its dehumanised and rather hypocritical spiritualism (cf. 618–27).

Where is Milton in all this? Insofar as Raphael repeats the papist 'touch not', Milton early on, though with considerable difficulties, had repudiated that kind of 'crabbed opinion'. Furthermore, Raphael responds to Adam's refusal to be fully abashed with warm approval, a smile like God's when Adam passed his previous 'trial'. What Raphael then says of angelic love is partially aetherialised,[35] but otherwise, as we have seen, it is more intense, more mutual than 'human' love and does not repudiate the physical. So this exchange dramatises a conflict between two conceptions of love. It is not clear that Milton is on the side of the angel (until the angel reveals he is on the side of man). If Adam's conception of love in Book VIII is closer to post-lapsarian love, and makes the fall more likely (as it clearly does) then we may ask, with Empson and many others, whether the Fall itself may not have been fortunate and encouraged by the hidden God of *Paradise Lost* as an immediate and considerable improvement on his attempt to create a 'pre-lapsarian' state.

Some allegedly 'modern' responses to both unfallen and fallen sexuality would thus become legitimate. 'Fallen readers' persist in finding 'unfallen' sex unsatisfactory, and fallen sex not perfect but better. Here is Eve being charmingly submissive:

> So spake our general mother, and with eyes
> Of conjugal attraction unreproved,
> And meek surrender, half embracing leaned
> On our first father, half her swelling breast
> Naked met his under the flowing gold
> Of her loose tresses hid: he in delight
> Both of her beauty and submissive charms
> Smiled with superior love, as Jupiter
> On Juno smiles, when he impregns the clouds
> That shed May flowers; and pressed her matron lip
> With kisses pure . . .
>
> (*Paradise Lost* IV. 492–502)

A sensuous and erotic description certainly, but one that has rarely received close scrutiny. There are, in fact, innumerable indications of tension. 'Unreproved' for instance: who would think of 'reproving' we may ask—and Raphael, for one, could give the answer. 'Meek surrender' sounds cloyingly abject, and again raises a question: what battle has she lost? Why does she '*half* embracing' lean with only '*half* her swelling breast' meeting his? Female students usually find the reference to 'superior love' rather absurd. It is worth pointing out here that Adam is delighted with his power, not his (or Eve's) wisdom: this is manipulative male love. The kiss sounds rather curious: 'pressed her matron lip/With kisses pure'. Did she 'press' back? The relationship is undoubtedly erotic, and much superior to Satan's enforced and anguished celibacy (significantly, as Empson noticed, seen as one of the most fiendish of God's punishments) which frames the description. But this relationship feels intolerable in many ways, flawed with unacknowledged antagonisms, negative responses, manipulative, unfree and half-concealed sexuality.

Their first act of love after eating the fruit is undoubtedly guilt-ridden, hectic and finally unfulfilling. But it is not necessarily less satisfying than pre-lapsarian sex. One of us had his education advanced immeasurably by a female student who cut through layers of neo-Christian apologetics with, 'but I like it like that'. She was, as the neo-Christians would gleefully retort, a very 'fallen' reader; indeed, and her insight was theoretically and experientially sound: Eve is *active* now as she never was in paradisal sexuality. Adam claims his senses are heightened and though Eve is still external, something for him to 'enjoy', to appropriate like the fruit, she is now a fully active partner:

> So said he, and forbore not glance or toy
> Of amorous intent, well understood
> Of Eve, whose eye darted contagious fire.
> > (*Paradise Lost* IX. 1034–6)

At least it is she herself who consciously directs her sexual activity—not those detached, sublimating, fictitious 'graces' (VIII. 60–63). Against this set the following description of paradisal love-making:

> > into their inmost bower
> Handed they went; and eased the putting off
> These troublesome disguises which we wear,
> Straight side by side were laid, nor turned I ween
> Adam from his fair spouse, nor Eve the rites
> Mysterious of connubial love refused
> > (*Paradise Lost* IV. 738–43)

Again, this is a much admired passage whose language merits closer attention than it has received. The happy couple were 'laid': who by? Adam is not seen to be doing anything, in this totally unfrank description. Eve does not 'dart contagious fire': she just does not actually refuse. Does she lie there and think of England, as Victorian wives were supposed to do? Most revealingly the language here works strongly to draw attention to Milton's inability to be frank about their sexual union, at the very point where he is repudiating such mystification (IV. 740–7). 'Mysterious' is the key word: why is he investing these 'rites' (!) with sacramental significance—the 'mystery' he himself tried to *rescue* marriage from, both in his published prose and in his *Christian Doctrine*, a 'mystery' which Blake so powerfully repudiates:

> Embraces are Cominglings: from the Head even to the Feet;
> And not a pompous High Priest entering by a Secret Place.
> > (*Jerusalem*, 69. 43–4)

Encouraged by Blake and many elements of his own work, we might be tempted to use Milton's own words against himself in *this* particular description of Adam and Eve—'austere hypocrite'.

Nevertheless, we would be very wrong to overlook the way Milton even here shows that he knows how inadequate prevailing sexual attitudes were. He also shows that either he knows about the inadequacies of Eden and its contradictions, or he is unable to free himself in practice of the very attitudes he is criticising—perhaps there is a mixture of both. The underlying uncertainty is central to Milton's work, and makes any attempt to offer final judgment on his 'position' in such matters not only deeply problematic but finally misguided.

He seems to confront contemporary life with two versions of Utopia. One is the repository of his most important revolutionary ideals, an imagined condition in which all contradictions will be magically resolved, New Jerusalem. This acted as a critique not only of the fallen 'state' but of Eden, the lesser Utopia, both politically and sexually.[36] It was a visionary focus for a revolutionary political and religious life which is also sexually radical. But the sexual critique is never fully articulated, and Milton gives great prominence to male supremacist stereotypes that at one level he knows must be superseded in the four-fold humanised world of the New Jerusalem. The radical Milton is pervasive but often covert. He must have been conscious of holding many radical views but he was unable, or unwilling, to express them and the confusions he was grappling with on the surface of his great poem. He may have meant the poem for a dimly envisaged 'fit audience though few' of extreme radicals surviving in 'Egypt', with the dominant (orthodox) ideology displayed sufficiently to allay the suspicions of those many unfit conformists whose heirs are Lewis, Fish, Patrides . . . It is certainly poor reading to abstract statements of a repressive sexual ethic in *Paradise Lost* and take them at their detached face value. But nor should we ignore Milton's inevitable complicity with orthodox sexist ideology. His thought includes an immense, yet insecure, advance over the course of his life, but there are limits to how far even a heroic individual can transcend his background and education, in thought and practice.

7

Historical Process, Individuals and Communities in Milton's Areopagitica

DAVID AERS and GUNTHER KRESS

In this chapter we explore one of Milton's best-known prose works, *Areopagitica* (1644). Our attention will focus on the way he envisages the relations between individuals and communities immersed in historical processes of discovery, choice and change so central to his case for 'the liberty to know, to utter, and to argue freely according to conscience'.[1] We hope our analysis will shed light on an important text written by a seventeenth-century revolutionary, contribute to the study of its great author's world-view and establish a form of inquiry which could be extended fruitfully to his other writings and those of his contemporaries.

We will begin with one of the most famous passages in Milton's prose. It has often been quoted to illustrate Milton's strenuously active version of individual virtue and responsibility. It is generally taken as demonstrating his emphasis on the individual's incessantly active struggle in a world shaped by constant acts of rational choice through which the individual and his community develop in both knowledge and virtue.

> Good and evil we know in the field of this World grow   1
> up together almost inseparably; and the knowledge of
> good is so involved and interwoven with the knowledge

of evill, and in so many cunning resemblances hardly
to be discern'd, that those confused seeds which were   5
impos'd on *Psyche* as an incessant labour to cull out,
and sort asunder, were not more intermixt. It was
from out the rinde of one apple tasted, that the
knowledge of good and evill as two twins cleaving
together leapt forth into the World. And perhaps this   10
is that doom which *Adam* fell into of knowing good and
evill, that is to say of knowing good by evill. As
therefore the state of man now is; what wisdome can
there be to choose what continence to forbeare without
the knowledge of evill? He that can apprehend and   15
consider vice with all her baits and seeming pleasures,
and yet abstain, and yet distinguish, and yet prefer that
which is truly better, he is the true warfaring Christian.
I cannot praise a fugitive and cloister'd vertue,
unexercis'd & unbreath'd, that never sallies out and   20
sees her adversary, but slinks out of the race, where
that immortall garland is to be run for, not without
dust and heat. Assuredly we bring not innocence into
the world, we bring impurity much rather: that which
purifies us is triall, and triall is by what is contrary.   25
That vertue therefore which is but a youngling in the
contemplation of evill, and knows not the utmost that
vice promises to her followers, and rejects it, is but
a blank vertue, not a pure; her whitenesse is but an
excrementall whitenesse; which was the reason why our   30
sage and serious Poet *Spencer,* whom I dare be known
to think a better teacher than *Scotus* or *Aquinas,*
describing true temperance under the person of *Guion,*
brings him in with his palmer through the cave of
Mammon, and the bowr of earthly blisse that he might   35
see and know, and yet abstain. Since therefore the
knowledge and survay of vice is in this world so
necessary to the constituting of human vertue, and
the scanning of error to the confirmation of truth,
how can we more safely, and with lesse danger scout   40
into the regions of sin and falsity then by reading
all manner of tractats, and hearing all manner of
reason?

                                              (CPW II. 514–16)

The argument is central in his overall defence of the liberty to
publish and debate issues freely. Since human purity, virtue and

the discovery of 'truth' in the fallen world can only come through each individual's strenuous and fully conscious combat with 'evil', 'falsity' and 'sin', any suppression of this vital struggle will endanger virtue more than vice. For vice, in Milton's view, has all the advantage of being sanctioned by the weight of inertia, dominant traditions, unexamined customs and human sloth.[2] This represents the traditional reading of the passage; the linguistic particulars of the argument, however, actually suggest a far more complex, tortuous and confused stance than commentators have suggested.

In grasping the substance and implications of Milton's position here, we will need to explore the meaning expressed through the organisation of language on the syntactic level. A number of striking linguistic features characterise this passage. Milton selects a number of abstract nouns and creates a discourse in which determinate human agents are conspicuously absent from the sequence he depicts. The passage opens with the claim that we know the abstractions 'good' and 'evil' as distinct, 'almost' but not quite inseparable entities which grow up as objects of human knowledge. (It is noteworthy that they are not treated as attributes or adjectives describing aspects of multifaceted human activity.) Although the claim overtly refers to a process involving growth it is striking that he presents this in a manner which precludes all reference to specific human agency in time. He does so by freely using the passive voice of verbs to delete agents, and by employing abstract rather than concrete nouns as the subjects (lines 1–6 in quoted passage). As commentators do not normally draw attention to these characteristics we will outline their main features rather carefully. The first point to notice is the basic relationship between an *abstract noun* such as "knowledge" and a core sentence, here "X knows Y". The writer can present his perception in either of two linguistic forms: he can select an abstract noun or he can choose to develop the core sentence, stating the agent (X), the action (knows), and the affected participant (Y). Following general linguistic usage, we call the abstract noun forms *nominalisations* to indicate that they may be derived from the full sentence form. The sentence form commits the writer to expressing the "knower" and the "known"; in addition the sentence form must be placed in a specific tense. These two requirements can be avoided by the use of the abstract noun "knowledge". Where a writer may find problems with the naming of specific human agents or of specific objects, the abstract nominal form enables him to eliminate these from the surface of the text. Where a writer may not wish to or be able to place an event in a specific time, and may wish to present it as outside history, avoiding the use of tense may prove desirable. Furthermore, the use of the nominalisation enables the writer to treat events and (temporally located) processes involving human agents as entities which can function as agents in their own right, initiating action in sentences which purport to describe the real historical world where humans live and die. So in Milton's text 'good' and 'evil' at first seem to be autonomous agents 'growing up', 'two twins' who 'leapt forth' from the apple rind Adam had tasted. This would be striking enough, but Milton has actually written that it is 'the knowledge . . . leapt forth' from the prohibited tree of 'knowledge'. This indicates how concrete processes of human discovery may become thoroughly reified, for in the chosen linguistic form these processes are transformed into an abstraction which has a bizarre life of its own, independent of the world of social being and human consciousness from which it has, in fact, been abstracted. If this is a common trait in the discourse it would suggest a writer who tended to forget that incarnate men immersed in specific situations make history, to forget that while abstract concepts are essential to our attempts to understand our world, they are not the reality being explored and can, indeed must, be subjected to a genuine dialogue with empirical evidence concerning the past and present. It would suggest a writer who, like Bacon's spider, spins out a self-generating conceptual universe which he wishes to substitute for the phenomena of the material world and social life.

The use of the passive voice to remove agency is fairly straightforward. For example: 'to be discerned', 'involved and interwoven' (*who* discerns, *who* involved and interwove . . .). If a writer employs this voice regularly (there are twelve instances of it in this passage) it is in itself a clear sign that he is either extremely uncertain about the responsible agents in his universe or that he has pressing needs to conceal the ones he knows.[3]

The passive voice and the deletion of the agent have one other consequence which becomes important in the text. The verb not only becomes 'passive', it also changes from describing a process to describing a state. Hence an action initially controlled by a specific agent can become the adjectival attribute of the abstract noun which had been the object of the process: 'a cloister'd vertue'. In this way the very processes and actions become absorbed into the writer's world of timeless abstractions.

In relation to our statements about the temporal effect of these characteristics we will briefly consider Milton's use of tense. The predominant tense in this passage is the so-called present tense: 'Good and evill we *know*' 'the knowledge of good *is* so involv'd', 'That vertue which *is* but a youngling', etc. We say so-called present tense, for the meaning of this form is not reference to "time now", but a reference to "all time". The effect of this tense therefore is to remove the statements to which it is attached out of the realm of historical and social time, and to give them the status of timeless or universally true statements. It is revealing therefore, to see where Milton uses this tense; as a generalisation we can say that those statements which deal with theoretically crucial points are in the present tense. Those parts of the argument are therefore removed from time, are not anchored in historical time, but are also presented as being beyond dispute, by virtue of their universal validity.[4]

We shall now move on to the sentences in which Milton gives his account of the procedures through which humans become virtuous and discover 'truth' (the passage runs from 'He that can . . .', i.e. lines 15ff.) The most obvious impression Milton gives is of the worthy man's strenuous activity and engagement with the material world, a model for all people, since that which purifies us is active trial against what is contrary. Milton condemns monkish withdrawal into the cloister, and praises running the race in the world's dust and heat with full apprehension of 'vice' and 'error'. Yet the obviously active verbs should not persuade us to conclude the discussion of this passage with such observations. There are important features which commentators have ignored.

Milton defines the Christian warrior he admires in the following sequence of verbs (our italics): 'He that *can apprehend* and *consider* vice . . . and yet *abstain*, and yet *distinguish*, and yet *prefer* that which is truly better'. Struck by the overall impression of activity and the energy in the passage, readers seem not to have attended to an extremely curious feature about these verbs.

Although these verbs have a transitive surface form (that is, they appear in subject-verb-object structures) in fact the processes are not, semantically, transitive. That is, they are not actions done by someone/thing to someone/thing. Nothing is 'transacted' from X to Y, indeed X alone is engaged in an activity, in which Y coincidentally and marginally also appears. We use the term non-transactive for such forms[5] to characterise their real semantic nature. The distinction draws attention to the seemingly active engagement on the surface, and the underlying self-contained reflexive nature of the processes. They also all, rather interestingly, involve mental processes with no particular consequences for 'virtuous' *practice,* and they all take the tense which eschews temporal dimensions and distinctions. The modal verb *can* which Milton uses here also disguises a centrally problematic issue. For inherent in this verb is the ambiguity about whether it is *ability* or *permission* to do something which the writer has in mind, an ambiguity which relates to some rather basic questions in Christian theology, including Milton's own. Staying with the passage under discussion, one may well wonder just what effects on ability the 'impurity' of original sin that we all allegedly bring into the world, may have; this topic itself preoccupied the devils in hell in *Paradise Lost,* God in heaven in that poem, and Milton in his *Christian Doctrine.* Similarly with the verbs in the sentences which immediately follow. They describe the kind of contemplative 'virtue' Milton claims he 'cannot praise' (the kind he had practised between leaving university and his growing involvement in the revolution, we might note), but they are presented in a form which also gives the 'virtue' he *can* praise. The syntactic agent is a nominal abstraction, 'virtue', and the praiseworthy virtue, we gather, *sallies out* and *sees* the adversary. She (for so virtue is now classified, though the 'true warfaring Christian' was made male) never *slinks out* of the race 'where the immortal garland is to be run for'. Once again the verbs are *non-transactive* and the agent (already an abstract noun) simply does not engage with the world in any concrete *practice.* She (it) may sally out, see and run a race, but effects nothing, engages in changing or preserving nothing. We now suspect that the verbs of physical activity ('sally out', 'run') are being used figuratively for purely mental notions;[6] and, however surprisingly, it thus ceases to be at all clear how the 'virtue' Milton admires differs from the 'fugitive and cloistered virtue' he condemns. Those favouring and teaching the cloistered life which culminates in the contemplative virtues have hardly seen monastic spirituality and labour as an 'unexercised and unbreathed' slinking out of the spiritual race for salvation, with its dust, heat and potent 'adversary'. This point is obvious enough but we believe that Milton lost sight of the present similarities between what he thinks he 'cannot praise' and what he thinks he can praise, similarities his linguistic choices disclose. He may have felt that the active impression the verbs convey included a statement of transactive relationships with the world and this mistake may have been encouraged by the figurative language he chose. For this imagery of individual spiritual struggle (battles and races) is traditional enough and was still alive for G.M. Hopkins, Roman Catholic and Jesuit, when he wished to contrast the exploits of the 'fighter' Christ or the martyr with the 'conquest' of those who appear noncombatants:

> But be the war within, the brand we wield
> Unseen, the heroic breast not outward-steeled,
> Earth hears no hurtle then from fiercest fray.
> Yet God (that hews mountain and continent,
> Earth, all, out; who, with trickling increment,
> Veins violets and tall trees makes more and more)
> Could crown career with conquest while there went
> Those years and years by of world without event
> That in Majorca Alfonso [a hall-porter] watched the door.
>> ('In honour of St Alphonsus Rodriquez',
>> 11.6–14)

Milton wishes to use traditional battle imagery in its figurative sense but simultaneously wants to literalise it: thus he seems to assume that one must 'sally out' (where?!) to 'see' 'the adversary' whereas in the register of his figurative language, as in Hopkins's, that adversary lives *within* the individual as well as around him. After all, Milton does assert that we actually 'bring impurity' into the world, we carry the 'adversary' within from birth. By drawing on the traditional spiritualisation of battle Milton saves himself from having to specify the relevant historical actors and battles, while by implying its literal usage Milton can convince himself and, it seems, many readers that he is talking about action appropriate to incarnate men with God-given vocations *in* the historical world.[7] And he is, indeed, overtly addressing a very earthy and specific Parliament of gentry, lawyers and merchants. Nevertheless, through our analysis we are coming to see that his language is more fit for dissolving historical time, place, social processes and practices than for engaging with these.

As we follow the supposedly active and emphatically practical virtue which Milton wants to recommend, the decisive linguistic features we have been describing recur. Having told us that what purifies us impure beings is trial by what is contrary, he offers an illustration from Spenser's *Faerie Queene,* putting forward his version of the Book of the Knight of Temperance (II) who allegedly proved 'that he might see and know and yet abstain'. The verbs 'see', 'know' and 'abstain' are once again verbs used *non-transactively*. With this major feature it is also worth noticing that these verbs play down the occasionally mixed responses and partial failures of Guyon in cantos 1, 7, 8 and 12 of Book two, together with his extremely violent *action* at the end of canto 12.[8] The choice of non-transactive verbs (with Miltonised Guyon) once more discloses insights about Milton's outlook which do not match his overt demand for active virtue exercised in the 'dust and heat' of the social world, as opposed to contemplative, cloistered virtue. For Milton's choice of 'see', 'know' and 'abstain' do not at all imply active, practical and consequently complex engagement with empirical existence, while his version of Guyon's progress evaporates the moral ambiguities which are so often at the heart of Spenser's poetic achievement and vision, despite his plain enough ambitions for a static and unambiguous scheme of ethical and political judgments. The non-transactive verbs which Milton selects in fact favour a *contemplative* posture, although this is just what he is attacking. Given this, it is not surprising that in the following sentences (lines 34ff.) he piles together nominalisations ('the knowledge and survey of vice . . . so necessary to the constituency of truth . . . the scanning of error . . . the confirmation of truth'), totally eliminating human agents and the temporal dismensions of human action. Whatever his overt claims, he perceives virtue and truth in terms of a contemplative and detached stance ('see', 'abstain') rather than of a *practice* which involves dialogue and transactive processes with the world of social and material existences.

Here we return to a phrase we passed over earlier but which

proves rather problematic when seen in its context—'that which purifies us is trial, and trial is by what is contrary' (see the whole sentence, lines 19–25). Because commentators appear not to have noted any difficulty here we will spell out just what it is. Milton claims that 'we bring *impurity*' (our italics) into the world with us 'not innocence'. He also claims 'that which purifies us is trial, and trial is by what is contrary'; since we (impure people) are purified by trial against our 'contrary' it seems we are purified by trial *against purity,* the 'contrary' of 'impurity'. We find that this position lacks coherence. Milton has argued that most writing should be freely published because if it does contain 'evil' and 'falsehood' this is no bad thing for it is through our apprehension of 'evil' and 'falsehood' that we learn to know 'good' and 'truth'. In this argument our intellectual and moral purification is by trial *against* what Milton takes to be 'impurity', *not* purity. If the necessary purifying trial *is* actually against purity, then Milton's argument for free publication of what he acknowledges may be judged as impure ('evil' and 'falsehood') collapses. Here he has a further difficulty: *how,* if we all bring 'impurity' (original sin affects all the faculties) into the world, are we to judge correctly concerning pure and impure? And *where* would we even find the pure contrary against which we should enter into purifying trial? Milton does not notice the initial incoherence, let alone these ramifications. It is as though he had been bemused by his own universe of abstractions, here compounded by an extraordinarily dense set of explicit and implicit negations (lines 19–24): 'cannot', 'fugitive', 'unexercised' (compare 'disexercising' in the last line on p. 491 of the Yale edition), 'unbreathed', 'never ', 'slinks out', 'immortal', 'not without', 'not innocence', 'impurity'. Like the marked use of non-transactive verbs we discussed above, these negative formulations are a linguistic manifestation of Milton's inability (or possibly conscious unwillingness?) to envisage the allegedly active virtue he praises and commends as specifically embodied and engaging with the world in dynamic and specific interchange. Tangled in his own web of negatives and the abstract nominals which he has endowed with agentive powers, absorbed in a self-generating conceptual universe, he quite fails to enter into dialogue with the empirical processes of human interaction which might have encouraged him to focus on the inadequacy and immediate incoherence of simple and fixed dichotomies like purity and impurity. The local incoherence we have noted is a symptom of the way such anti-empirical procedures always tend, at some stage, to collapse into plain nonsense, although a particularly significant kind of nonsense which reveals a great deal about a writer's version of his world and the relationship between conceptual activity and social, historical being.

For all the claim about the complexity of distinguishing 'good' and 'evil' in this world (lines 1–7) the model with which Milton chooses to illustrate this is curiously simple and static. He likens the labours of intellectual and moral exploration to the task of sorting out the different kinds of seed, which Venus imposed on Psyche. The seeds are not planted and the model eliminates any movement in the objects of knowledge; it also precludes any possibility that the classifying concepts which humans use to explore the world are provisional ones developed in the face of the changing, fluid and often ambiguous realities that confront us. The relationships and materials we are supposedly learning to know are turned by Milton into static and totally explicit 'knowledge' which is merely a matter of separating fixed entities into two apparently straightforward categories, 'good' and 'evil'. It is appropriate that in the myth on which Milton draws, the task Venus set was successfully accomplished by ants.[9]

Even when Milton offers a more dynamic model of individual quest and discovery many similar features recur. In another much quoted passage he asserts that when God gave Adam reason, 'he gave him freedom to choose, for reason is but choosing'. This is a remarkably impoverished version of rational exploration, which, whether we follow it in the work of great historians, poets or philosophers, is far more and other than 'but choosing' between distinct entities. Milton's own illustration of the rational and free activity for which we were apparently created runs as follows:

> God therefore left him free, set before him a provoking object, ever almost in his eyes: herein consisted his merit, herein the right of his reward, the praise of his abstinence.

(PCW II. 527)

This contrasts starkly with the subtle exploration he carried out years later in *Paradise Lost,* but it accords with the tendencies we have noted so far in this chapter. The model depends on *non-transactive* verbs and culminates, as in the earlier distortion

of Guyon's story, in an ideal of abstention from action in response
to a very simple dichotomy (abstain and live, or eat and die:
Genesis 2–3). It is also quite as static as the one based on Psyche
and the seeds of grain she had to separate. God may have created
'passions within us, pleasures round about us', which are the very
'ingredients of virtue' *(CPW* II. 527), but Milton reduces the
activities of practical reason and individual moral development in
the human world to the one decision to abstain from one fixed
'object' quite unequivocally and directly forbidden by 'God'.
Nevertheless, Milton does want to suggest more than this and in
mentioning the God-created 'passions within us, pleasures round
about us', he offers a generous vision of divine plenitude which
challenges the mean-minded anxiety of repressive governments
and their laws of censorship:

> God pours out before us even to a profuseness all desirable things, and
> gives us minds that can wander beyond all limit and satiety. Why
> should we then affect a rigor contrary to the manner of God and of
> nature, by abridging or scanting those means, which books freely
> permitted are, both to the trial of virtue, and the exercise of truth.
>
> (528)

This is more like those aspects of *Paradise Lost,* books IV and
VII, so often celebrated in commentaries on that poem. Yet
although Milton does insist that 'the matter' of 'sin' and 'virtue' is
the same human energy (527), he continues to select *non-
transactive* verb forms and to eschew the construction of any
dialogue, or dialectical relationship, between human consciousness and social being (it is instructive to compare Marvell here, a
contemporary whose work often manifests the kind of dialectical
thought we have in mind).[10] This procedure has consequences for
his grasp of the present. For instance, he asks why men wish to
affect a rigour contrary to God's and nature's generosity, and
proclaims that books are means 'to the trial of virtue and the
exercise of truth'. We can applaud the liberal sentiments here yet
there are important lacunae in the statement. When he writes of
'the exercises of truth' he treats 'truth' as an autonomous agent
(exercising him/her/itself and being exercised as a horse is
exercised by its trainer). This way of perceiving once again rules
out the two-way exchange in which human knowledge is generated, criticised, revised and extended, the exchange between

specific individual consciousness and equally specific realities in the social and material world. Milton's approach also blinds his readers (and himself) to many vital aspects of the contemporary battle of ideas in which he himself had joined so vigorously. These struggles were, after all, abstract expressions of the real, conflicting, historical and social relationships in his England. The role of ideas and religion, for instance, in the gentry's determination to maintain and tighten their own control in the counties was lost on neither themselves nor their opponents. For them the free play of critical ideas and the institutional implications of such free play (as over tithes)[11] meant a serious threat to their version of community, order and religion. They considered that the theoretical and practical exercises of their social subordinates were of considerable importance to their own well being, knowing that the battle of ideas was not simply part of an autonomous field of inquiry but related to the public world where people worked, rebelled, loved and fought. Phrases like 'the exercise of truth', so characteristic of Milton's discourse, are deeply misleading in the way they systematically eliminate human actors and their historical relationships. A writer who habitually uses such forms probably lacks categories for treating historical change and action, even when, as in Milton's case, they are most obviously inherent in his topic—the human production of knowledge.

The next extended model that Milton offers for thinking about individual pursuit of true knowledge is most memorable for its passionate insistence on individual responsibility as against uncritical faith in traditions and existing institutions (p. 543, lines 5–13).

> Truth is compar'd in Scripture to a streaming fountain; if her waters flow not in a perpetuall progression, they sick'n into a muddy pool of conformity and tradition. A man may be a heretick in the truth; and if he beleeve things only because his Pastor sayes so, or the Assembly so determins, without knowing other reason, though his belief be true, yet the very truth he holds, becomes his heresie. There is not any burden that som would gladlier post off to another, then the charge and care of their Religion.

These moving statements about the moral responsibility individuals have to 'exercise' their own critical reason are typical of radical Protestants and one of the most valuable convictions they have bequeathed to us. Nonetheless, the passage does contain features related to those we have been analysing. The 'truth' that humans can discover is presented as an agent which may flow 'in a perpetual progression' or 'sicken into a muddy pool', seemingly, once again, in autonomous fashion. Milton's image implies no dialogue or dialectic between the objective realities pursued by humans and the consciousness of the human inquirers. Somehow the fountain of truth can sicken (like an animate being) 'into a muddy pool of conformity and tradition'. Later Milton tells us that 'Truth' once came into the world (with Christ, p. 549) and what he probably refers to here is the processes of change initiated by Jesus and brought about by human actions, ideas and relationships. Protestants were not given to regarding the history of Christianity since its Golden Pauline age in terms which encourage nuanced attention to such complex processes, but here Milton is not just generalising about the reign of Antichrist and the Whore of Babylon. He is in fact talking about the Protestant epoch itself, warning Presbyterians and their supporters against inquisitorial methods. Yet even here Milton's language betrays the compulsion to turn the *practices* of human individuals and groups into objectified *states*. So he writes of 'a muddy pool of conformity and tradition'. We sympathise with his description of uncritical intellectual and religious conformism to dominant traditions in terms of individual and collective stagnation, yet we still see that behind the nouns 'conformity and tradition' Milton simply obscures the real practices and commitments of diverse groups in his world. Particularly he obscured those middling gentry who had supported Parliament with the aim of gaining (and regaining) control of 'their' counties from encroachment by monarch and state church, but were determined not to relinquish control of government or religion in any sphere to subordinate social groups.[12] To create a form of discourse which blocked out the practices and convictions of vital groups such as this was to create a form incapable of illuminating those processes in which human beings strove to change and order their world.

We now move to a discussion of the extended model of the human pursuit of 'truth' which Milton composed around the myth of Osiris and Isis (pp. 549–51).

Truth indeed came once into the world with her divine   1
Master, and was a perfect shape most glorious to look
on: but when he ascended, and his Apostles after him
were laid asleep, then strait arose a wicked race of
deceivers, who as that story goes of the *Aegyptian*   5
Typhon with his conspirators, how they dealt with the
good *Osiris*, took the virgin Truth, hewd her lovely
form into a thousand peeces, and scatter'd them to the
four winds. From that time ever since, the sad friends
of Truth, such as durst appear, imitating the carefull   10
search that *Isis* made for the mangl'd body of *Osiris*,
went up and down gathering up limb by limb still as
they could find them. We have not yet found them all,
Lords and Commons, nor ever shall doe, till her Masters
second comming; he shall bring together every joynt   15
and member, and shall mould them into an immortal
feature of lovelines and perfection.

The first sentence (lines 1–9) again establishes that the notion of a
dialogue, a dialectic between knowing mind(s) and field to be
known is alien to Milton (it had not been alien to Chaucer and it
was not to Marvell).[13] The fact that a great many human beings
did *not* find the poor carpenter Jesus accompanied by 'a perfect
shape most glorious to look on', that the gospels themselves
make this plain and that the early Christian appropriation of the
suffering servant sequence in Isaiah emphasises the *absence* of
any platonically 'perfect shape most glorious to look on', this is
all eliminated by Milton. He effects the elimination in a linguistic
strategy familiar enough to us by this stage, one which avoids any
statement concerning relevant human agents and specific temporal processes—'Truth . . . was a perfect shape most glorious *to
look* on'. The form discourages readers (and Milton himself) from
asking *who* precisely was looking *when* and *where,* and then from
raising the tricky but relevant questions about the problematic
nature of *interpreting* the known, about the relations between a
knower and known immersed in time and space. Instead of
perceiving the development of Christianity after the death of the
Apostles in terms of the actions and relationships of human
beings living through changing circumstances, he substitutes an
immediate magical arising of a demonic 'race of deceivers'

possessing irresistible power. These wicked deceivers are not even motivated in their nasty attack on the 'glorious' but forlorn platonic abstraction 'the virgin Truth' somehow still wandering about in Palestine (or was it Rome?). Again, one sees the attractiveness for Milton of abstract actors like 'the virgin Truth' in place of actual human individuals or groups, and their empirical practices. They are a considerable help in dismissing historical processes and avoiding the need to engage in any serious dialogue with people and movements. And they encourage his imposition of self-confirming fictions on the phenomena he appears to consider. Not that he wants to acknowledge this. In fact, he often wishes to give the appearance that his text *does* relate to objective historical processes and is empirically anchored—for example, in his account of the Inquisition, or here in referring to the alleged activity of the 'deceivers' as an event in human time—'*when . . . then . . . from that time*'.

In the rest of the quoted passage he continues to use the Osiris myth to disclose his views about the human pursuit of true knowledge. 'Truth' is presented as a dismembered body whose limbs we ('the sad friends of Truth') gradually gather together 'till' Christ's second coming. The image of 'Truth' as a dismembered corpse clashes rather bizarrely with that of 'Truth' as the perpetually flowing fountain (discussed above). Yet we can easily see its appeal to the author who had presented the human quest for ethical knowledge in terms of Psyche (or the arts) sorting out different kinds of grain seeds. Despite Milton's emphasis that 'reformation' must continue (549), that the quest for 'truth' is to continue 'till' the second coming, the image he selects implies that in fact 'we' ('friends of Truth') know perfectly well what 'truth' is. 'We' apparently know the total 'shape' without any need to attend to problems concerning human perception or any need to meditate on the different accounts given by 'the friends of Truth' across generations and in different classes and cultures. Our task is 'gathering up limb by limb' the parts of the body we know so well, 'to unite those dissevered pieces which are yet wanting to the body of Truth' (549, 550–1). Once more (as in the seed image) the phenomena humans engage with are presented in a model which makes them static and ignores any questions concerning the selection of appropriate concepts and categories for the exploration being undertaken. It precludes any consideration of the dialectical and changing relations between perceivers and perceived. And it evaporates the historicity of the relations even while asserting the open-ended and historical nature of the pursuits which only Christ will complete.

Not that Milton stays with this model for the rest of the text. Later (pp. 561–3) he envisages 'Truth' not as a dismembered corpse being reassembled by her 'sad friends' but as a (female) battler:

> And though all the windes of doctrin were let loose to play upon the earth, so Truth be in the field, we do injuriously by licencing and prohibiting to misdoubt her strength. Let her and Falshood grapple; who ever knew Truth put to the wors, in a free and open encounter.
>
> *(CPW* II. 561)

Here 'Truth' is apparently alive and ready for battle. Once more an abstract noun is personified and made an actor. Readers unsympathetic with Milton's stance could well have reminded him that the conditional he admits *('so* Truth *be* in the field, we do injuriously by licencing and prohibiting') is, by his own earlier account, not fulfilled. Truth lies dead and dismembered, not at all ready for battle in the field. So, such readers might have protested, 'we' are indeed justified in our 'misdoubt' of 'her strength', and in doing all we can to prevent what we take to be licentious, blasphemous incitement to social and religious revolution which many gentry (and others) fear as anarchy and violent chaos. Leaving aside such protests for the moment, let us concentrate on the model Milton is deploying here. By making 'Truth' (as an abstract noun) the actor 'in the field', in a battle against 'Falsehood' (another abstract noun), Milton achieves a number of effects. At a stroke he gets rid of all the diverse and perplexing phenomena of contemporary social existence and religious conflicts. In their place he puts a battlefield in which a powerful abstraction ('Truth') grapples with one which is *(a priori)* defined as weaker in our world ('Falsehood'). The author then confidently assures the gentry and citizens in Parliament, to whom he directs his address, that 'we' need not doubt who the victor will be. The multi-layered processes of reality are thus dissolved in an idealist fantasia. Furthermore, he then asserts, as an unquestionable truism, that history also bears out his claim that 'Truth' always defeats 'Falsehood', at least 'in a free and open encoun-

ter'. It is one thing to express an act of totally blind faith in the
'final' justice and coherence of the ultimate apocalypse and divine
judgment: from such acts of faith are traditional theodicies
composed.[14] But Milton is here doing something else. He claims
that no-one has ever found incidents of 'Truth put to the
worse'—that is, within human history. The statement, to say the
least, is foolish. But one can see why Milton and many readers
might overlook its folly. For *despite* the overt appeal to history,
the very abstractionism of the terms ('Truth . . . a free and open
encounter', 'Falsehood') delivers the statement from any dialogue with past or present social existence, delivers it from any
possible historical verification or falsification. What the author
would count as 'Truth' being put to the 'worse', or as 'a free and
open encounter' and within what social practice or intellectual
discipline, we cannot tell. Furthermore, we recall how a few
pages earlier Milton informed us that 'Truth' had not only been
put to the worse but hacked to pieces by a wicked race of
deceivers. Presumably he would now allege that this historical
'event' had not been in a free and open encounter, but one has no
means of knowing. In fact his mode of discourse (and his models)
dissolve social existence and resist concrete engagement with
historical relations and processes. The risk of such discourse is
that it encourages dangerous self-deception. It invites author and
reader to evade the dynamic contradictory realities of the present
(here, for instance, the convictions of the middling gentry and
their power, the social implications of radical religious convictions over tithes, etc.), and to impose some self-satisfying ideal
construct. Or it invites us to exalt and sublimate some human
individuals or groups into 'Truth' and the civil war into 'the wars
of Truth' (562) with a unified abstraction, 'Truth', fighting a
homogenous contrary, 'Falsehood'. It is contemptuous of the
fluidity and ambiguity which permeate human relationships
across time, and provides no directions for subjecting the informing concepts and categories to empirical checks from actual
events and developments. It is also lacking in any procedure
which might encourage self-reflexivity, critical reflexion on the
role of the specific and contingent individual writer in constructing the discourse, in organising the categories and concepts with
which to interrogate the present and the past.[15]

There is one more model we shall consider before closing this

part of the chapter. It comes after Milton has been celebrating
London as the 'mansion house of liberty', the home of 'belea-
gured [not dismembered now, we note] Truth' in the last days of
fallen history when the final harvest of John 4:35 'need not be five
weeks', for 'had we but eyes to lift up, the fields are white
already' (p. 554). Milton pleads for charity and toleration towards
Protestant enthusiasm and invokes the Jews who constructed the
Temple. This, he believes, will serve as a model for the present
rulers of England in their attitude to all groups of Protestant
reformers:

> Yet these are the men cry'd out against for schismaticks   1
> and sectaries; as if, while the Temple of the Lord was
> building, some cutting, some squaring the marble, others
> hewing the cedars, there should be a sort of irrationall
> men who could not consider there must be many schisms and   5
> many dissections made in the quarry and in the timber, ere
> the house of God can be built. And when every stone is
> laid artfully together, it cannot be united into a contin-
> uity, it can but be contiguous in this world; neither can
> every peece of the building be of one form; nay rather the   10
> perfection consists in this, that out of many moderat
> varieties and brotherly dissimilitudes that are not vastly
> disproportionall arises the goodly and the gracefull
> symmetry that commends the whole pile and structure. Let
> us therefore be more considerat builders, more wise   15
> in spirituall architecture, when great reformation
> is expected.

(CPW II. 555)

Milton's boundless delight and faith in the exuberant energy of
God's 'Englishmen', apparently elected by God himself 'to the
reforming of Reformation' (p. 553) runs through the long paragraph of which our quote is a very small portion (pp. 551–5). But
he is also offering a version of individual and collective action to
Parliament as a guide in the present. As such it has some
noteworthy features. We will take the Old Testament source first
(1 Kings 5 and 6), then Milton's model and finally its implied
application to the 'mansion house of liberty' in 1644. In the
Biblical text King Solomon explicitly *commanded* the Jews to
prepare stone before they brought it to the building-site ('so that
there was neither hammer nor mace nor any tool of iron heard in

the house, while it was in building', 1 Kings 6:7, see *CPW* II. 555, n.244) and he himself *organised* the whole process. Indeed, as one has come to expect in texts written by and for members of the possessing and managerial groups in societies, the men who actually did the work are continuously deleted during chapter 6, and in their place the single hero, the one royal architect and commander stars. For instance: 'So he built the house, and finished it; and covered the house with beams and boards of cedar. And then he built chambers against all the house . . . And he built the walls of the house within with boards of cedar . . . And he built twenty cubits on the sides of the house . . . So Solomon overlaid the house within with pure gold: and he made a partition . . .'. In noting the conservative uses of 1 Kings 6:7 (quoted earlier) the Yale editor comments on 'Milton's technique of reversing a damaging received inference from a scriptural text by enlarging the scope of reference' (555, n.244). But Milton has done far more than enlarge the scope of reference from one verse to two chapters. He has tried to appropriate a text which is quite explicit about the absolute rule and control of King Solomon, both architectural and executive. Furthermore, the Old Testament text makes it clear that here it is only King Solomon whom God addresses in connection with building the temple, not any of those involved in doing the actual physical work. Fairly obviously this does not suit Milton's purposes and in his rendering of the story he simply deletes Solomon, the King and controller. Who then does he present as governor(s), architect(s) and executive agents? Attempting to answer the question we can begin by looking at the way he uses the verb 'build' in the first sentence. It appears in the phrase, 'while the Temple of the Lord .was building' (non-transactive) and in the final phrase 'ere the house of God can be built' (passive). This contrasts plainly enough with the source we quoted from (1 Kings 6). Milton has selected a linguistic form which enables him to use a verb of physical process without specifying any physical agents. (The Old Testament, we remember, made it clear that the workers were unquestioningly under the King's command and then banished them from the text, attributing all the activity of construction to Solomon). He does, like the book of Kings, refer to the manual workers, 'some cutting, some squaring the marble, others hewing the cedars', but in their brief appearance they are not perceived in any chain of command and power. This, in terms of traditional (and present) attitudes to social work is certainly rare and has thoroughly subversive implications.[16] But Milton does not think it through or attend to the manifest problems which any proponent of traditional assumptions and practices about the structures of command in the realm of human labour would have raised. Instead, as he thinks of the activity of construction, he returns to the passive voice and deletes the crucial agents ('when every stone *is laid artfully together,* it cannot *be united . . .*'). He does say that the building will never be completed 'in this world', yet in the same sentence he asserts that there '*arises* the goodly and the graceful symmetry' of 'the whole pile and structure'. The choice of 'arises' again makes the constructors as invisible as any overall architect(s). (We may remember the way the palaces of evil magicians like Busyrane in the *Faerie Queene* arise and vanish, or the sights generated by Comus, or by Satan in *Paradise Regained*.) Certainly, how the 'pile and structure' can stand gracefully and symmetrically, its design fully comprehended, while the workers have not yet united the parts 'into a continuity' is hard to envisage. As a model for thinking about collective human activity, physical and intellectual, it thus has glaring defects, all of them revealing about the author's outlook. When he applies his model to the contemporary 'mansion house of liberty' and his admirable wish to defend free discussion of ideas, the problems he faces are rather considerable, although he himself seems quite oblivious of this fact. He asserts that only 'irrational men' could fail to see that processes of construction mean there 'must be many schisms and many dissections made in the quarry and in the timber'. The workers cut marble and hewed wood: Milton turns this into 'schisms' and 'dissections', that is, into religious and political decisions made by diverse contemporaries to separate from the dominant traditions of Christian doctrine and ecclesiastical order. Yet he also keeps some of the literal first terms of the model from which he is extrapolating, so that these 'schisms' are 'made in the quarry and in the timber'. By whom are the present schisms 'made'? What could Milton possibly mean by schisms 'made in the quarry and in the timber'? And precisely what is the distinction between quarry and temple-site in *1644?* A rather irresponsible mixture of figurative and literal application of the model is undoubtedly part of the confusion here.

But the problem goes deeper than this. The form of discourse precludes any specific answer to these questions. Indeed, it discourages readers from even putting them, although they are central to the issues with which Milton is supposedly dealing—the necessity of the liberty of publishing in the progressive enhancement of 'reformation, liberty and order'. His text does indeed express his personal values and his faith in the happy outcome of 'schisms' and 'brotherly dissimilitudes' in a 'goodly and graceful symmetry'. But in branding as 'irrational' those who believed that the increasing diversity and dedicatedly partisan commitment of competing groups would lead into yet more destructive conflict, further misery and merely different kinds of tyranny under new tyrants, he was publicly claiming the role of rational critic engaged with the objective realities of the situation in the 1640s—'Let us', he invited the nobles, gentry and citizens gathered in Parliament, 'be more considerate builders, more wise in spiritual architecture, when great reformation is expected.' Yet this defender of reason, teacher of wisdom, has little to offer in terms of inquiry and substantial argument concerning the present religious, social and political grounds and effects of the 'schisms' towards which he gestures. Nor does he offer any explanation of why the spiritual illumination of '*a Nation of Prophets*' (554, 556) should necessarily entail *schisms*, with their social and political ramifications. Gradually it becomes clear that once more Milton has developed a model which seems concerned with the changing phenomena of the present world but actually excludes all engagement and dialogue with the empirical realities of human relationship, action and changing conflict. Even his serious (albeit highly abstract) commitment to 'free conscience and Christian liberties' is put in a manner which encourages an important question we have not yet asked: in Milton's mind who or what is represented by the utterly passive substances cut up, squared, hewed and 'laid artfully together'? Are they people, peoples' lives, ideas and religious convictions? It is difficult to see what else they could represent and the implications of this are rather disturbing. While Milton pleads for toleration for the expression of all *Protestant*

viewpoints, ('I mean not tolerated Popery, and open superstition, which . . . should be extirpated . . .', p. 565), he seems to
envisage the activists so briefly glimpsed ('some cutting, some
squaring the marble, others hewing the cedars') as able and
entitled to work on an inert mass of human materials in the cause
of 'spiritual architecture', of 'great reformation'. Who, concretely, on what grounds, and by whom, is to be assessed as inert
matter in need of being cut, squared, hewed and passively placed
in a structure over which those placed there have absolutely no
control? Milton and his model are too idealist to face such major
concrete issues relating to human relations and to historical
practice. This is one of the ironies of his discourse since it is
offered as an intervention at a particular moment in a religious
and political revolution.

Some readers may perhaps feel that we are making too much of
what seems a fairly casual image. Milton was hardly a writer of
casual images, especially images intended to support a central
part of an argument. But even if this were a casual image, it would
still have the significance we are describing. Even, or particularly, clichés used quite unreflectingly, encapsulate ways of
seeing in a condensed form. The very fact that they are generally
regarded as banal and uncontentious, devoid of significance,
makes them excellent vehicles for conveying unexamined positions and assumptions. Moreover, the way in which this particular image meshes so perfectly with the other linguistic processes
and strategies which we have analysed confirms that we are not
dealing with an insignificant and extrinsic image. Rather, we are
dealing with the encapsulation of a fundamental ideological
stance, with its attendant problems. There is a choice in such
matters and it might be worth recalling how Marvell used a
similar basic model but absorbed it into his own vision, one
habitually more aware of the dialectical relation between knowing
mind and the phenomena to be known, far more aware of the
fluidity, *un*fixity both in historical processes and in the concepts
with which people organise their dialogues with history. In his
'First Anniversary' Marvell contemplates the achievements of
Cromwell by 1655 and after recollecting the myth of Amphion's
magical construction of Thebes, presents Cromwell's recent
attempts to establish constitutional order in these terms:

All other Matter yields, and may be rul'd;
But who the Minds of stubborn Men can build?
No Quarry bears a Stone so hardly wrought,
Nor with such labour from its Center brought;
Non to be sunk in the Foundation bends,
Each in the House the highest Place contends,
And each the Hand that lays him will direct,
And some fall back upon the Architect;
Yet all compos'd by his attractive Song,
Into the Animated City throng.

The Common-wealth does through their Centers all
Draw the Circumf'rence of the publique Wall;
The crossest Spirits here do take their part,
Fast'ning the Contignation which they thwart;

And they, whose Nature leads them to divide,
Uphold, this one, and that the other Side;
But the most Equal still sustein the Height,
And they as Pillars keep the Work upright;
While the resistance of opposed Minds,
The Fabrick as with Arches stronger binds,
Which on the Basis of a Senate free,
Knit by the Roofs Protecting weight agree.
                                        'First Anniversary'

Marvell's attention to the dynamic nature of historical change has
encouraged him to transform the basic architectural model even
while retaining it. We know that building materials are inert, but
Marvell shows us that we must change our picture of them if we
are to use building as a model for thinking about social order.
With this purpose he animates the structure and evokes a
two-way relationship between the 'architect' (Cromwell) and the
self-interested, diverse 'minds of stubborn men' who form the
Commonwealth. The poet does not celebrate or want Milton's
'schisms and many dissections', and he is now happy to have a
specific architect and constitutional ruler, Cromwell. Yet it is
Marvell, not Milton, who creates a brief image of a social
framework within which contradictory human commitments can
be enacted and acknowledged, he who creates a dialectical model
which takes us beyond the static, one-dimensional nature of
Milton's.[17]

So for all the energy and apparent orientation to historical change and present events in *Areopagitica* our analysis has shown that Milton's discourse employs a range of linguistic strategies and guiding models which *resist* engagement with the phenomena of social existence, including those which are absolutely central to his own address. He dissolves the processes of reality in a discourse which lacks any means of treating the *interaction* between individual consciousness and social being, any way of subjecting its abstractions and assertions to genuine engagement with the determinate evidence of past and present events and the diverse interests of contemporary groups or individuals making their country's history in highly specific circumstances. Are these features characteristic of radical puritan prose, are they shared by other writers, or are they idiosyncratic? Are they characteristic of Milton's work at all stages of his life or only in the period around 1644? Do the great poems manifest similar syntactic features and if they do, to what effect in that different mode? These seem to us just some of the questions our chapter raises although a detailed exploration is beyond the scope of the present book.

In the second and briefer part of the chapter we focus on what seems a real problem for Milton, in fact a real problem for any intellectual who discovers that the way things are is not the best of all possible ways, who lives in a period of open, violent conflicts, and notices contemporaries producing diverse religious, social and political programmes. What community does he address? Who precisely does Milton perceive as the audience for his radical utterances in 1644, and where does he see his own social basis? Defining the community to which one belongs and exactly whom one is addressing is peculiarly problematic in periods of accelerated changes when received groupings and ideas come to seem inadequate and anomalous. Furthermore, alignments and any individual's perceptions of his affiliations are likely to change in such a period, as the overall circumstances and relationships change. In this section we wish simply to propose a method of textual enquiry into such problems by taking just one major work which represents Milton's response to a historical situation at one specific moment. We believe that our approach can contribute to mapping any writer's relations to wider communities over a range of texts and moments. In a detailed study of Milton these would need to be considered.

One of the most direct ways of exploring such a sense of community is by looking at the writer's use of pronouns (especially 'we'/'them'), since this should express his self-location in terms of the groups his own perspectives allow him to notice. On the opening page of the 1644 edition of *Areopagitica* Milton mentions that 'the thought of whom it *[Areopagitica]* hath recourse to' is present to him in the act of writing (p. 487), and the tract is explicitly addressed 'To the Parliament of England'. Milton presents himself as one of those responsible 'private persons' concerned with that increasingly important concept in political ideology, 'the public good', and so setting out to advise the present 'triennial Parliament' (488, 486). The 'I' which features so prominently in the opening pages (486–491) encourages one to expect Milton to organise his text along the basic structure of 'I' (individual champion of 'liberty', 487): 'you' (parliament—patron of 'liberty'). This itself would be an interesting example of address in a period when conflict was being articulated in more and more consciously ideological forms, when status, tradition and customary authority were losing their force in argument. Indeed, Milton implies that he, the private individual, without any specific social status or class other than what he can convey by his control of *words* and *ideas,* by his *ideological* discourse, is 'the voice of reason' (490) deserving attention *as such*. Here he speaks as one of the new class of ideologue whose history is currently being illuminated by the work of a number of scholars.[18] But this is not the only, or probably even the predominant, stance he adopts. He soon uses the pronoun 'we' (487). For example,

> *we* are already in good part arrived [i.e., at 'the utmost bound of civil liberty'], and yet from such a steep disadvantage of tyranny and superstition grounded into *our* principles as was beyond the manhood of a *Roman* recovery
>
> ['we' and 'our' italicised by us]

He attributes this arrival to God and 'your faithful guidance and undaunted Wisdom, Lords and Commons of England' (487). Here the word 'we' seems to stand for all the people of England, the elect 'Nation' about which Milton had such exalted views at this stage of his life and with whom he here identified himself. On p. 553, for instance, 'us' is God's 'English-men' (with the only exception being 'our obdurat Clergy'), while those who were in opposition to the dominant group in the Parliament by 1644, or those attempting to be 'neuters', simply have no presence in this scheme. However, Milton shifts the referents of the pronoun *we*. A few pages on, Milton writes, 'We should be wary therefore what persecution we raise aginst the living labours of public men' (493; similarly 521, lines 5–8). This use identifies him with the current *rulers* who are applying the censorship over the elect nation. This is partly a sensible tactical move—it implies that Milton understands the practices of the group he addresses and is one of them, sharing their values, aspirations and difficulties, therefore unlikely to be advocating anything against their (our) real interest, identical with God's and his nation's of course (so too p. 564, where he identifies himself with the new inquisitors!). It is also more than an opportunist tactic. Milton was himself a leisured intellectual who *never* in his life *had* to work for a living, *never* had to sell his labour-power and *never* had to join in a degrading scramble for patronage.[19] He did have genuine class and cultural affinities with many men in the revolutionary parliament, however far removed his religious and political ideology was from most of its members even by 1644, let alone by the end of the civil wars. When he mentions 'the common people' he mentions them as a group of whom he is definitely not a member:

> Nor is it to *the common people* less than a reproach; for if *we* be so jealous over *them*, as that *we* dare not trust *them* with an English pamphlet, what do *we* but censure *them* for a giddy, vicious, and ungrounded *people* . . . That this is care or love of *them*, *we* cannot pretend . . .
>
> (536–7)

'We' is Parliament and Milton, 'they' the common people; what becomes of the 'we' who represented 'the whole Nation' (535, 536, later 553) is not at all clear.[20] It seems to disappear under the real pressure of major class and status differentiations which are not openly acknowledged in the text. That it should vanish is hardly surprising for the notion of 'one Nation' in a society divided by antagonistic classes has always been a rather unilluminating one when the questions have involved understanding that society. Milton's own position emerges in yet another light two paragraphs further on. Having described his tour of Italy, his visit to Galileo and other 'learned men' and their complaints against the Inquisition, he notes that he has now heard very similar arguments in England among 'as learned men' against parliamentary censorship of publication. What is more, these 'learned men', ones, he reassures Parliament, 'who honour you and are known and respected by you', importuned John Milton to write a tract against 'an undeserved thraldom upon learning' (the *deserved* one, we suppose, is a Roman Catholic 'learning', though we doubt that Milton would have extended the courtesy of calling this 'learning', rather than 'superstition'). He thus proclaims that there is a community to which he belongs and one which Parliament should respect:

> That this is not therefore the disburdening of a particular fancy, but the common grievance of all those who had prepared their minds and studies above the vulgar pitch to advance truth in others, and from others to entertain it, thus much may satisfy. And in their name I shall for neither friend nor foe conceal what the general murmur is . . .
>
> (539)

So he claims to represent an *intellectual elite*, 'above the vulgar pitch', propagators of 'truth' in lesser mortals. He does not show any signs of having reflected on the social basis or role of this self-proclaimed elite nor its relationship to the powerful commercial and landed elites in England. Instead he proceeds to merge it into what seems a far more inclusive grouping as he claims that these learned men murmur,

> that if it comes to inquisitioning again, and licencing and that we are so timorous of our selves, and so suspicious of all men, as to fear each book, and the shaking of every leaf, before we know what the contents are, if some who but of late were little better then silenced from preaching, shall come now to silence us from reading, except what they please, it cannot be guessed what is intended by some but a second tyranny over learning: and will soon put it out of controversy that Bishops and Presbyters are the same to us both name and thing.
>
> (539)

By referring to the complaints of the 'learned' elite as 'the general murmur' Milton implies that they are not limited to a small, self-interested group. Now the pronoun 'we'(*'we* are so timorous of ourselves', and 'before *we* know what the contents are') seems to include not only Parliament (whose anxiety Milton signals) but also 'the whole Nation' again (535, 536). It even includes 'the common people' (536) and all those whose minds and studies are *not* 'above the vulgar pitch' (539). This is a motley collection to unify, and one immediately fragmented by the division between 'some' who recently suffered censorship, and 'us' whom these 'some' are now threatening to silence (through the agency of Parliament) in their apparent wish to establish 'a second tyranny over learning'. Here Milton uses 'us' to unite all those who see themselves threatened by Presbyterian ideologues who have acquired significant political influence and sympathy among many county gentry who disliked both Laudian church and toleration of local sectarian congregations. But it seems that the 'us' will be the literate minority of English men and women, for he picks out the Presbyterian wish to 'silence us from reading'. The stance seems to imply an individual or group, who believes that the most important liberty and tyranny centres on the activity of 'reading', and while we shall return to this matter later, here it seems fair to note that 'us' has again been narrowed down to involve a special group, although Milton has not overtly indicated this.

This is predictable, because no-one who introduces himself as serving grand abstractions like 'the public good' and 'the Country's liberty' (486, 487) is going to admit that he is actually preoccupied with sectional interests, especially if they conflict with other interests which must be branded as sectional and divisive (as the Presbyterian ones are in the passage above). Yet the shifts in the groupings indicated by Milton's use of pronouns suggest a reluctance or inability to focus on the implications of these difficulties which is much more than tactical cunning. It may be helpful to indicate the extent of Milton's shifting. In the space of the nineteen lines which we are discussing here, the first person pronoun (and its cognates) stands for six recognisably distinct groupings. Viz: 1. I = Milton, the private man; 2. I = representative of those with minds above the vulgar pitch; 3. I = the spokesman for the 'general murmur'; 4. We = all of us who have the power to prevent this threatened tyranny; 5. Us = all of us, every Englishman; and 6. a use of us = those above the vulgar pitch, but excluding parliament, that is, similar to 2. The same applies to the second and third person pronouns.

In dealing with the passage about 'learned men' it is pertinent to take a later statement where Milton threatens Parliament while seemingly praising it. He tells its members that their own 'free, and human government' has sponsored 'liberty . . . enfranchised, enlarged and lifted up our apprehensions', before offering his first threat: 'You cannot make us now less capable, less knowing, less eagerly pursuing of the truth, unless you first make yourselves, that made us so, less the lovers, less the founders of our true liberty . . . you cannot suppress that . . .' (559). Here Milton reverts to the pronouns 'we', 'us', 'you' in which 'we' is the mass of 'the whole Nation' (535, 536, 551–9 *passim*) and 'you' the liberating leaders who 'enlarged and lifted up our apprehensions'. (Like other 'learned men' Milton would in fact hardly have felt indebted to an English Parliament for having his intellectual powers improved, so we should probably emphasise the *tactical* role of the 'we' here in which the 'learned' writer gracefully submerges his distinction in the putative unity of the elect nation). The next threat is more overt. He warns that if the members of Parliament suppress the 'liberty' which they have introduced they will lose all support which, Milton insists, was *not* primarily in defence of material and political interests ('for cote and conduct . . .') against the encroachments of Charles's rule.[21] However, he does hastily, and wisely, add 'I dispraise not the defence of just immunities', a concession to one of the chief motives in arousing the country gentry against the monarch.

But after this pragmatic concession he makes a brief statement which is central to his overall outlook: 'Give me the liberty to know, to utter, and to argue freely according to conscience, above all liberties' *(CPW* II. 560). Wage labourers in the hardships of the 1640s, subsistence farmers with copyhold tenures subjected to rack renting as well as traditional feudal impositions, the mass of servants or, at the other end of the society, well-to-do country gentry defending their political, social, economic and religious power in their localities, none of these would think that the liberty of learning was *'above all* liberties'. As we have already suggested, Milton's freedom from ever having *had* to work as a hired labourer (whether manual or intellectual), his freedom from the labour market, his freedom from the pressures and commitments affecting those in the commercial sector of society or the landed gentry, this social and economic freedom is a shaping factor in his statement about the most valuable liberty and in his whole experience. It is, however, one he seems largely unable to bring into self-reflexive consciousness, unable to acknowledge how fundamental such freedom was to his own intellectual, aesthetic and religious achievement. We believe that this is as much a matter of imaginative failure and intellectual closure as of any inevitable product of class background, and here it is worth considering the letter his friend Moses Wall wrote to him in 1660:

> You complain of the non-progression of the nation, and of its retrograde motion of late, in Liberty and spiritual Truths. It is much to be bewailed; but yet let us pity human frailty when those who had made deep protestations of their zeal for our liberty both spiritual and civil, and made the fairest offers to be asserters thereof, and whom we thereupon trusted; when those being enstated in power, shall betray the good thing committed to them, and lead us back to Egypt, and by that force which we gave them, to win us Liberty, hold us fast in chains what can poor people do? You know who they were that watched our Saviours sepulcher to keep him from rising. Besides, whilst people are not free but straitened in accommodations for life, their spirits will be dejected and servile. And conducing to that end [of liberty] there should be an improving of our native commodities, as our manufacturers, our fisheries, our fens, forests and commons, and our trade at sea which would give the body of the nation a comfortable subsistence, and the breaking that cursed yoak of tithes would help much thereto. Also another thing I cannot but mention, which is that the Norman Conquest and tyranny is continued upon the nation without any thought of removing it: I mean the tenure of land by copyhold, and holding for life under a lord (or rather Tyrant) of a manor, whereby people care not to improve their land by cost upon it, not knowing how soon themselves or theirs may be outed it [ejected], nor what the house is in which they live for the same reason. And they are far more enslaved to the lord of the manor than the rest of the nation is to a King or supreme magistrate![22]

Much of this is in close accord with the powerful social criticism and analysis developed by Winstanley, but we thought it of particular interest to quote from a letter actually received by Milton himself, and written by a friend replying to one of his own letters.[23] Wall's attention to the realities of domination in England

and to the actual life-processes and daily circumstances of a wide range of people highlights features in his friend's approach with which we have been dealing. For, unlike Wall's, Milton's orientation involves the dissolution of concrete social reality in particular human communities where, and where alone, the individual develops his specific identity and lives his life. This dissolution is rather indicative of his inability to make the advantages and limitations of his own social and economic position a topic for serious examination. Even Wall's impressively intelligent letter seems not to have persuaded him to do this or reconsider his approach, for his diagnosis of the defeat of the 'good old cause' (in *The Ready and Easy Way*, for example) shows no signs that he learnt from Wall.

Both Wall's brief letter and especially the sustained commentary and analysis in Winstanley's extensive writings, argue that 'liberty' (including the kinds of religious and intellectual liberties Milton proclaimed so bravely) had to have some basis in the daily lives of all people; that individual freedoms and fulfilments need political and social dimensions which include the sphere of work and a certain level of overall material security. The way Milton dissolved the dialectical relations between individual and social circumstances and discounted the extremely diverse actualities of life confronting God's Englishmen, is an important aspect of his version of liberty, individual, and community. It is also very much part of those static, anti-historical, anti-empirical tendencies of his outlook on which we focused in the first part of this chapter. Studying his prose we need to remember the issues raised by *Areopagitica* and discussed in the present chapter as we meet the admirable, challenging phrases about liberty. Phrases such as the one maintaining that Christ 'has won for *us all* proper freedom . . . not of religious liberty alone, but also of political' (*CPW* IV. 374, our italics).[24] The 'us' may seem to be 'the whole Nation', or rather all Christians, but in the same work he shows how easily 'us all' becomes the 'few': 'those who long for liberty or can enjoy it are but few' *(CPW* IV. 343). Perhaps so, and circumstances in 1651 were different to 1644. But, recalling Wall's letter, one would like to know more (something at least!) about the empirical content of this 'liberty', the quality of relationships being offered, who is doing the offering and why all but the 'few' should have withdrawn active support from the 'good old cause'. Yet Milton's approach, in *Areopagitica*, to historical processes, individual and community, is one which, as we have attempted to show, systematically screens such considerations; and although his later work is beyond the scope of the present chapter, we do not believe that Milton ever fully penetrated this particular and highly complex screen.

8

Satan and the Revolution of the Saints

BOB HODGE

What is the relation between the politics of *Paradise Lost* and Milton's political commitments in the Civil War? The problematic answer that occurs most readily is that the poet seems to contradict the polemicist. Milton, regicide in the war on earth, seems fiercely on the side of order and authority in the war in heaven. One way of resolving this apparent contradiction traditionally has been to see Satan as the real hero of the poem. Milton was 'of the Devil's party without knowing it' in Blake's famous phrase. But this is not entirely satisfactory as a solution. Why did he not know it? How could he not know it? If he was so obtuse that he did not notice that he had totally changed sides, why did no-one else seem to notice? On the contrary, the 1688 edition, coinciding with the successful 1688 revolution, was ushered in with a list of 500 names, mostly notables of the Whig establishment.[1] Milton became the supreme poet for this establishment, who were the new standard-bearers for a version of Milton's Good Old Cause. Were all these worthies so subtle that they saw beneath the overt betrayal to Milton's subconscious support of Satan?

However, I do not think Milton did inadvertently repudiate two decades of political commitment in this his greatest poem. The apparent contradiction between poetry and life reflects contradic-

184

tions in his ideology. Ideology can systematically invert reality, and a poem can present an image of that inversion, and also its negation, the negation of a negation, no longer recognisable as either reality or ideology. In Milton's ideology 'liberty' could mean the repressive rule by his own party, 'rebellion' could mean respect for traditional authority, or any other opposition to the revolutionary cause, and 'faithfulness' or 'loyalty', a revolutionary commitment to the new order. Such an extreme form of double-think, to use Orwell's vivid term, shows an ideology under acute strain. To understand this very complex poem, we need to be able to relate the key ideological terms to the political realities to which they refer, and we need also to realise what the underlying contradictions were that necessitated such strange transformations.

> But unheroic as bourgeois society is, it nevertheless took heroism, sacrifice, terror, civil war and battles of peoples to bring it into being. And in the classically austere traditions of the Roman republic its gladiators found the ideals and art forms, the self-deceptions they needed in order to conceal from themselves the bourgeois limitations of the content of their struggles and to keep their enthusiasm on the high plane of the great historical tragedy. Similarly, at another stage of development, a century earlier, Cromwell and the English people had borrowed speech, passions and illusions from the Old Testament for their bourgeois revolution.[2]

This comes from Marx's brilliant analysis of Louis Napoleon's rise to power in the aftermath of the 1848 revolution, where Marx is reflecting back on the revolution of 1789. The distinction he is making here, between the revolutionary and post-revolutionary condition of the bourgeoisie, is an important one. For Marx, the idea of bourgeois heroism is something of a contradiction in terms, a paradox liable to collapse into farce with a Louis Napoleon, but a paradox which the bourgeoisie must pass through if they are to achieve rule.

Milton lived in another of the heroic ages of the bourgeoisie. Walzer has shown in more detail how a revolutionary ideology was forged out of the Old Testament.[3] Milton's art in practice fuses the two stages of development mentioned by Marx, having roots in epic as well as the Bible. Both kinds of literature provided Milton with images of 'heroism, sacrifice, terror, civil war and battles of peoples', and both served the bourgeoisie to conceal 'the bourgeois limitations of the content of their struggles'.

We can see something like this opposition, between the heroic and unheroic aspects of the bourgeoisie, between bourgeois and revolutionary consciousness, underlying the course of events of the civil war. The war began basically as a limited bourgeois revolution, masquerading as a defence of ancient rights. Disaffected members of the aristocracy figured in the leadership, giving the revolution respectability, and lower-class support was mobilised. But the 'many headed monster' terrified many of the larger propertied bourgeoisie, whose aims had been sufficiently realised by the early 1640s. So a split developed in the bourgeoisie, between the majority and a revolutionary minority, who continued to draw dangerously on lower-class support as they pushed through a far more radical programme than the bulk of the bourgeoisie wanted, in religion or politics.

This primary opposition in fact expressed itself in a whole series of conflicts: between the peace party and the war party in the early stages of the war, between the Presbyterian and Independent factions in the events leading up to the execution of the King, and within the Independents themselves, between the moderates and the more revolutionary minority, and between the MPs and the army. Even within an individual the same opposition might occur, tugging him in two directions: hence the vacillations of a Cromwell or a Fairfax. The fundamental split in consciousness and strategy left both factions of the bourgeoisie caught in a contradiction. As Milton said, the Presbyterians had effectively unkinged the king, and weakened the old order, but then wished to set this discredited king between them and a thorough-going revolution. Milton mocked the contradiction mercilessly. But the Independents for whom Milton was apologist based their position on a contradiction too, as a military elite claiming to represent the popular will when they lacked the support even of their own class. Cromwell attempted to serve the interests of the bourgeoisie and win their support, ruthlessly suppressing the Levellers, but the majority of the bourgeoisie in 1660 cravenly (as Milton thought) preferred to sacrifice parts of their revolution for some of the economic and political gains they had made.[4]

Milton's judgment on his fellow-revolutionaries was harsh, as can be seen from a revealing discussion which he wrote for his *History of Britain,* but deleted from the published work. In the *History* he had seen a parallel between the failure of the Ancient Britons to take advantage of the departure of the Romans, and his own countrymen's failure to seize the opportunity presented by the success of the civil war. He sees it both times as failure of will, compounded by a failure of leadership.

> Some indeed were men of wisdom and integrity. The rest, and to be sure the greatest part whom wealth and ample possessions or bold and active ambition rather than merit had commended to the same place, when once the superficial zeal and popular fumes that acted their new magistracy were cooled and spent in them, straight every one betook himself, setting the commonwealth behind and his private ends before, to do as his own profit or ambition lead him. Then was justice delayed and soon after denied, spite and favour determined all: hence faction, then treachery both at home and in the field, everywhere wrong and oppression, foul and dishonest things committed daily, or maintained in secret or in open. Some who had been called from shops and warehouses without other merit to sit in supreme councils and committees, as their breeding was, fell to huckster the commonwealth; others did thereafter as men could sooth and humour them best.[5]

Milton here acknowledges with manifest distaste the utterly bourgeois nature of the majority of his fellow revolutionaries. They were only petty tradesmen who 'huckster the common-wealth', or men of greater wealth and 'ample possessions', the larger bourgeoisie who manipulated justice with even greater freedom now they were in the ascendancy, or men of 'bold and active ambition', thrusting New Men without any coherent ideology.[6] To these Milton opposes the kind of leader he desired, the 'few' who proved unable to leaven this mass:

> men more than vulgar, bred up as few of them were, in the knowledge of ancient and illustrious deeds, invincible against money, and vain titles, impartial to friendships and relations.[7]

This is a dedicated elite, highly trained, and indifferent to ties of friendship or family. They also must be fed on 'the knowledge of ancient and illustrious deeds', the images of past heroism which Marx observed nourished the revolutionary ardours of the bour-geoisie.

In books XI and XII of *Paradise Lost*, Michael gives Adam a lesson in history. The bare narrative comes from the Bible, but as expanded by Milton it becomes myth, the distillation of Milton's decades of thinking about politics. At the beginning of book XII Michael gives two alternative accounts of the basis of political power. The first takes the story of Nimrod as its starting point (three uninformative verses from Genesis, expanded to 20 lines of verse). Michael starts off presenting a brief idyll of justice and equality after the flood. Men then

> With some regard to what is just and right
> Shall lead their lives, and multiply apace,
> Labouring the soil, and reaping plenteous crop.
>   (XII. 16–18)

Michael is clearly less than ecstatic about their virtue. These are fallen men. But it is important to note that the Fall is not used to justify rule. It only explains why a figure like Nimrod with his crew will inevitably emerge. The ideal life, if only men could have persisted in it, was a rural, proto-Leveller paradise, in which everyone labours, and no-one pre-empts rule.[8] This situation does not last. Men will dwell:

> Long time in peace by families and tribes
> Under paternal rule; till one shall rise
> Of proud ambitious heart, who not content
> With fair equality, fraternal state,
> Will arrogate dominion undeserved
> Over his brethren, and quite dispossess
> Concord and law of nature from the earth.
>   (XII. 23–9)

In this state of nature there is paternal rule, but this does not (as in Filmer for instance) justify any other kind of rule outside the family. The political conceptions that underlie this account are reminiscent of those in the *Tenure of Kings and Magistrates*.

Nimrod also helps us to place Satan politically, since he is linked with him through a number of clear allusions. Nimrod attempts to build Babel ('Confusion named' XII. 62) as Satan had Pandaemonium built in Hell. God strikes the builders of Babel with confusion of tongues, 'a hideous gabble' (line 56) as God reduces the devils' speech to 'a dismal universal hiss' (X.508). The mortar for his building came from 'the mouth of hell'

(XII.42). The connection establishes Satan as the archetypal tyrant-figure.[9] Other images scattered through the poem reinforce this connection, most notably in the famous introduction to book II:

> High on a throne of Royal state, which far
> Outshone the wealth of Ormus and of Ind . . .

It may seem paradoxical that the Great Rebel is also the archetypal tyrant. The paradox works both ways. Nimrod the first tyrant is also called a rebel, though there was no king or lord for him to rebel against:

> And from rebellion shall derive his name.
> Though of rebellion others he accuse.
>
> > (XII.36–7)

Milton here relies upon a dubious etymology which derived Nimrod's name from a Hebrew verb meaning 'to rebel', and does not otherwise justify the paradox. The point is that to rule over others is closely associated with rebellion against God. The heavenly perspective allows this ideological switch, whereby tyrants, or rulers, become rebels, and rebels (if they are saints, like Milton) become loyalists.[10]

This particular paradox occurs at other important points in Milton's poetry. In August 1653 he did a translation of psalm 2. In this psalm, God rebukes 'the kings of the earth' and 'the princes in their congregations', and proclaims his Messiah. In the authorised version, the announcement is given as: 'Yet have I set my King upon my holy hill of Sion'. Milton gives this a parenthetical gloss:

> but I, saith he,
> Annointed have my king (though ye rebel)
> On Sion my holy hill.

Here also, the opposition of kings and princes to God's Messiah makes them the real rebels. God's speech in heaven announcing the creation (or elevation) of Messiah echoes this psalm (V.735). This speech precipitated the war in heaven. Satan's rebellion foreshadows the reaction of earthly kings and princes to God's decrees. So rule-as-rebellion is very close to the original sin.

Adam cannot understand how a Nimrod could emerge, so

Michael gives an explanation. But where the Nimrod myth came from the political world of *Tenure*, the explanation comes more from *Ready and Easy Way*, with the fierce contempt of that work for the majority of men.

> Since man permits
> Within himself unworthy powers to reign
> Over free reason, God in judgment just
> Subjects him from without to violent lords;
> Who oft as undeservedly enthrall
> His outward freedom: tyranny must be,
> Though to the tyrant thereby no excuse.
>   (XII. 90–6)

These 'violent lords' are the heirs of Nimrod and Satan, and remote ancestors of the powerful magnates Milton was prepared to entrust the revolution to, in the dark days of 1659–1660.[11] In this explanation the Fall fulfils a different role. In the previous account it explained why Nimrods emerged. Now it justifies the subjection of the majority of men to such tyrants, though Milton still disapproves of tyrants. The men so castigated no doubt included the faint-hearted non-revolutionary bourgeoisie, whom Milton abused in similar terms for longing to thrust their necks back into the yoke of servitude. There is a crucial difference between the Nimrod myth and its ostensible gloss. In the first, the rule of powerful magnates is repudiated as an offence against the law of Nature. In the second it is the divinely sanctioned consequence of the sinful nature of the majority of men.

In this history, Milton considers three revolutionaries, i.e. men who opposed the fundamental principles of such states, and who have the qualities Milton wanted for the leaders of his own revolution. Those leaders, he compained, were 'few'. These exemplary figures are entirely isolated. They are Enoch 'The only righteous in a world perverse' (XI. 701), Noah, 'the only son of light/In a dark age' (XI.808–9) and Abraham, 'A nation from one faithful man to spring' (XII.113). The fortunes of these three are significantly different. Enoch's denunciation would have proved fatal, if God had not snatched him to safety. In human terms his revolution is unsuccessful, though God approves of him. Noah also denounces his society, but God this time endorses the denunciation by destroying all Noah's enemies with a flood.

Abraham adopts an alternative strategy, by withdrawing entirely and founding a new nation—like the radical puritans who colonised New England.

A revolutionary is liable to be attracted by this myth, of the solitary just man vindicated by divine power in a total triumph over his enemies. In this myth 'raised consciousness' is sufficient guarantee of final success. The failed revolutionary will find it especially attractive. His revolution is assured, and is dependent on no-one else's help. Isolation instead of being his source of weakness confirms his strength. The myth celebrates a revolution that dispenses with any social basis: a pure and utterly impossible revolution. But Milton has the honesty to place these recurring revolutions in a history where God-given successes inevitably lapse back into the *status quo,* revolutions are always eroded, and the counter-revolution prevails.

The War in Heaven is Milton's great dramatisation of the perfect revolution, presented, by characteristic inversion, as the exemplary counter-revolution. This inverse relationship between heaven and earth directly embodies the typical use of millenarian rhetoric by the 'armed Saints' in the Civil War. We can see the process clearly in Milton's well-known climax to the early *Of Reformation* (1641). He looks forward to

> that day when thou the Eternal and shortly-expected King shall open the clouds to judge the several kingdoms of the world, and distributing national honours and rewards to religious and just commonwealths, shall put an end to all earthly tyrannies, proclaiming thy universal and mild monarchy through Heaven and Earth. Where they undoubtedly that by their labours, counsels, and prayers have been earnest for the common good of religion and their country, shall receive, above the inferior orders of the blessed, the regal addition of principalities, legions and thrones into their glorious titles, and in supereminence of beatific vision progressing the dateless and irrevoluble circle of eternity shall clasp inseparable hands with joy, and bliss in over measure for ever.[12]

Christ's coming is imminent, as the Millenarians believed, and will be a political event, not just a spiritual one. Christ's kingdom does not re-inforce the principle of Monarchy on earth; 'Just commonwealths' are rewarded, but 'all earthly tyrannies' are destroyed. The crucial distinction between tyrant and king is left obscure here, but Charles was to find out soon enough how he was classified. It is interesting that the principle of hierarchy is retained, and all the titles and degrees will remain, but will belong now to the earnest aristocracy of the saints (really a meritocracy of course). What is envisaged here is a total revolution which retains all the forms of the old hierarchical order, the tiaras preserved intact for the new ruling class to wear: a revolution that will be nearly invisible.

But *Of Reformation* is an early work, written before Milton had lived through the events of the civil war. By the time he wrote *Paradise Lost* he knew that this revolution could not remain invisible. Also, he had been exposed to the more radically egalitarian ideas of the Levellers, which had begun to filter through into his thought by *Tenure* in 1649. The attitude to hierarchy in the poem is both more ambiguous and more obscure.

At first sight, Heaven does of course seem based on the principle of hierarchy. There undoubtedly is order and hierarchy in Heaven. At a number of points, Raphael alludes to differences of ranks. On the occasion of Messiah's elevation he describes the host of heaven, ordered

> Under their hierarchs in orders bright.
> Ten thousand thousand ensigns high advanced,
> Standards and gonfalons twixt van and rear
> Stream in the air, and for distinction serve
> Of hierarchies, of orders, and degrees;
> Or in their glittering tissues bear emblazed
> Holy memorials, acts of zeal and love
> Recorded eminent.
>
> (V. 587–94)

So there are leaders, 'hierarchs', and differences of rank indicated by standards, though these standards can record acts of virtue as well as insignia of rank. God begins his address with what can be taken to be the official rank order of pre-war heaven: 'Thrones, Dominations, Princedoms, Virtues, Powers' (line 601). This list is repeated twice by Satan (V. 772, X. 460), and by Abdiel once (V. 840).

But the important point to notice here is the difference in the attitudes of God and Satan to this list. The effect of God's decree is to subvert this traditional order. Satan offers himself as its defender. He begins his speech:

> Thrones, Dominations, Princedoms, Virtues, Powers,
> If these magnific titles yet remain
> Not merely titular, since by decree
> Another now hath to himself engrossed
> All power, and us eclipsed under the name
> Of king anointed.
>
> (V. 772–7)

He sees correctly that God is a leveller. He does not at this stage know what God's ultimate plan is, a state of absolute equality, with even Christ's regal sceptre laid aside (III. 349–50), but he has shrewd suspicions.[13] His followers also are motivated by respect for traditional values, by unthinking allegiance to status rather than by personal ambition:

> all obeyed
> The wonted signal, and superior voice
> Of their great potentate
>
> (V. 704–6)

Their real sin is blind obedience, not pride or rebellion.

Of course, we must be slightly sceptical about Satan's absolute reverence for hierarchy. Raphael says that he is 'of the first, / If not the first archangel' (V. 659–60). Where this puts him is not entirely clear, but he is certainly not next in line to the heavenly crown. The highest rank he is given, until his elevation to a 'Throne' in book II ('by merit raised', II. 5) is 'Prince'. This is a high rank, but below both 'Thrones' and 'Dominations'. Among his followers is Moloch, whose name means king, who is described as 'horrid king' (I. 392) and 'sceptred king', the 'strongest and the fiercest' of the rebel angels (II. 43–4). Moloch is the quintessential 'violent lord', whose contribution to the infernal debate is predictably mindless and blood-thirsty. Other 'Thrones' in Satan's army are Adramalech and Asmadai, 'Two potent Thrones' (VI. 366).

So Satan's position is ambiguous. As Lewis notes, 'he wants hierarchy and does not want hierarchy'.[14] But his upward movement is the exception in the ranks of the devils, whereas fluid meritocracy is the rule in heaven. None of God's principal angels has the rank of 'Throne'. The highest ranking good angel is

Michael, who is a prince (VI. 44). Gabriel, who seems to be his second-in-command, is given no rank, but is described as 'in military prowess next' (VI. 45), appointed entirely on merit. It is usually assumed that Raphael (discussed in chapter 7 'Rational Burning') is a high-ranking archangel, but he is described as a 'virtue' once, and as a 'power' on another occasion, (V. 371, III, 249) the two least significant orders named by God.

Abdiel is the clearest example of the irrelevance of rank as far as God and Milton are concerned. He is referred to as a 'seraph' (V. 896) but in Milton this gives no indication of rank. Seraphs in Satan's status-obsessed army are mere gunners (VI. 579, 604). Raphael also is a seraph, but as we have seen, that may not be proof of high rank. Abdiel seems to have no troops in the war in heaven, yet both in the Satanic parliament and in battle he confronts Satan as an equal, and defeats him.[15]

Before the military confrontation, Abdiel is said to step forth 'from his armed peers' (VI. 127), which may seem to give him rank. But 'peers' means 'equals'. Milton glosses the word in this way in a passage in *Tenure:*

> The peers and barons of England had a legal right to judge the King: which was the cause most likely, for it could be no slight cause, that they were called his peers, or equals . . . And so much I find both in our own and foreign story, that Dukes, Earls, and Marquesses were at first not hereditary, not empty and vain titles, but names of trust and office, and with the office ceasing, as induces me to be of opinion, that every worthy man in Parliament, for the word Baron imports no more, might for the public good be thought a fit Peer and judge of the King.[16]

By virtue of this radical version of the history of the English and foreign nobility, Abdiel is a 'Baron' and 'peer', fit to judge the highest in the land. His real rank is given by his name, which means 'servant of God'. All God's elect are his servants, so that Abdiel's victory over Satan stands for the equal right and capacity of all God's servants to triumph over the tyrant Satan.

Abdiel uses precisely the kind of argument Milton used on earth to justify rebellion, but its revolutionary force does not appear because it is set against the background of a political world conceived in terms of the same ideology. Satan accuses the army of the Saints of being feudal lackeys, contemptibly servile. Abdiel indignantly repudiates this charge:

> Unjustly thou depravst it with the name
> Of servitude to serve whom God ordains,
> Or Nature; God and Nature bid the same,
> When he who rules is worthiest, and excels
> Them whom he governs. This is servitude,
> To serve the unwise, or him who hath rebelled
> Against his worthier, as thine now serve thee,
> Thyself not free, but to thyself enthralled.
>
> (VI. 174–81)

This seems like an argument for loyalism, but it is that only if the rulers are naturally superior. C. S. Lewis saw the real drift of the argument clearly enough:

> The idea, therefore, that there is any logical inconsistency, or even any emotional disharmony, in asserting the monarchy of God and rejecting the monarchy of Charles II is a confusion. We must first enquire whether Charles II is, or is not, our natural superior. For if he is not, rebellion against him would be no departure from the hierarchical principle.[17]

But Lewis blurs the issue slightly by replacing Charles I with the less disturbing Charles II, who we all know was naughty with Nell Gwynn and died in his bed. Otherwise, he is showing clearly how an appeal to the principles of spiritual hierarchy could justify an attack on all existing hierarchical systems. Here is Milton's answer to an enquiry whether Charles I or II is likely to be our natural superior:

> Indeed, if the race of Kings were eminently the best of men, as the breed at Tutbury is of horses, it would in some reason then be their part only to command, ours only to obey. But kings by generation no way excelling others, and most commonly not being the wisest or the worthiest by far of whom they claim to have the governing; that we should yield them subjection to our own ruin, or hold of them the right of our common safety . . . we may be sure was never the intent of God.[18]

So Abdiel's conditions would in practice exclude a hereditary ruling class. They would lead to either a meritocracy or a democracy, depending on whether the elite is sufficiently recognisable or not. Abdiel clearly believes the former. Who decides who is 'worthiest' is left unclear, as it commonly is with theories of revolutionary elites. The appeal to 'God' (or 'Nature') is a convenient way of not dealing with this problem.

At one point Satan accuses Abdiel of being 'seditious' as well as servile (VI. 152). This accusation seems outrageous, since it is Satan not Abdiel who is seditious. But in human terms, Satan is probably correct. If everyone who joined the rebel council did so because they owed Satan neo-feudal allegiance (cf. V. 705–6) then Abdiel's presence there makes him Satan's man. His opposition to Satan is therefore disloyalty, sedition. We saw the same paradox with Nimrod:

> And from rebellion shall derive his name,
> Though of rebellion others he accuse.
> (XII. 36–7)

There it seemed odd to call tyranny 'rebellion': here in the anti-world of heaven it seems odd to call Abdiel 'seditious'. But it is the same paradox, and the same ideology, seen from a different perspective.

Satan is the most interesting angel on either side, as every reader of the poem has always realised. This could not be simply because he is a devil. Moloch, Belial, Mammon etc. are devils too, but they are not especially interesting. Satan is the only angel who is aware of moral problems. He alone acknowledges an inner life whose intensity is nearly overwhelming, and must be held in check by strength of will. He shows the heroism that makes the counter-revolution formidable, and the complexity of feeling that both undermines it and makes its failure something to regret.

He is also curiously drawn to disguises and role-playing, first as 'stripling Cherub', then as toad, then serpent, and finally as a 'plebeian angel militant / Of lowest order' (X. 442). The first three of these could be justified tactically, but the last seems gratuitous. A Moloch would never have contemplated any of these. Everyone else's behaviour is bound by his angelic status. Satan sometimes seems socially insecure—he behaves like a touchy aristocrat, standing uneasily on his dignity when the lowly Ithuriel and Zephon apprehend him—but he has an impressive capacity to get inside all classes of angelic society. Milton presumably valued this quality in Satan, since the only other person who changes status in the poem is Messiah. Messiah changes more completely, actually becoming man, where Satan can at best adopt a disguise. So Messiah transcends his class where Satan only briefly takes a holiday from his. But no-one else has even that degree of mobility.

This reading does not in the least dispose of the famous 'problem of Satan'. Any reading which simply disposed of this problem would be unconvincing for that reason, since it is evident to every reader that Satan is a problematic creation, embodying something that Milton found immensely but illicitly attractive. That something is not 'evil' because Milton's Satan clearly is not evil. Nor is it rebellion, because Satan stands for much that is best in the old patrician class, along with the heroic abilities hoped for in the new. He is the doomed champion of the old order, romanticised embodiment of what Milton felt was a richer civilisation than the bourgeoisie could show, with something of the heroism that the ordinary bourgeois so lamentably lacked. The myth was compounded out of the deficiencies of his own class as much as from the virtues of the old order. Milton's admiration for this fiction perhaps lay behind his capitulation in *Ready and Easy Way,* where he proposes that

> the nobility and chief gentry from a proportionable compass of territory annexed to each city, may build, houses or palaces befitting their quality, may bear part in the government, make their own judicial laws, or use these that are, and execute them by their own elected judicatures and judges without appeal, in all things of civil government between man and man.[19]

If the revolution has failed, better such a composite elite than the contemptible mass of the bourgeoisie.

The failure of Milton's revolutionary hopes shaped the poem as decisively as their success. But 'failure' is a relative term. The Restoration was not failure for the bourgeoisie as it was for Milton. The revolutionary aspirations had been repudiated by the class out of a sense of their immediate interests. 1688 showed that those interests had been too narrowly conceived but Milton was dead by then.

Of the angels, Abdiel is closest to the post-revolutionary Milton. Even after he rejoins God's army he remains essentially isolated. In his exchange with Satan, he justifies his absolute confidence through his trust in God.

> Who out of smallest things could without end
> Have raised incessant armies to defeat
> Thy folly; or with solitary hand
> Reaching beyond all limit at one blow
> Unaided could have finished thee, and whelmed
> Thy legions under darkness
>
> (VI. 137–41)

God here is a source of irresistible power, which releases the revolutionary from dependence on anyone else, allowing revolution without compromise, without concessions to the need for a political base. Abdiel in fact is surrounded by allies at this point, but he never mentions them as a source of confidence. God is a guarantee of 'incessant armies' raised out of 'smallest things'. For a later revolutionary it might have been History not God that guaranteed future successes through irresistible armies formed from smallest things.

But Abdiel's victory on this occasion proved inconclusive. The army of the saints itself is unable to win a decisive victory. Milton arranges the battle so that it is a stalemate, then has Christ sweep to victory on his own. This creates a strain in the narrative that many have noticed. It involves a logical difficulty—God seeming to contradict himself—but more important is the emotional dissonance between the two parts of the narrative, the sense in the first part that human effort and united action matter, whereas in the ultimate victory they do not.

God's opening command celebrates united action in a holy cause:

> Lead forth to battle these my sons
> Invincible, lead forth my armed saints
> By thousands and by millions ranged for fight:
> Equal in number to that godless crew
> Rebellious, them with fire and hostile arms
> Fearless assault, and to the brow of heaven
> Pursuing drive them out from God and bliss
>
> (VI. 46–52)

This vision of a multitude of 'armed saints' sweeping to an irresistible victory is the vision that inspired the 'Army of the Saints' in Milton's time.[20] But things did not work out like this, either on earth or in heaven. God's sons in heaven are 'invincible', unconquered, but they do not conquer and do not themselves drive the foe out of heaven. They are left standing ineffectively (but happily) by. Not only can they not achieve victory on their own, they are not even allowed to follow Christ into battle, or fight under his banner. This is an image of the total impotence of all joint human action in a totally successful revolution. The revolution has been entrusted to the last and greatest of the solitary righteous men. This carries the polarisation of the 'bourgeois revolution' to its ultimate extreme, a repudiation not only of the bourgeoisie but even of their revolutionary elite. Milton is celebrating a revolution that transcends class, in a myth that itself transcends its time and place, giving all revolutionaries, bourgeois and proletarian alike, an image in art of their necessary illusions.

NOTES

Abbreviations

ELH	English Literary History
HLQ	Huntington Library Quarterly
MLN	Modern Language Notes
MS	Milton Studies
UP	University Press

Chapter 1
MARLOWE, MARX AND MACHIAVELLI: READING INTO THE
PAST   pp. 1–22

1. *Brecht on theatre: the development of an aesthetic* (ed. and tr. John
   Willett, London: Eyre Methuen 1964.
2. L. Althusser and E. Balibar, *Reading 'Capital'* (tr. B. Brewster)
   London: New Left Books 1970, 18.
3. Ibid, 26.
4. Ibid, 28–9.
5. For a twentieth-century revolutionary's appreciation of the continuing relevance of Machiavelli's thought, see A. Gramsci, *Prison
   Notebooks*, tr. Q. Hoare and Nowell Smith, London: Lawrence and
   Wishart 1971; especially 125–36.
6. See E. Meyer, *Machiavelli and the Elizabethan Drama*, Weimar
   1897.
7. L.C. Knights, *Drama and Society in the Age of Jonson*, London:
   Chatto and Windus 1937.

Chapter 2
DARKE TEXTS NEED NOTES: VERSIONS OF SELF IN
DONNE'S VERSE EPISTLES pp. 23–48

1. J.F. Danby, *Elizabethan and Jacobean Poets*, London: Faber 1964
   (originally published as *Poets on Fortune's Hill*, 1962) chapter 1.

2. 'Donne's assumption is the relationship of a poet to patron as of nothing to everything, and out of this he spins his conceits direct. He makes metaphysics out of the poet and patron relations, and a poet-patron relation out of metaphysics', *Elizabethan and Jacobean Poets*, 39.

3. See R.C. Bald on this period in *John Donne: A Life*, Oxford UP 1970, chapter 8; see too Donne himself in his letters: *Life and Letters of John Donne*, ed. E. Gosse, 2 vols., 1899, reprint London: Smith 1959, especially vol. I, 114–15, 166, 181, 185–7, 191.

4. All quotations are from *Donne's Poetical Works*, 2 vols., ed. H.J.C. Grierson, Oxford UP 1912, reprint Oxford UP 1966, referred to hereafter as Grierson. This quotation is from vol. I. We have also used W. Milgate's edition of *The Satires, Epigrams and Verse Letters*, Oxford UP 1967.

5. Grierson, vol. II, 156–7; cf. Milgate, 256–7.

6. See M.H. Curtis, 'The Alienated Intellectuals of Early Stuart England', *Past and Present*, 23 (1962), reprinted in *Crisis in Europe* ed. T. Aston, London: Routledge 1965. On Donne's desperate wish for 'incorporation' see the letter to Goodyer in Gosse, vol. I, 191–2.

7. One of the best studies of this issue is by R. Ellrodt, *L'inspiration personnelle et l'esprit du temps chez les poètes métaphysiques anglais*, 3 vols., Paris 1960, see vol. I, especially chapters 3–4.

8. As Danby suggested, Donne is obsessed with his nothingness (note 2, above). For examples of the explicit social causes of his sense of being *nothing,* and its remedies, see especially prose letters in Gosse, vol. I, 181, 167, 191–2, and on loss of employment as death, for example, 291; also volume II, 28, 42; and the verse epistles to the Countess of Bedford and the Countess of Salisbury.

9. See previous note.

10. In contrasting Donne with Jonson, very much at Donne's expense, Danby, like other commentators, misses these rich complexities in Donne's stance.

11. Nor is the manner in which the concept of self is being explored in these poems confined to Donne. That questions about value in just the way we are discussing were current in the milieu from which Donne received his training, are suggested by Shakespeare's *Troilus and Cressida* which includes, among its central preoccupations, a study of conflicting versions of value and their relation to social fabric and metaphysical frameworks.

12. James I, 1609 speech to Parliament, in *The Political Works of James I,* ed. C.H. McIlwain, Cambridge, Mass. 1918, reprint 1966, 307.

13. There remain important connections to be examined with the political Petrarchianism cultivated under Queen Elizabeth and discussed in L. Forster, *The Icy Fire,* Cambridge UP 1969. The theological vocabulary in patron poems has also been studied by B.K. Lewalski in *Donne's Anniversaries,* Princeton UP 1973; relevant here are chapters 1 and 2: her approach (well illustrated in

comments on p. 46) tends to isolate the metaphysical and the social in a way which we think distorts both areas.

14. It is worth noting how Donne is contemptuous of the market contingencies which donate those very same social eyes he actually covets so strongly!

15. M. H. Curtis, op.cit., 299, 312, where he also refers to G.E. Aylmer's study, *The King's Servants,* London: Routledge and Kegan Paul 1961, chapters 3–4. For Walzer see *The Revolution of the Saints,* London: Weidenfeld 1966, chapters 1–4.

16. Curtis, op.cit. 308–11.

17. Walzer, op.cit.

18. Walzer, op.cit. 130–32; see chapters 4–6 passim.

19. Probably it is worth drawing attention to the relevance of the work of the Frankfurt School to this area of study. See especially: M. Horkheimer, *Critical Theory,* New York: Seabury Press 1972; T. Adorno, *Minima Moralia,* New Left Books 1972; and 'Society' in *Salmagundi,* 10–11 (1969–70), 144–53; H. Marcuse, *One Dimensional Man,* London: Routledge and Kegan Paul 1964.

20. On Donne's early life see especially R.C. Bald, *John Donne,* chapters 1–4.

21. Not always so subtle: see the letters to Rochester which Gosse sadly called "somewhat ignominious" in the *Life and Letters of John Donne,* cited earlier, vol. II, 22–3, 28; on this episode see Bald (extremely sympathetic to Donne), *John Donne,* 272–4, 313–14.

22. Curtis, op cit. 312.

23. Raymond Williams, *Country and City,* London: Chalto and Windus 1973 27–34.

24. See, especially, I. Meszaros, *Marx's Theory of Alienation,* London: Merlin Press 1970, chapter 4; B. Ollman, *Alienation* Cambridge UP 1971, part three. Also relevant here is C.B. Macpherson, *The Political Theory of Possessive Individualism. Hobbes to Locke,* Oxford UP 1962.

25. Walzer has some suggestive speculations on this topic in his conclusion to *The Revolution of the Saints.*

26. L. Stapleton, 'The Theme of Virtue in Donne's Epistles', *Studies in Philology* 55 (1958), 187–200, reprinted in *Essential Articles for the Study of John Donne's Poetry,* ed. J.R. Roberts, Sussex: Harvester Press 1975, 451–2. On the date of 'Sir, more then kisses', see Milgate, op cit., 227–8. and Grierson, op.cit., vol. II, 140–1.

27. Stapleton, article cit., 452.

28. There is no space here to contrast the profound explorations of such issues in Marvell's *Upon Appleton House.*

29. The conclusion of a classic contemporary stoic poem, Ben Jonson's fine *To the World* ('False world, good night') provides an essential contrast here.

Chapter 3
VEXATIOUS CONTRARIES: A READING OF DONNE'S
POETRY   pp. 49–74

1. *Life and Letters of John Donne,* ed. E. Gosse, reprint London: Smith 1959, vol. I, 104, 114–15, 291; hereafter referred to as *Letters* in text and notes. On these events see R.C. Bald, *John Donne. A Life,* Oxford UP, 1970, chapter 7; hereafter cited as Bald.
2. The letter is dated September 1608 by Gosse; on Donne and Goodyer see Bald, 158–73 and references in his index, 664–5. We have made one change to Gosse's text: where he alters the 1651 text to 'as I thought might [have] employed' we have reverted to his source.
3. Spelling modernised; for Donne's family and his early life, see Bald, chapters 2–4.
4. For an extremely relevant and detailed linguistic analysis of the world created in *A nocturnall,* see Gunther Kress, 'Poetry as Anti-Language: A Reconsideration of Donne's *Nocturnall Upon S. Lucies Day*', *Journal for Descriptive Poetics and Theory of Literature,* 3 (1978), 327–44.
5. *Revaluation,* 1936, Harmondsworth: Penguin 1967, 18.
6. For some more detailed comments on this 'traditional culture' and an exceptional imaginative challenge to it in the fourteenth century, see David Aers, *Chaucer, Langland and the Creative Imagination,* London: Routledge and Kegan Paul 1980, chapters 5 and 6.
7. See Donne's awareness of this fluidity in, e.g. *The Second Anniversary,* ll. 381–400, *Elegie III, Womans constancy, The Indifferent, Confined Love, Loves Alchymie, Farewell to love;* and the relevant comments in P. Cruttwell, *The Shakespearian Moment,* New York: Random House 1960, chapter 2.
8. Here again see Gunther Kress's analysis cited in note 4.
9. See similarly, W. Sanders, *John Donne's Poetry,* Cambridge UP 1971, 67.
10. For an important discussion of these matters see H. Marcuse, *Eros and Civilization,* Boston, Mass: Beacon Press 1955, Tunbridge Wells, Kent: Abacus 1972.
11. We write that the couple *seem* involved in action not only because of the use of the present tense but also because throughout the stanza Donne chooses a number of verbs which suggest that the lovers are passive rather than themselves agents: e.g. 'wee are made such by love' (lovers passive), 'wee in us finde' ('finde' not used as transactive verb), we 'prove mysterious' (hard to classify but certainly not attributing agency or conscious action to the lovers); it is the sexual activity pointed to in 'Wee dye and rise' that constitutes their action, but action in a closed world and presented as a mystically non-temporal and sublimated form of sexual exchange.

12. *The Sermons of John Donne,* ed. G.R. Potter and E.M. Simpson, 10 vols., University of California Press 1953–62, V. 293, modernised.
13. Quotations from *Devotions upon emergent occasions,* University of Michigan, Ann Arbor paperback 1965, 30, 31, 33, 108–9, 138.
14. See L. Stone, *Crisis of the Aristocracy,* Oxford UP 1965, chapter 11; and L. Stone, *The Family, Sex and Marriage in England 1500–1800,* Weidenfeld and Nicolson 1977; and the work cited in note 6.
15. Here we have not the space to recapitulate and develop Gunther Kress's analysis cited in note 4 above, of *A nocturnall* but it is accessible.
16. Obviously enough we disagree with L.L. Martz's reading of Donne as a fundamentally conventional Roman Catholic meditative poet, as we do with Halewood's different version of Donne as a straightforward Augustinian protestant teacher—respectively, *The Poetry of Meditation,* revised ed. Yale UP 1962, chapters 1,2,3, and 6 passim, and *The Poetry of Grace,* Yale UP 1970, especially 24–32, 74–84. In their concern to absorb Donne into the traditions they favour, neither of these critics is closely concerned with the minute particulars of the poems, although it is obviously there that the man's vision resides. Likewise they seem to share little of our sense of the way Donne's particular, thoroughly individual experience and sensibility permeate his poetry.
17. For example *Caelica,* numbers 98–100, 102, 109 and many others; on Greville see especially R.A. Rebholz, *The Life of Fulke Greville,* Oxford UP 1971 and R. Waswo, *The Fatal Mirror,* University of Virginia Press 1972, chapter 4.
18. For example, *Paradise Lost,* III. 173–202, XII, passim; *Christian Doctrine,* I.4, 14, 17–18, 21, 23, 27 etc; on this topic see especially C. Hill, *Milton and the English Revolution* London: Faber 1977, especially chapters 18–21, 28–9.

Chapter 4
THE LANGUAGE OF SOCIAL ORDER: INDIVIDUAL SOCIETY AND HISTORICAL PROCESS IN *KING LEAR*   pp. 75–99

1. On this topic see especially J.F. Danby, *Shakespeare's Doctrine of Nature,* London: Faber 1961 and W.R. Elton, *King Lear and the Gods,* San Marino, California: Henry Huntington Library and Art Gallery 1966.
2. The linguistic theory underlying the analyses in the book is based on G.R. Kress and R.I.V. Hodge, *Language as Ideology* London: Routledge and Kegan Paul 1979; extensive descriptions of different types of texts along these lines may be found in R. Fowler, R. Hodge, G. Kress and A. Trew, *Language and Control,* London: Routledge and Kegan Paul 1979.
3. The system of pronominal usage as forms of address is set out clearly

in Brown and Gilman's 'The Pronouns of Power and Solidarity' which is most readily accessible in P.P. Giglioli (ed.), *Language and Social Context,* Harmondsworth: Penguin 1972. Oversimplifying somewhat, the forms of address were governed by the two dimensions of power and solidarity, the 'power-laden' pronoun being 'you' and its cognates (we, our, us, etc.), the pronoun of solidarity being 'thou' and its cognates (my, thy, I, etc.). The system was not reciprocal, so that the powerful received 'you' from inferiors, but gave 'thou' in return; though the powerful could give 'you' to inferiors—as Lear does initially to Cordelia.

4. On the uses of this ideology, and the problems it posed for its users in the later Middle Ages, see D. Aers, *Chaucer, Langland and the Creative Imagination,* London: Routledge and Kegan Paul 1980, chapter one; R. Hilton, *Bond Men Made Free,* London: Temple Smith 1973, 221–33; and Hilton, 'Idéologie et ordre Social dans l'Angleterre médiéval', *L'Arc,* vol. 72, 32–7.

5. Lawrence Stone, *The Family, Sex and Marriage in England 1500–1800,* London: Weidenfeld and Nicolson 1977, 502–3; also Elton, *King Lear and the Gods,* 131–5. Our reading of *King Lear* seems to support Stone: Gloucester seems between Stone's 'sixteenth century' and his 'early seventeenth century'. Had he lived longer he might have leapt from pseudo-pagan England to pseudo-Catholic but very puritan Vienna and met Angelo in *Measure for Measure.*

6. On Edmund's 'nature' and the social significance he held for Shakespeare, see especially Elton, *King Lear and the Gods,* chapter 6 and J.F. Danby, *Shakespeare's Doctrine of Nature,* London: Faber 1949 31–5.

7. The extent to which real subversive opposition to the bourgeois and capitalist world in the eighteenth century was based on people's feelings, myths, and ideology concerning a tradition being violated by 'new' practices is documented in E.P. Thompson's works, and in essays in *Albion's Fatal Tree,* ed. D. Hay, et al., Harmondsworth: Penguin 1977.

8. Lawrence Stone's work is illuminating about the transitions in family relations at this period, and shows why Shakespeare was so preoccupied with parent-child relationships in a way quite absent from the work of Langland, Gower, Chaucer, or the Gawain-poet.

Chapter 5
MINE EYES DAZZLE: FALSE CONSCIOUSNESS IN
WEBSTER'S PLAYS pp. 100–21

1. A. Harbage, *Shakespeare and the Rival Traditions,* New York: Macmillan 1952, 25.

2. G. King, *Natural and Political Observations and Conclusions upon*

the State and Condition of England, 1696, ed. G.E. Barnett, Baltimore 1936, 31.

3. E.H. Phelps-Brown and S.V. Hopkins, 'Seven centuries of the prices of consumables compared with builders' wage rates' in *Economics* 26, 1956. See also C. Lis and H. Soly, *Poverty and Capitalism in Pre-Industrial Europe*, Sussex: Harvester 1979.

4. Webster, *Works*, ed. F.L. Lucas, London 1927, III. 315.

5. First raised, very hesitantly, by Lucas in his introduction to the *Works*, authoritatively endorsed by C. Leech in *John Webster*, London 1951.

6. See, e.g., L. Stone, *Crisis of the Aristocracy*, Oxford 1965, and his *Family, Sex and Marriage in England 1500–1800*, London: Weidenfeld and Nicolson 1977.

7. M. Marcovic, *The Contemporary Marx*, Spokesman Books 1975, 59.

Chapter 6
'RATIONAL BURNING': MILTON ON SEX AND MARRIAGE
pp. 122–51

1. Good examples of the kind of work we have in mind are: C.S. Lewis, *Preface to Paradise Lost*, Oxford UP 1942; C.E. Fish, *Surprised by Sin*, University of California, 1976; C.A. Patrides, *Milton and the Christian Tradition*, Oxford UP 1966, 165–86 especially; J. Halkett, *Milton and the Idea of Matrimony*, Yale UP 1970, chapter 4; and most recently a typical expression by B.K. Lewalski, 'Milton on Women—Yet Once More', *MS*, 6(1974), 3–20, to which see M. Landy's most pertinent reply, 'A Free and Open Encounter: Milton and the Modern Reader', *MS*, 8(1976), 3–36.2.

2. On this topic, useful introductions are those by B. Ollman, *Alienation*, Cambridge UP 1971, and I. Mészáros, *Marx's Theory of Alienation*, London: Merlin Press 1970.

3. See: K. Thomas, 'Women and the Civil War Sects', *Past and Present* 13, 1958, reprinted in *Crisis in Europe*, ed. T. Aston, London: Routledge 1965, 317–40; P. Higgins, 'The Reactions of Women', chapter 5 in *Politics, Religion and the English Civil War*, ed. B. Manning, London: Arnold 1973; W. Notestein, 'The English Woman, 1580–1650', *Studies in Social History*, ed. J.H. Plumb, London: Longmans 1955, 69–107; L. Stone, *Crisis of the Aristocracy* Oxford UP 1966, chapter 11; and important suggestions in L.B. Wright, *Middle-Class Culture in Elizabethan England*, University of North Carolina Press 1935, 202–9 and 465–503, where he argues that changes in social organisation and a corresponding increase in 'burgher writers' 'had greatly increased women's liberties'. This relevant area needs far more intensive research, and what has been done needs attention from literary critics. For the case that the

overall position of women in the seventeenth century can actually be judged as deteriorating if compared with the position of women in the American colonies see R.G. Thompson, *Women in Stuart England and America,* London: Routledge 1974; on the topic in general Laurence Stone's recent work is most useful: *The Family, Sex and Marriage in England, 1500–1800,* London: Weidenfeld and Nicolson 1977.

4. R. Baxter, *A Christian Directory,* London 1673, 529, spelling modernised.

5. J. Dod and R. Cleaver, *A Godly Force of Household Government* London 1630 edition, spelling modernised.

6. Similarly William Gouge, *Of Domestical Duties* (first edition 1622) strongly discouraged any familiarity of speech between husband and wife, warning against the use of terms of affection or even letting the wife use the husband's Christian name (see L.B. Wright, *Middle Class Culture,* 222).

7. See similar accounts, evidence and references showing that women were normally and explicitly envisaged as commodities and useful property: R.G. Thompson, *Women in Stuart England and America,* op.cit., 48–51, 116–22, 162–7; E.S. Morgan, *The Puritan Family,* 1944, Harper and Row 1966, 38–54; C. Hill, *The World Turned Upside Down,* London: Temple Smith 1972, 247–51; J.T. Johnson, *A Society Ordained by God: English Puritan Marriage Doctrine in the First Half of the Seventeenth Century,* Nashville, Tenn. Abingdon 1970, 23–4, 32–5.

8. W. and M. Haller, 'The Puritan Art of Love', *HLQ,* 5 (1941–2), 235–72.

9. We could follow Milton himself and add atheism—*Complete Prose Works,* Yale UP, in process, II. 269, etc. Of all the psychic consequences, perhaps the outstanding critique is contained in Blake's *Four Zoas.*

10. M. Weber, *The Protestant Ethic and the Spirit of Capitalism* tr. T. Parsons, 1930, London: Unwin 1971, 103–4. For a useful commentary on the group organisation and psychology of puritans, see M. Walzer, *The Revolution of the Saints,* London: Weidenfeld 1966, and on puritanism and the family, 183–98. (For caveats on his argument about Calvinist politics see Quentin Skinner, *Foundation of Modern Political Thought,* Cambridge UP 1978, vol. II.)

11. For the economic basis and philosophical manifestations see C.B. Macpherson, *Possessive Individualism,* Oxford UP, 1962.

12. Like other militant Protestants, however, he could certainly see the relation between the traditional externalisation and reification of grace and God in human institutions and the social realities involved here.

13. Compare Blake's continual emphasis that 'All deities reside in the human breast' *(Marriage of Heaven and Hell,* pl.11). There are many examples of seventeenth-century versions of this position

explored by C. Hill in *The World Turned Upside Down*, op.cit., which includes an appendix on Milton and Bunyan; see his major study of *Milton and the English Revolution*, London: Faber 1977.

14. Quotations of Milton's prose are from the Yale edition of the *Complete Prose Works (CPW)*, but we have modernised the spelling. On the commonplace connection of family and state see for example Dod and Cleaver quoted earlier, R.G. Thompson, *Women in Stuart England and America*, op.cit., chapter 7, E.S. Morgan, *The Puritan Family*, op.cit., chapter 6, C. Hill, *Society and Puritanism*, London; Secker and Warburg 1964, chapter 13. On the whole broader topic, see L. Stone, *Family, Sex and Marriage in England, 1500–1800*, Weidenfeld and Nicolson 1977.

15. Another interesting effect is that in Milton's analogy 'government', at least when it is resisted, does not include any people either—as though there is no *human* opposition to the revolutionary elite. Of course a dominant social group normally seems to itself to represent the universal welfare of society—see chapter 8.

16. In *The Ready and Easy Way* see especially *CPW* VII. 442–3, 458–9, where the revolutionary elite of the Saints is explicitly made into a traditional property elite.

17. See K. Thomas, 'Women and the Civil War Sects', note 3 above.

18. Milton is obscure here, concealing his failure to deal with the problem of children by the vague gesture at the 'ancient civil law'. It is clear that he only envisages upper-class marriages here (based on marriage contracts and transactions of property [see note 7 above] and fails to meet his 'Answerer'. See also G.E. Howard, *A History of Matrimonial Institutions*, 1904, II. 56–9, 71–96.

19. *Twelve Serious Questions* (1644), quoted in *CPW* 722,n.5.

20. See D. Masson, *The Life of John Milton*, London, 1859–1880, III. 189–92, and references in W.R. Parker, *Milton*, 2 vols., Oxford UP 1968, II. 919–20, n.6. On the connections between Milton and antinomian positions see Christopher Hill's stimulating study in *Milton and the English Revolution*.

21. John Holland, *Smoke of the Bottomless Pit, or, A More True and Fuller discovery of the Doctrine of those men which call themselves Ranters: or, The Mad Crew* (1651), quoted in W. Cohn, *The Pursuit of the Millenium*, Herts: Paladin 1970, 293. On the Ranters see A.L. Morton, *The World of the Ranters*, London: Lawrence and Wishart 1970.

22. *A Single Eye All Light, no Darkness* . . . 1650, in Cohn, op.cit., 312–13. See C. Hill's works cited above in notes 7 and 20.

23. *The Works of Gerrard Winstanley*, ed. G. Sabine, 1941, London: Russell and Russell 1965, 400–1.

24. *CPW* I.890

25. For the seventeenth century, see C.B. Macpherson, *Possessive Individualism*, cited earlier. As the next paragraph notes, St Augustine had an extremely pertinent comment on the aspect of Milton's

argument which maintains that what Adam wants is an asexual companionship: 'If it was company and good conversation that Adam needed it would have been much better arranged to have two men together, as friends equally, not a man and a woman', *De Genesi ad Litteram,* IX. 5.9 *(P. Lat.,* 34, 396; see too *CPW* II. 596, n.26).

26. Poetry quoted from *The Poems of John Milton,* ed. J. Carey and A. Fowler, London: Longmans 1968.

27. Typological connections must not, of course, be confused with equations. It is also worth noticing how even in asserting Eve's *activity* Milton seems to dissociate the arrow-shooting from the subject, the woman (VIII.60–3), by bringing in the graces; the syntax, however, does remain ambiguous.

28. On the subject of angelology see R.H. West, *Milton and the Angels,* University of Georgia Press 1955, especially chapters 5–9.

29. On angelic eating see West, 106, 138–40, 164–9; Empson makes an interesting connection between this half-promise and Satan's temptation to Eve in her dream (V.79), see *Milton's God,* London: Chatto and Windus 1965, 150.

30. On angelic sex, see especially West, 169–74, 88–9, 106, 124. West himself treats Raphael's redness here as a sign his disclosure is 'embarrassed' (171–2), though most commentators have simply accepted Milton's own gloss here, that red is 'love's proper hue' (e.g. E.L. Marilla, 'Milton on Conjugal Love Among the Heavenly Angels', *MLN,* 68 [1953], 485–6). It is also taken, in Fowler's words, as 'the colour of angelic ardour' (gloss to VIII. 618–20, in the Carey and Fowler edition—note 26), and West, 146, links this passage with IV. 977ff. Raphael is *not* red to represent the traditional Cherubim since he is named as a *seraph* (V.277), a *virtue* (V.371) or an *angel* or *archangel* (see West, 134).

31. For all exegetes, and Hume editing *Paradise Lost* in 1695, the famous text on marriage in heaven at Matthew 22:30 settled any speculation about heavenly sex (West, 171–2). This reflects the traditional confusion of sexuality, procreation and marriage (evidenced in the title of Marilla's article, n.30). Milton's implicit approach to the text is fascinating: for him it seems to licence the fact that angelic sexuality is unfettered by any institutional restraints (such as conventional marriage and its market) and is the direct expression of spontaneous affection. This is a vision of liberated sexuality which transcends the socio-economic and ethical nexus which had traditionally contained and controlled Eros. There is not space to develop this discussion here, but there is suggestive material in H. Marcuse, *Eros and Civilisation,* Abacus edition 1972. For Blake here, see D. Aers, 'Blake and the Dialectics of Sex', *ELH,* 1977, and for earlier treatment of relevant issues by Chaucer, D. Aers, *Chaucer, Langland and the Creative Imagination,* op.cit., chapters 5 and 6.

32. For good measure, the reader's sympathies with Adam can be chastised as ghastly signs of his own corruption, out of which 'Milton' is allegedly educating him into a new Christian ortho-doxy—e.g. S.E. Fish, *Surprised by Sin*, University of California Press 1971. Contrast P. Lindenbaum's discussion in 'Lovemaking in Milton's Paradise', *MS*, 7 (1975), 293–8 suggesting limitations in Raphael's views from a perspective different to our own.

33. Compare *Christian Doctrine*, I.5, I.6, I.7 *(CPW*, VI. 267–8, 282, 301–4): here Milton emphasises that creation is *not* by Christ but by the Father *through* Christ.

34. Bush, notes to VIII. 521–59, 596ff.

35. John Carey unkindly calls it 'gasseous love' in his *Milton*, New York: Evans 1969.

36. For a clear statement of this schema see for example *Tetrachdon, CPW*, II. 587–8, on the liberating supersession of Adamic paradise through Christ.

Chapter 7
HISTORICAL PROCESS, INDIVIDUALS AND COMMUNITIES
IN MILTON'S AREOPAGITICA pp. 152–83

1. Throughout we quote Milton from the *Complete Prose Works of John Milton*, Yale University Press, still in process: we cite the edition as *CPW* and refer in the text to volume and page or, if the volume has been clearly stated *(Areopagitica* is in volume two) just the page number. Here CPW, II. 560. The literature on Areopagitica is substantial, but we have found the following especially interest-ing: Don M. Wolfe, *Milton in the Puritan Revolution*, Cohen and West 1941, chapter 3; K.W. Stavely, *The Politics of Milton's Prose Style*, Yale UP 1975, chapter 3; W. Haller, *Liberty and Reformation in the Puritan Revolution*, Columbia UP 1955, chapter 5; C. Hill, *Milton and the English Revolution*, London: Faber 1977, chapter 10. For the linguistic analysis see G.R. Kress and R. Hodge, *Language as Ideology*, London: Routledge and Kegan Paul, 1979 and R.G. Fowler, R. Hodge, G.R. Kress and A.A. Trew, *Language and Control*, London: Routledge and Kegan Paul 1979.

2. As he continually makes clear in *Doctrine and Discipline of Divorce, Tetrachordon, Christian Doctrine* and throughout his work pertain-ing to politics, marriage, religious organisation and theology.

3. Compare Tony Trew's analysis of the way in which English news-papers reported how white police killed black people in Salisbury: Tony Trew, 'Theory and Ideology at Work', chapter 6 in R.G. Fowler, R. Hodge, G.R. Kress, A.A. Trew, *Language and Control*.

4. For an extended discussion of tense on these lines see G.R. Kress 'Tense as Modality', *UEA Papers in Linguistics*, 5, 1977; also J. Lyons, *Semantics, Vol. II*, Cambridge UP 1978.

5. See Kress and Hodge, *Language as Ideology* and Kress, ed. Halliday, *System and Function in Language,* Oxford UP 1976, chapters 2 and 11 for detailed discussion.

6. See 1 Corinthians 9: 24–5 and *CPW* II.515, note 103.

7. B.M. Berry's discussion of pre-Civil War puritan sermons seems very relevant to Milton's confusion (sleight of hand?): *Process of Speech,* John Hopkins UP 1976, chapter 12. This is an outstanding study of Milton and his contexts.

8. In our view the Yale editor misrepresents the relations between Spenser and Milton when he asserts that Milton here changes Spenser's use of the Palmer to suit his 'more strenuous and (it may be suspected) more realistic' psychology based on the role of active choice and reason'(516, note 108).

9. Doubtless Ramistic ants! See the comments on Ramistic logic and Milton in R.I.V. Hodge, *Foreshortened Time: Marvell and 17th Century Revolutions* Cambridge: Brewer 1978, chapter 1; and the study by W.J. Ong, *Ramus, Method and the Decay of Dialogue,* Harvard UP 1958.

10. See Hodge, *Foreshortened Time,* passim.

11. On tithes, see C. Hill, *Economic Problems of the Church,* Oxford UP, reprinted 1968, part 2, especially chapter 3; M. James, 'The political implications of the tithes controversy', *History* (June 1941) 1–18, and B. Reay, 'Quaker opposition to tithes', *Past and Present,* 86 (1980), 98–120.

12. The literature on this subject is large: a most usefully particularised study is P. Clark, *English Provincial Society from the Reformation to the Revolution,* Sussex: Harvester 1977; more generally, L. Stone, *The Causes of the English Revolution,* Routledge and Kegan Paul 1972.

13. See D. Aers, *Chaucer, Langland and the Creative Imagination,* op.cit., and Hodge, *Foreshortened Time.*

14. For some extremely penetrating commentary on theodicies, see L. Kolakowski, *Marxism and Beyond,* London: Pall Mall Press 1969, 107–77.

15. On this subject see A.W. Gouldner, *The Dialectics of Reason and Technology,* London: Macmillan 1976; and Aers, *Chaucer, Langland and the Creative Imagination,* chapter 4.

16. See Morris's explorations of such issues in the utopian novel *News from Nowhere,* chapter 26, but passim.

17. See Hodge, *Foreshortened Time,* op.cit.; C. Hill, 'Society and Andrew Marvell' in his *Puritanism and Revolution,* 1958, Herts: Panther 1968, chapter 13; A.M. Patterson, *Marvell and the Civic Crown,* Princeton UP 1978, especially see p. 236. On the metaphor of building the temple see the important discussion in J. S. Coolidge's *The Pauline Renaissance in England,* Oxford UP, 1970, chapter 2; also cf. 1 Peter 2:5 where the stones are as animate as in Marvell's model.

18. See especially Gouldner, *Dialectics of Reason and Technology*, cited, note 15; M. Walzer, *Revolution of the Saints*, op.cit.; C. Hill, *Society and Puritanism*, 1964, Panther 1969, 215–16, 479–80; our own chapters on Donne in this volume: Donald Hanson, *From Kingdom to Commonwealth*, Harvard UP 1972.

19. See C. Hill, *Milton and the English Revolution* and *The World Turned Upside Down*, 1972, Harmondsworth: Penguin 1975, 395–404.

20. On Milton's attitude to 'the people' see Hill, *Milton and the English Revolution*, 160–62, 168–70. With the attitude to the 'nation' and 'the people' in *Areopagitica*, contrast the despairing anger in the preface to *Eikonoklastes* five years later, with its contempt for 'the people' as an idolatrous and 'mad multitude', and its hope for only a 'few', a 'sole remainder' elected by God from the perverse generation of the present. See *CPW* III. 337–49.

21. Contrast, for instance, P. Clark, *English Provincial Society*, op.cit.

22. Moses Wall's letter is printed in *Life Records of John Milton*, ed. J.M. French, Rutgers UP 1949–1958, see May 1659, 267–8, modernised spelling and punctuation.

23. For Winstanley, whose works should be read carefully by all students of seventeenth-century literature, culture and society, see *The Works of Gerard Winstanley*, ed. G. Sabine, 1941, Russell and Russell 1965: with Wall's letter compare pp. 506–7, 158–9, 190–1, 316, 389 ff., 538. There is a substantial paperback selection of Winstanley's work, with a fine introductory essay by Christopher Hill, *Winstanley: The Law of Freedom and other writings*, Harmondsworth: Penguin 1973.

24. See too the splendid statement in the preface to his *Christian Doctrine*, *CPW* VI. 118; and C. Hill, *Milton and the English Revolution*, op.cit.

Chapter 8 SATAN AND THE REVOLUTION OF THE SAINTS pp. 184–99

1. On Whig championing of Milton, see J. W. Good, *Studies in the Milton Tradition*, Illinois, 1915, 28.

2. K. Marx, *The Eighteen Brumaire of Louis Napoleon*, 1852, in *Selected Works*, London: Lawrence & Wishart 1968, 97.

3. M. Walzer, *The Revolution of the Saints*, Cambridge, Mass. 1965; see also W. Lamont, *Godly Rule*, London: Macmillan 1969.

4. On fears of lower-class action, see especially C. Hill, 'The many headed monster . . .' in *From the Renaissance to the Counter Reformation*, ed. C. H. Carter, Cape 1966. The best account of the conflicts between Presbyterians and Independents, and within the Independent alliance, is D. Underdown, *Prides Purge*, Oxford 1971. Underdown isolates what he calls the 'revolutionary minority', inside and outside Parliament, and shows a number of ways in which

MPs in this group differ significantly in wealth and social background from the rest of Parliament.

5. *History of Britain*, 1670, in *Complete Prose Works*, V, Yale UP (hereafter *CPW*) 443–5. This parallel is usually ascribed to 1647, but for no strong reason. It would be very interesting to know exactly when Milton was roused to make this judgment on his fellow revolutionaries.

6. Milton was basically right. See e.g. Underdown, *op. cit.*, whose figures for the 'revolutionary minority' show that 65 percent of them bought confiscated lands, a greater percentage than for other groups who acquiesced in the revolution. Underdown's status-breakdown of the revolutionaries is: 20 per cent greater gentry, 30 per cent county gentry, 30 per cent lesser gentry, and 20 per cent merchants or merchant gentry. He estimates that at least 35 per cent had an income of less than £500 p.a., and 30 per cent lacked the advantages of higher education at either University or the Inns of Court: exactly what Milton feared.

7. *History, CPW* VI. 451.

8. In Milton's Eden, all things are held in common except wives, cf. IV. 750–2.

9. This identification is a commonplace in Milton's criticism. See M. Hughes, 'Satan and the "Myth of the Tyrant"', in *Ten Perspectives on Milton*, Yale UP 1965; see also C. Hill, *Milton and the English Revolutionary*.

10. This inversion, whereby supporters of Charles were described as rebels, was widespread, cf. e. g. *Two Declarations of the Lords and Commons assembled in Parliament*, 16 August 1642, 7, Royalist supporters "have traitorously and rebelliously levied war against the King'. See also *A Declaration of the Lords and Commons . . .*,23 October 1642, 9–10, and *A Declaration of the Lords and Commons . . .*, 9 August 1642, 3.

11. See especially *The Ready and Easy Way to Establish a Free Commonwealth*, 1660.

12. *CPW* I. 616.

13. It is interesting that God's ultimate plan sounds like an argument for absolute monarchy, and would be that if God was an earthly King: again, ideological inversion, which however shows the real affinity between absolutist monarchy and an egalitarian state. Underwood, *Op. cit.* p. 29 suggests that in counties where rule was concentrated in one or two families, the transfer of power was more revolutionary.

14. C. S. Lewis, *A Preface to Paradise Lost*, Oxford UP 1942, 194.

15. R. H. West, in his *Milton and the Angels*, University of Georgia 1955, argues that Milton carefully avoids all available rank orders, and uses none of them consistently. Strangely, he didn't conclude from this that Milton might not be committed to the *principle* of hierarchy either: he suggests that Milton was merely keeping all options open, as he did with science.

16. *CPW* III. 219–20.
17. op. cit. 75.
18. *Eikonclastes* 1649, *CPW* VII. 458–9.
20. For an enlightening analysis of Milton's syntax (and in particular the use Milton uses of the passive construction) in relation to his ideology of sainthood see Boyd M. Berry, *Process of Speech: Puritan Religious Writing and Paradise Lost,* Johns Hopkins UP 1976.

INDEX

215